THE ARTFUL TABLE

GREAT FOOD FROM THE DALLAS MUSEUM OF ART LEAGUE

DALLAS MUSEUM OF ART

The Artful Table

First published in 1995
by the Dallas Museum of Art League

Dallas Museum of Art
1717 North Harwood
Dallas, Texas 75201

ISBN 0-936227-14-1
Library of Congress Card Catalog Number 95-068019

Designer and creative consultant   Carol Haralson
Photography stylists   Carol Haralson and Julie Cochran
Food writer and editor   Alicia Cheek
Photography   Tom Jenkins with assistance from Alex Contreras
Project consultant   Robert V. Rozelle

A PUBLIC ART MUSEUM must rely on the goodwill and support of many different constituencies. For the Dallas Museum of Art, no single organization has been more faithful in its support or has provided greater service to the institution and the community it serves than the DMA League. Since its founding in 1938, the League has funded the acquisition of almost 100 works of art, established a $1-million endowment fund for the DMA's Education Department, and provided major funding to reinstall the Museum's arts of Africa and arts of Asia and the Pacific. The publication of *The Artful Table* is the latest tangible evidence of that historic support.

The League, which currently numbers approximately 900 members, serves as the Museum's ambassador to the community, and its dedicated volunteers have, over the years, contributed countless hours of service. Members of the League bring warmth and life to the Museum. *The Artful Table* is symbolic of their devotion of time, effort, and talent to the institution. The quality, beauty, and diversity of this cookbook parallel the character of the Museum itself.

A precedent for this publication was first published in 1977. *The Gallery Buffet Soup Cookbook* was produced in response to repeated requests for recipes from the Museum's restaurant, which the League itself founded, managed, and staffed, beginning in 1969. This latest cookbook is both something old and new. It represents not only a continuing tradition of volunteerism, but also a new and glorious collection of recipes shared by League members and their families and friends. Featuring exquisite photographs of objects from the Museum's decorative arts collection, this book is a feast for the eye as well as the palate.

Dozens of League members contributed to the creation of *The Artful Table*. To all of these dedicated and energetic volunteers, we at the Dallas Museum of Art express our deep admiration and gratitude. Producing *The Artful Table* was a labor of love and vision. The fruits of that labor now exist for all to enjoy as a tribute to volunteerism and triumphant goodwill.

JAY GATES
DIRECTOR
DALLAS MUSEUM OF ART

THIS COOKBOOK IS BEAUTIFUL, but like any work of art, it is not completely original. As artists draw on the accomplishments of their predecessors—or rebel against them—so do we as cooks benefit from the instruction and inspiration of our beloved mothers, grandmothers, aunts, and friends. We love, and often try to replicate, the wonderful tastes of favorite dinners from around town, around the country, and around the world. Our preferred chefs, books, and magazines have spiced our dishes and added zest to our lives. We are indebted to all of those who have flavored the bounty we call our own. To them, we say thank you and offer in return to our sons and daughters, our families and our friends the heritage and art of our tables.

This book, in fact, reflects our lives. We do not offer only one style of cooking, for we come from different areas of the country. Our recipes mirror the great cultural variety of our city and our Museum. This rich diversity of origins and sources has been enhanced by our sharing of the long, amiable hours of planning, testing, and tasting in the creation of our book. We thank all friends and family who played such a great part in creating and perfecting the recipes. Our new or deepening friendships—and the satisfaction of seeing our book surpass our dreams—are all the thanks we need. We must recognize and thank, however, the many who have enriched our recipes with their expertise and love.

In particular, we thank the superb and cordial staff of the Dallas Museum of Art, especially Jay Gates, the DMA's Director, who opened all doors for our efforts; Charles Venable, Chief Curator and Curator of Decorative Arts, for his splendid eye and good-humored assistance; Tom Jenkins, Museum Photographer, whose artistry and limitless patience command our deepest respect and gratitude; and Kimberley Bush, Karen Zelanka, Ginger Reeder, Gary Wooley, Alex Contreras, and Ron Moody. Many friends outside the Museum made invaluable contributions to the creation of this book. We are especially indebted to Sherry Ferguson, a professional who as a volunteer polished and perfected our selections.

Finally, this book could not have been possible without the indulgence, tasting expertise, and loving support of our husbands: Conrad McEachern, Sloan Leonard, Frank Macari, Steve Cochran, and John Cheek.

To all we offer our love and gratitude. *Bon Appétit!*

CAROL MCEACHERN, MARY LOIS LEONARD,
BARBARA MACARI, JULIE COCHRAN, ALICIA CHEEK

DECORATIVE ARTS
AT THE DALLAS MUSEUM OF ART

W HILE PROVIDING THE READER with wonderful recipes, this book also offers up a visual feast of exquisite illustrations featuring selections from the DMA's decorative arts holdings. Given the variety and breadth of the pieces depicted, few perusers of this volume will believe that every item from the Museum collection seen here, with very few exceptions, has been acquired in the last decade. This book documents the fact that the growth of the decorative arts at the DMA has been nothing short of meteoric.

Before the early 1980s, Dallas did not collect in the area of European and American decorative arts. The arrival of the Wendy and Emery Reves Collection was a catalyst for change, however. Famous for its impressionist paintings, this collection also contained over 1,000 objects from Europe and China. Suddenly the Museum had significant holdings in the areas of textiles, glass, metalwork, porcelain, furniture, and frames.

The impact of the Reves gift went well beyond the mere presence of decorative arts objects in the DMA. Shortly after Wendy Reves decided to donate her extraordinary collection, local decorative arts enthusiasts approached the Museum with ideas of how to build on this new foundation. For example, they suggested acquisitions be made in the American decorative arts to balance the new European holdings. Thanks in large part to the generosity of the Tri Delta Charity Antiques Show, enough support existed by the opening of the Reves galleries in 1985 to purchase the well-known Faith P. and Charles L. Bybee Collection of 18th- and 19th-century American furniture. Faith Bybee was so pleased with the reception her collection received in Dallas that she subsequently gave scores of objects to the DMA, including textiles, ceramics, glass, metalwork, and additional furniture.

In the late 1980s and early 1990s, Dallas's decorative arts holdings continued to expand. The Karl and Esther Hoblitzelle Collection of British and Irish silver was given in 1987, making 18th-century silver one of the highlights of the Museum. Between the gifts of an anonymous donor and those from the Barbara and Hensleigh Wedgwood Collection, Dallas has acquired an impressive array of English ceramics made by Britain's most renowned potter, Josiah Wedgwood. Similarly, the Dallas Glass Club has donated over 200 examples of American glass. Dozens of other objects have been added by gift or purchased singly. Especially noteworthy has been the building of a fine survey of American silver made in the 19th and early 20th centuries. The wonderful array of spoons featured in this book, for example, comes from this collection.

Overall, the extraordinary growth seen in the area of the decorative arts during the past ten years reflects the countless acts of private and public generosity that have so transformed the DMA. As in the area of decorative arts, donors have broadened the Museum's holdings in many fields to the point that an entire level of new galleries was added to the building in 1993. Of the many who have made this amazing growth possible, the Dallas Museum of Art League has always been in the forefront. On behalf of all those who have benefited from its efforts, I hope this beautiful volume will serve as a salute to the League's generous spirit, as well as provide food for body and soul.

CHARLES L. VENABLE
CHIEF CURATOR AND CURATOR OF DECORATIVE ARTS
DALLAS MUSEUM OF ART

Appetizers

Marinated Shrimp and Artichokes

Serves 8 to 10

2 cans (13¾-ounce) water-packed artichoke
  hearts, drained and quartered
1½ pounds medium shrimp, cooked, peeled and
  deveined

5 tablespoons minced fresh chives
½ cup olive oil
½ cup vegetable oil
½ cup white wine vinegar
1 egg (or ¼ cup pasteurized egg substitute)
2½ tablespoons Dijon mustard
2 teaspoons fresh rosemary
  (omit if fresh not available)
½ teaspoon salt
½ teaspoon freshly ground pepper

Layer artichokes, shrimp and chives in large bowl. Combine remaining ingredients in blender and mix until consistency of heavy cream. Pour marinade over shrimp mixture and refrigerate at least 6 hours before serving. (Can be made 1 day ahead.)

BEAUTIFUL AS A FIRST COURSE SERVED ON BIBB LETTUCE OR RADICCHIO. GARNISH WITH CHERRY TOMATOES AND BLANCHED SNOW PEAS.

SERVE MARINATED SHRIMP AND ARTICHOKES STUFFED IN LARGE TOMATOES FOR A LUNCHEON. ACCOMPANY WITH SLICES OF CANTALOUPE OR HONEYDEW AND HOT PARMESAN PUFFS (PAGE 62).

FARMERS' MARKET BRUSCHETTA

SERVES 12 TO 16

14 ripe plum tomatoes, seeded, chopped and drained
3 tablespoons minced garlic
¾ cup chopped fresh basil
¼ cup chopped fresh Italian parsley
2 tablespoons fresh lemon juice
pinch crushed red pepper flakes
salt and pepper to taste
30 slices (¼-inch thick) French bread
6 cloves garlic, halved

Combine tomatoes, minced garlic, basil, parsley, lemon juice and seasonings in large bowl. Toss well and set aside for at least 4 to 5 hours. (Can be prepared 1 day in advance.)

Just before serving, lightly toast bread and rub with garlic. Place bowl with tomato mixture on large platter and surround with toasted bread.

THIS IS WONDERFUL SERVED WITH FRESH MOZZARELLA CHEESE.

BRUSCHETTA MIXTURE IS ALSO AN EXCELLENT TOPPING FOR OMELETTES OR PASTA.

ARTICHOKE, ARUGULA AND BEEF CROSTINI

YIELDS 36

2 jars (6-ounce) marinated artichoke hearts, drained
1 clove garlic
¼ cup white wine vinegar
½ cup olive oil
salt and pepper to taste
1 baguette, thinly sliced and lightly toasted
2 bunches arugula, stems removed, washed, spun dry and cut into shreds
2½-pound fillet of beef, roasted rare and thinly sliced
36 Parmesan curls formed with vegetable peeler

Purée artichoke hearts, garlic, vinegar, oil, salt and pepper in blender. (Can be made 3 days ahead and kept refrigerated.) To assemble, spread each toast slice with artichoke purée. Top with arugula, slice of beef and Parmesan curl.

WHEN WATERCRESS IS IN SEASON, IT'S A NICE ALTERNATIVE TO THE ARUGULA. THINLY SLICED ROMA TOMATOES CAN BE USED IN PLACE OF THE BEEF.

TOP WITH CHOPPED PARSLEY OR MINCED RED ONIONS FOR ADDITIONAL COLOR AND FLAVOR.

CAJUN GRILLED TENDERLOIN WITH MUSTARD-HORSERADISH CREAM

SERVES 20 AS AN APPETIZER OR 8 AS AN ENTRÉE

MARINADE
4 tablespoons Tabasco sauce
4 tablespoons Teriyaki sauce
2 tablespoons Worcestershire sauce
1 tablespoon Creole seasoning

1 tenderloin of beef (about 3½ pounds)

MUSTARD-HORSERADISH CREAM
1 cup heavy cream
¼ cup Dijon mustard
¼ cup horseradish, drained in fine sieve
juice of ½ lemon

Combine Tabasco, Teriyaki, Worcestershire and Creole seasoning in bottle with shaker top (for convenience). Shake marinade generously over tenderloin. Marinate at room temperature for 1 to 1½ hours.

To prepare sauce, pour cream into bowl and whip until stiff. Fold in mustard, horseradish and lemon juice. Refrigerate, covered, until serving time.

Prepare coals for grilling. Remove meat from marinade and grill until rare (24 to 30 minutes). Allow meat to sit for 10 minutes before slicing.

For a cocktail buffet, meat can be cooked several hours ahead and served at room temperature.

Meat can be kept warm by wrapping tightly in heavy-duty foil. (If wrapped, it is best to slightly undercook meat as it will continue to cook for a short time in foil.)

Slice thinly and serve on cocktail buns accompanied by Mustard-Horseradish Cream.

IF GRILLING OUTSIDE ISN'T CONVENIENT, YOU CAN ROAST THE TENDERLOIN IN AN OVEN FOR 30 MINUTES AT 450 DEGREES FOR RARE MEAT.

HOT CRAB CRISPS

YIELDS 50 TO 55 ROUNDS

1 cup mayonnaise
½ cup finely chopped green onion
1 cup freshly shredded Parmesan cheese
4 drops Tabasco sauce
1 tablespoon fresh lemon juice
8 ounces fresh crabmeat
2 baguettes, thinly sliced

Combine mayonnaise, onion, cheese, Tabasco and curry powder, mixing thoroughly. Fold in crabmeat. Place bread rounds on cookie sheet and crisp for about 10 minutes in 300-degree oven. Spread crab mixture on rounds and bake at 350 degrees for 15 minutes, or until bubbly and lightly browned.

FOR VARIATIONS ADD GARLIC OR REPLACE PARMESAN WITH SHARP CHEDDAR AND ADD ⅛ TEASPOON CURRY POWDER. YOU CAN ALSO MAKE **CRABMEAT MUSHROOMS.** STUFF MIXTURE INTO MUSHROOM CAPS AND BAKE AT 350 DEGREES FOR 15 TO 20 MINUTES.

GREEN PEPPERCORN PÂTÉ WITH CALVADOS AND CURRANTS

SERVES 8 TO 10 (3 CUPS)

2 stalks celery with leaves
1 teaspoon salt
12 whole green peppercorns
6 cups water
1 pound chicken livers
¼ teaspoon cayenne pepper
1 cup (2 sticks) unsalted butter
2 teaspoons dry mustard
½ teaspoon freshly grated nutmeg
¼ teaspoon ground cloves
¼ cup coarsely chopped yellow onion
1 clove garlic
¼ teaspoon white pepper
¼ cup Calvados (apple brandy)
½ cup dried currants

Add celery, salt and peppercorns to water in saucepan. Bring to a boil; reduce heat and simmer for 10 minutes. Add chicken livers and simmer very gently for 10 minutes, or until still slightly pink inside. Drain livers, discarding celery and peppercorns.

Place livers in food processor and add cayenne, butter, dry mustard, nutmeg, cloves, onion, garlic, pepper and Calvados. Purée until very smooth.

Stir in currants and transfer pâté to a 3- or 4-cup crock or terrine. Smooth surface, cover, and refrigerate at least 4 hours. Bring to room temperature for 30 minutes before serving. Serve with thinly sliced French baguettes or melba toast.

ROASTED STUFFED MUSHROOMS

YIELDS 24

24 large mushrooms, cleaned and stems removed
½ pound hot Italian sausage (bulk, or casing removed from link)
1 cup shredded Monterey Jack cheese
½ cup picante sauce
¼ cup thinly sliced green onions

Place mushroom caps in large, shallow baking dish. Brown sausage in skillet, stirring to break up large pieces. Drain and mix with cheese. Fill mushroom caps with sausage mixture. (Can be prepared to this point 1 day in advance.) Spoon picante sauce over mushrooms and bake at 375 degrees for 15 minutes or until heated through. Top with onions before serving.

STERLING SILVER SERVING SPOON, *BIRD'S NEST* PATTERN, DESIGNED 1869, GORHAM MFG. CO., PROVIDENCE, RI, 1991.101.10

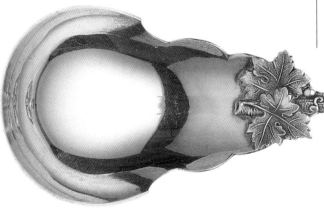

The liquid from steeping dried mushrooms is a flavorful addition to soups and sauces. To remove any grit, be sure to strain the liquid through cheesecloth.

BAKED OYSTERS WITH ITALIAN HERBS

SERVES 8 TO 10 AS AN APPETIZER

OR 6 AS AN ENTRÉE

½ cup (1 stick) butter
½ cup olive oil
½ cup chopped green onions
¼ cup chopped fresh parsley
2 tablespoons minced garlic
1⅓ cups Italian breadcrumbs
½ cup Parmesan cheese
¼ teaspoon salt
½ teaspoon coarsely ground pepper
¼ teaspoon cayenne pepper
1 teaspoon dried basil
1 teaspoon dried oregano
4 pints oysters, well drained on paper towels

Heat butter and oil in a large skillet. Add onions, parsley and garlic, cooking until tender.

Combine breadcrumbs, cheese, salt, peppers, basil and oregano. Add mixture to skillet and combine well. Remove from heat and add oysters. Stir gently and transfer to large, shallow baking dish. Bake 20 minutes at 425 degrees or until brown. Serve immediately.

ENAMELED
PORCELAIN
SAUCE TUREEN
AND STAND, CA.
1770-80, CHINA;
1985.R.881.A-C
STERLING AND
SILVERGILT
BERRY SPOON,
NARRAGANSETT
PATTERN,
DESIGNED 1884,
GORHAM MFG.
CO.,
PROVIDENCE,
R.I., 1991.76

BAKED CHÈVRE WITH TOMATOES AND NIÇOISE OLIVES

SERVES 12

1 medium onion, chopped
3 tablespoons olive oil
4 cups (about 2½ pounds) peeled, seeded, chopped and drained tomatoes
1½ teaspoons chopped garlic
1 teaspoon salt
freshly ground pepper to taste
¼ cup chicken stock or white wine
8 ounces chèvre (goat cheese), room temperature
1 tablespoon chopped fresh parsley or fresh basil
½ cup Niçoise olives, halved

Sauté onion in olive oil for 2 to 3 minutes. Add tomatoes, garlic and seasoning. Continue cooking 2 to 3 minutes over medium heat. Add stock and simmer, stirring frequently, for 20 to 25 minutes, until all liquid has disappeared.

Mold the chèvre into a 4-inch circle about 1½ inches thick. Place in medium-sized quiche dish or pie plate. Spoon tomatoes all around. Bake at 400 degrees until cheese just starts to melt, about 15 minutes. Scatter parsley or basil and olives on top. Serve with garlic toast.

SAUSAGE CHEESE TARTLETS

YIELDS 5 DOZEN

2 cups cooked sausage, drained on paper towels and crumbled
1½ cups grated sharp Cheddar cheese
1½ cups grated Monterey Jack cheese
1 package (0.4-ounce) ranch-style dressing mix
1 can (2.5-ounce) chopped black olives
½ cup finely chopped red bell pepper
1 package won ton wrappers, cut into quarters
olive oil

For filling, combine sausage, cheeses, dressing mix, olives and bell pepper in large bowl and mix well. (Filling can be prepared a day in advance, covered, and refrigerated. Bring to room temperature before using.)

Lightly rub miniature muffin tins with olive oil. Press won ton wrapper in each cup and lightly brush wrapper with oil. Bake 5 minutes at 350 degrees until golden. Remove wrappers from muffin tins and transfer to baking sheet. (Wrappers can be baked early in the day.) Fill wrappers with sausage mixture. Bake 10 minutes at 350 degrees, or until bubbly and heated through. Serve immediately.

IF YOU PREFER, YOU CAN USE MILD (SOMETIMES CALLED SWEET) ITALIAN SAUSAGE INSTEAD OF HOT SAUSAGE IN THE SAUSAGE CHEESE TARTLETS. MIX WITH MOZZARELLA CHEESE AND TOP WITH A SMALL AMOUNT OF BASIL PESTO (PURCHASED, OR PAGE 147). BAKE AS DIRECTED. THIS FILLING CAN BE USED IN MUSHROOM CAPS AS WELL.

PORTABELLA AND PORCINI TART

SERVES 8 TO 10

CRUST

6 tablespoons unsalted butter, cut into pieces
2 tablespoons vegetable shortening
1¼ cups flour
¼ teaspoon salt
4 tablespoons ice water

FILLING

1 box (⅞-ounce) dried porcini mushrooms
2 tablespoons olive oil
2 tablespoons unsalted butter
1 medium red onion, chopped
½ cup chopped Italian parsley
¼ pound portabella mushrooms, sliced
¾ pound white domestic mushrooms, sliced
1 tablespoon tomato paste
1 cup beef broth, warmed
salt and pepper to taste
3 large eggs, beaten
½ cup Parmesan cheese

For crust, cut butter and shortening into flour and salt until it resembles coarse meal. Add water and mix lightly with a fork. Knead dough, flatten, brush with flour and wrap in plastic wrap. Chill 1 hour. Roll out and place in 10-inch tart pan. Prick shell and chill for 30 minutes. Line with foil and fill with pie weights or dried beans. Bake at 425 degrees for 15 minutes. Remove foil and weights. Bake an additional 5 minutes, or until lightly browned. Cool.

To prepare filling, soak porcini mushrooms in warm water to cover for 30 minutes. Drain, rinse well, chop coarsely, and set aside. Heat oil and butter in saucepan. Add onion and parsley and sauté for 10 minutes. Add all mushrooms and tomato paste, cooking 5 minutes. Pour in broth and season with salt and pepper. Simmer for 30 minutes until most of broth has evaporated. Pour into a bowl and allow to cool. Stir in eggs and Parmesan, blending well. Correct seasoning. Pour into cooled tart shell and bake 30 minutes at 375 degrees. Allow to rest 15 minutes before cutting.

GRILLED BRIE WITH PESTO

SERVES 4 TO 6

1 cup fresh basil leaves, packed
¾ cup fresh shredded Parmesan cheese
   (divided use)
2 cloves garlic
3 tablespoons pine nuts
¼ cup olive oil
2 baguettes, sliced into ¼-inch thick rounds
2 tablespoons chopped sun-dried tomatoes
2 Danish Brie cheeses (4½-ounce)

To make pesto, place basil, ¼ cup Parmesan, garlic, pine nuts and oil in food processor and purée until smooth and thick. Place baguette slices on cookie sheets and spread with pesto, reserving about ¼ cup. Sprinkle with sun-dried tomatoes and remaining Parmesan.

Bake at 400 degrees for 8 minutes, or until crisp and golden brown.

Brush the Brie cheeses on both sides with the reserved pesto and lightly grill on both sides. (If preferred, bake in 400-degree oven for 10 minutes.) The cheese should be warm and soft to the touch. To serve, place warm Brie in center of serving plate and surround with baguette slices.

BRIE IS A FRENCH COW'S MILK CHEESE THAT ORIGINATED IN THE ILE-DE-FRANCE REGION AROUND PARIS. IT IS IVORY TO PALE YELLOW IN COLOR AND COVERED WITH A WHITE RIND. WHEN RIPE, THE CHEESE SHOULD BE CREAMY, NOT RUNNY, AND DELICATE IN FLAVOR. SINCE ROUNDS OF FRENCH BRIE ARE NOT MADE IN SMALL SIZES, THE SMALLER DANISH ROUNDS ARE USED FOR GRILLED BRIE WITH PESTO.

THE ARTFUL TABLE

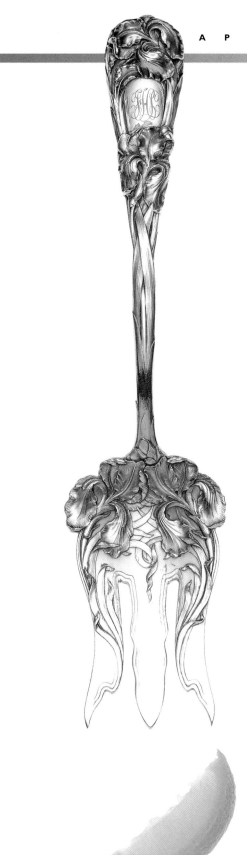

STERLING SILVER
SALAD SERVING
FORK, *NEW ART*
PATTERN,
DESIGNED 1904,
WILLIAM B.
DURGIN, CO.,
NEW HAMPSHIRE,
1993.57.2;
MATCHING
SPOON ON PAGE
3 (TITLE PAGE),
1993.57.1

HERBED BRIE EN CROÛTE

SERVES 6

CHEESE

1 wheel (17.6 ounces) ripe Brie cheese, chilled
⅓ cup minced shallots (about 2 large)
2 tablespoons chopped fresh chives
2 teaspoons dry white vermouth
¼ teaspoon white pepper
½ package (17¼-ounce) frozen puff pastry sheets,
   thawed

GLAZE

1 egg, beaten with 1 teaspoon water to blend

Cut off top rind of cheese and discard.
Combine shallots, chives, vermouth and pepper in a small bowl and mix until blended. Press shallot mixture firmly over top of cheese.

Roll out pastry on lightly floured surface to an 11-inch square. Lay pastry over cheese, folding under to enclose cheese completely. Turn cheese over; press pastry seams together, sealing tightly. Turn cheese right side up and place on baking sheet. Wrap in plastic and refrigerate at least 30 minutes. (Can be prepared to this point 1 day ahead.)

Brush top and sides of pastry with egg glaze. Bake 25 minutes at 400 degrees, until pastry is golden brown. Let stand 30 minutes. Serve with crackers or crusty bread and apple slices.

TRY SUBSTITUTING SUN-DRIED TOMATOES AND BASIL PESTO (PAGE 147) FOR THE HERBS.

SMOKED SALMON CHEESECAKE

SERVES 16 TO 20

CRUST
1 cup grated Parmesan cheese
1 cup breadcrumbs
½ cup (1 stick) melted butter

CHEESECAKE
1 tablespoon olive oil
1 red onion, chopped
1 red bell pepper, chopped
½ green bell pepper, chopped
  (optional, for color)
½ teaspoon salt
¼ teaspoon freshly ground pepper
28 ounces cream cheese, room temperature
4 eggs
1 teaspoon Creole seasoning
½ cup heavy cream
1 cup cubed smoked Gouda cheese
  (about 5 ounces)
1 pound smoked salmon, cut into slivers

To prepare crust, combine Parmesan, breadcrumbs and butter until thoroughly blended. Press mixture into bottom of 10-inch springform pan. Bake at 350 degrees for 8 minutes. (This can be done ahead and set aside.)

Heat oil in medium skillet over high heat. Add onions and bell peppers. Sauté for 2 minutes, stirring and shaking skillet. Stir in salt and pepper and continue cooking for 1 minute. Remove from heat.

Using electric mixer, beat cream cheese with eggs until thick and frothy (about 4 minutes). Add Creole seasoning, cream and vegetables. Beat until thoroughly incorporated and creamy (1 or 2 minutes). Fold in Gouda and salmon and beat 1 more minute. (Salmon and Gouda should still be in easily visible pieces.)

Pour filling over crust in springform pan. Bake at 350 degrees for 1 hour and 15 minutes or until firm. Allow to cool at least 2 hours before removing sides of pan. Serve chilled or at room temperature. (In order to transfer cheesecake from pan bottom to a tray, it must first be refrigerated until firm.)

Cheesecake keeps well in refrigerator and can be made 1 or 2 days before serving. Recipe can be halved and baked in 7-inch springform pan. Check for doneness after 50 minutes.

SERVE AS AN APPETIZER OR AS A LUNCHEON ENTRÉE WITH A SALAD OF MIXED FIELD GREENS.

FOR VARIETY, SUBSTITUTE CRAB OR SHRIMP FOR THE SALMON.

FONDUTA WITH GOAT CHEESE, SPINACH AND SUN-DRIED TOMATOES

A SUMPTUOUS ITALIAN VERSION OF CHEESE FONDUE. SERVES 8.

1 tablespoon minced garlic
4 tablespoons butter
4 tablespoons flour
2 cups half and half
4 ounces goat cheese, crumbled
1 cup grated Quattro Formaggio
  or Provolone cheese
½ cup crumbled Gorgonzola cheese
1 cup spinach chiffonade, packed (see note)
½ cup sun-dried tomatoes, soaked ½ hour in
  hot water to cover, drained and chopped
pepper to taste

Sauté garlic in butter for 2 minutes. Add flour, stir and cook 3 minutes longer, but don't let it color. Heat half and half until hot (do not boil), add to flour and whisk until smooth. Simmer a few minutes longer until slightly thickened. Reduce heat. Add cheeses, continuing to whisk until smooth. (Can be made in advance to this point, then carefully reheated.)

Fold in spinach, sun-dried tomatoes and pepper. Keep warm, but do not allow to boil. Serve with crostini, crackers, bread cubes or vegetables.

NOTE: CHIFFONADE IS THE TECHNIQUE OF TIGHTLY ROLLING LEAFY VEGETABLES OR HERBS, THEN CUTTING THEM CROSSWISE INTO VERY THIN STRIPS USING A SHARP KNIFE. THE LEAVES FORM LONG, THIN SHREDS WHEN THEY ARE UNROLLED.

FONDUTA IS DELICIOUS THINNED A LITTLE AND USED AS A SAUCE FOR BAKED PASTA. CHICKEN CAN BE ADDED TO CREATE A HEARTIER ENTRÉE.

CRAWFISH WITH SHERRIED CREAM

SERVES 10

1 pound cooked crawfish tails, cleaned,
  prepackaged (available frozen in most grocery
  stores)
¾ cup (1½ sticks) butter (divided use)
½ cup chopped fresh parsley
1 bunch green onions, chopped
3 tablespoons flour
1 pint heavy cream (can use half and half, if
  preferred)
3 tablespoons dry sherry
salt and cayenne pepper to taste
½ teaspoon lemon juice

Sauté crawfish tails in 4 tablespoons butter for 5 minutes, to heat through. (Be sure to include all fat packed in bag along with tails.) Set aside.

In remaining butter, sauté parsley and green onions for 3 to 4 minutes. Blend in flour to make a roux, cooking 2 to 3 minutes longer. Gradually add cream, sherry, spices and lemon juice, stirring constantly. When sauce is thickened slightly, add crawfish. Place in chafing dish and serve hot with crackers or melba toast.

CRAWFISH WITH SHERRIED CREAM SERVES 3 TO 4 AS AN ENTRÉE SERVED OVER RICE.

IF YOU PREFER TO SERVE INDIVIDUAL CANAPÉS, YOU CAN DECREASE THE AMOUNT OF CREAM AND SPREAD THE MIXTURE ON MELBA TOAST ROUNDS.

TOMATO TART WITH OLIVES AND CHEESES

A VERSATILE DISH THAT WORKS AS AN APPETIZER, A SAVORY ACCOMPANIMENT TO GRILLED STEAK, OR AS A LUNCHEON ENTRÉE.

SERVES 8

10-inch pastry shell
2 medium tomatoes, sliced thick (about 4 slices each)
1¼ teaspoons salt (divided use)
¼ cup flour
¼ teaspoon freshly ground black pepper
2 tablespoons olive oil
½ cup sliced Calamata olives
¾ cup minced green onions
3 ounces Provolone cheese, thinly sliced
2 eggs slightly beaten
1 cup grated Cheddar cheese
1 cup heavy cream

Prick pie crust with fork and bake at 425 degrees for 12 minutes. Remove from oven and set aside. Reduce oven temperature to 375 degrees.

Sprinkle tomato slices with ½ teaspoon salt and drain on paper towels for 15 minutes, turning once. Mix together the flour, ¾ teaspoon salt and pepper. Dip tomato slices in flour mixture and sauté briefly in olive oil, being careful not to let tomato slices fall apart.

Line pastry shell with olives, onions and Provolone cheese. Top with tomato slices. Combine eggs, Cheddar cheese and cream. Pour over tomatoes.

Bake 45 minutes or until set. Cool 5 minutes before slicing. Serve warm or at room temperature.

FOR A REDUCED-FAT VERSION OF THE TOMATO TART, SUBSTITUTE ½ CUP PASTEURIZED EGG SUBSTITUTE PLUS 1 EGG WHITE FOR THE EGGS, REDUCED-FAT CHEDDAR FOR THE CHEDDAR AND EVAPORATED SKIMMED MILK FOR THE HEAVY CREAM.

STERLING SILVER AND SILVER GILT SALAD SERVING SPOON AND FORK, CA. 1880, GORHAM MFG. CO., PROVIDENCE, RI, 1989.4.1-2

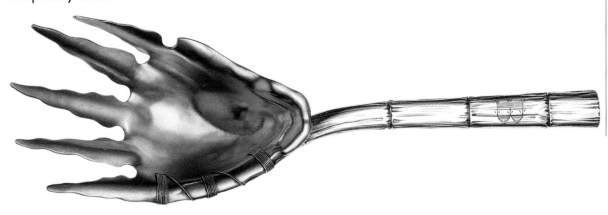

FRESH CORN CAKES

BEAUTIFUL PRESENTATION AS A
FIRST COURSE OR AS A SIDE DISH.
YIELDS ABOUT 28 SMALL CAKES.
(SERVE 2 PER PERSON)

6 medium-sized ears of corn
4½ tablespoons flour
4 large eggs
1 teaspoon salt
¼ teaspoon freshly ground white pepper
½ cup heavy cream
¼ cup (½ stick) melted butter, plus extra butter
  for cooking
sour cream (optional garnish)
caviar (optional garnish)
pico de gallo (optional garnish)

Cut corn off ears with sharp knife. Using back of knife, scrape each ear to extract as much pulp as possible.

Mix all ingredients thoroughly, starting with corn pulp and flour. Grease skillet with small amount of butter. Using about 3 tablespoons batter for each cake, cook over medium-high heat until lightly browned on both sides.

These can be made ahead of time, cooled on a rack, then stacked in overlapping rows on lightly greased cookie sheet. Cover with foil and reheat 5 to 10 minutes in warm oven when ready to serve.

Garnish with sour cream and caviar, or pico de gallo.

THE DELICATE FLAVOR OF THESE CORN CAKES MAKES
THEM AN IDEAL ACCOMPANIMENT TO VEAL CHOPS OR
GRILLED QUAIL OR DOVE.

GLAZED AND SPICED PECANS

STORE THESE IN THE FREEZER FOR
UNEXPECTED GUESTS.
YIELDS 3 CUPS

2 tablespoons butter
3 cups pecan halves
½ cup light brown sugar
1 teaspoon paprika
2 teaspoons chili powder
1 tablespoon ground cumin
3 tablespoons apple cider vinegar
salt to taste

Melt butter in large skillet over medium heat. Add pecans and sauté until lightly browned, about 3 minutes. Add sugar and cook until lightly caramelized. Stir in paprika, chili powder and cumin. Add vinegar and continue cooking until all liquid has evaporated. Season with salt. Spread pecans on cookie sheet and bake at 350 degrees until crisp, about 3 to 5 minutes.

GLAZED PECANS MAKE A PIQUANT ADDITION TO MIXED GREEN SALAD.

INSTEAD OF PECANS, TRY GLAZING ALMONDS, WALNUTS OR HAZELNUTS.

SMOKED CHICKEN WITH RED CHILE MAYONNAISE IN RADICCHIO CUPS

SERVES 10 TO 20

RED CHILE MAYONNAISE
½ to 1 dried red chile, minced
1 large clove garlic, minced
1 teaspoon fresh lime juice
¼ teaspoon ground cumin
¼ teaspoon sugar
¼ teaspoon salt
¾ cup mayonnaise

SMOKED CHICKEN AND RADICCHIO CUPS
1 celery root
2 tablespoons fresh lime juice
2 heads radicchio
2 cups shredded smoked chicken
1 bunch fresh cilantro, for garnish

Fold chile, garlic, lime juice, cumin, sugar and salt into mayonnaise. Stir until well blended. Cover and refrigerate until ready to use.

Peel and shred celery root. Toss with lime juice to prevent discoloration. Cut off root end of radicchio to facilitate separating leaves. Rinse leaves and pat dry. Cut leaves in half or thirds if they are large. Several hours before serving, combine chicken with celery root mixture and Red Chile Mayonnaise. Rinse cilantro and carefully remove leaves; set aside.

At serving time, fill radicchio cups with chicken mixture and garnish each with a cilantro leaf.

TRANSFER-PRINTED PEARLWARE, *TEXIAN CAMPAIGNE WARE*, CA. 1846-52, LION POTTERY & JAMES BEECH & CO., STAFFORDSHIRE, ENGLAND, 1992.B.224.5; PRESSED GLASS SUGAR AND CREAMER, *TEXAS BICENTENNIAL* PATTERN, DESIGNED BY JERRY BYWATERS, 1992.501.1-2; PRESSED GLASS GOBLET, *DEER DOE WITH LILY OF THE VALLEY* PATTERN, U. S., 1992, 404; COMMEMORATIVE SPOON, 1936, U.S.

TEXIAN CAMPAIGNE WARE WAS PROMOTED AS DEPICTING SCENES FROM THE WAR BETWEEN THE U.S. AND MEXICO (1846-48). HOWEVER, THE IMAGES APPEAR TO BE STOCK 19TH-CENTURY MILITARY SCENES. NEVERTHELESS, AMERICAN CONSUMERS FOUND THE WARE APPEALING BECAUSE OF ITS SUPPOSED NATIONALISTIC CHARACTER AND ITS ASSOCIATION WITH THE NEW STATE OF TEXAS.

CHICKEN SATAYS WITH SPICY PEANUT DIPPING SAUCE

YIELDS 32 SATAYS

CHICKEN SATAYS

2 whole skinless boneless chicken breasts

32 bamboo skewers (7-inch), soaked in water to cover for 15 minutes

salt and pepper

¾ cup sweetened flaked coconut

2 teaspoons peeled chopped fresh ginger root

2 teaspoons curry powder

2 tablespoons fresh lime juice

½ cup hot water

SPICY PEANUT DIPPING SAUCE

½ cup peanut butter

2 tablespoons water

4 tablespoons soy sauce

¼ cup dark sesame oil

2 tablespoons sherry

4 teaspoons rice wine vinegar

¼ cup honey

4 cloves garlic, minced

3 teaspoons minced fresh ginger

2 tablespoons hot pepper oil

ENAMELED
PORCELAIN
COMPARTMENTED
SERVICE ON
LACQUER TRAY,
CA. 1790-1810,
CHINA, 1985.R.1033

Cut chicken lengthwise into ½-inch strips; thread onto skewers and season with salt and pepper.

To make marinade, combine coconut, ginger root, curry, lime juice and hot water in blender and mix until smooth. Strain through fine sieve, pressing hard on solids. (Marinade can be made 2 days ahead and stored covered in refrigerator.)

Place chicken in large, non-metallic, shallow dish and pour marinade over, coating well. Marinate chicken, covered and chilled, for 1 to 3 hours. (Do not let chicken marinate longer or meat will break down.)

To make Spicy Peanut Dipping Sauce, combine all ingredients in blender or food processor and purée until mixture is smooth. If necessary, thin with hot water, 1 tablespoon at a time.

Remove chicken from marinade and grill over hot coals about 1½ minutes on each side, or until cooked through. Serve with Spicy Peanut Dipping Sauce.

SPICY PEANUT DIPPING SAUCE IS WONDERFUL WITH RAW VEGETABLES OR EGG ROLLS.

SPICY SPINACH DIP WITH LEMON-CUMIN PITA TOASTS

SERVES 8 TO 10

DIP

2 to 3 tablespoons finely chopped jalapeños

¾ cup chopped green onions

1 package (10-ounce) frozen chopped spinach, thawed and squeezed dry

2 cups chopped tomatoes

8 ounces cream cheese, softened

2 cups (8 ounces) shredded Monterey Jack cheese

⅓ cup half and half

PITA TOASTS

2 teaspoons lemon pepper

2 teaspoons cumin

½ cup softened butter

6 pita bread pockets

To prepare spinach dip, mix all ingredients together and pour into buttered ovenproof dish. (Can be prepared 1 day ahead to this point and refrigerated.) Bake at 400 degrees for 10 to 15 minutes (20 to 25 minutes if mixture has been refrigerated), or until bubbly.

For pita toasts, blend lemon pepper and cumin into softened butter. Separate pita pockets into halves and cut into triangles. Spread each piece with butter mixture. (Can be prepared to this point several hours ahead.) Bake at 350 degrees for 8 to 12 minutes, or until crisp.

FILO PALMIERS WITH MUSHROOM FILLING

YIELDS 4 DOZEN

1 pound mushrooms, minced
3 tablespoons butter
1 tablespoon oil
½ cup minced yellow onion
1 cup minced green onions
¼ teaspoon Tabasco
½ cup sour cream
2 tablespoons minced fresh dill (or 1 tablespoon dried)
½ teaspoon salt
¼ teaspoon pepper
1 package (1-pound) filo pastry, thawed
9 tablespoons butter, melted

Place mushrooms in a dish towel and squeeze out moisture. Heat butter and oil in skillet. Sauté mushrooms and onions until moisture has evaporated, about 15 minutes. Remove from heat and stir in Tabasco, sour cream, dill, salt and pepper. Allow to cool.

Place filo leaves under a damp dish towel to keep moist. (This is the key to keeping the pastry pliable and easier to work with.) Place 1 filo leaf on a sheet of waxed paper and gently brush with melted butter. Place second filo leaf directly over first and brush with butter.

Filo can be tricky to work with until you get the hang of it, but you have plenty of leaves in case you ruin a few. If you have a few tears in the first 2 layers, you can always add a third or fourth layer to strengthen it. Remember to brush each layer with melted butter.

Spread a 1-inch wide strip of mushroom mixture on one of long sides of prepared filo. Roll up jelly-roll fashion, starting with side of strip that mushrooms are on. Place roll, seam-side down, on buttered baking sheet. Repeat process to make a total of 4 rolls, brushing each with butter. (The 4 rolls can be prepared to this point and frozen up to 6 months.) Bake 45 minutes at 350 degrees until crisp and golden. Allow rolls to cool 5 minutes before cutting on an angle into 1-inch slices.

AN ALTERNATE PREPARATION IS TO PLACE A SPOONFUL OF MUSHROOM FILLING IN THE CENTER OF A 3-INCH SQUARE OF 2 OR 3 LAYERS OF FILO. FOLD PASTRY OVER TO FORM A TRIANGLE AND SEAL EDGES BY CRIMPING WITH A FORK. YOU CAN ALSO STACK 2 OR 3 SHEETS OF FILO AND CUT THEM INTO 2½-INCH WIDE STRIPS. PLACE A SPOONFUL OF FILLING AT ONE END AND FOLD UP "FLAG STYLE" TO FORM A TRIANGLE.

SAVORY HORS D'OEUVRE TOASTS

THESE FREEZE BEAUTIFULLY AND ARE WONDERFUL TO KEEP ON HAND. YIELDS 75 TO 80 PIECES

FOR THE TOASTS

2 loaves thin-sliced, firm white bread

Cut 2 circles from each slice of bread (use cookie cutter). Toast bread for about 10 minutes at 350 degrees.

Prepare any of the following toppings. Directions are the same for each one. Combine all ingredients and mix well. Spread prepared mixture on toast rounds. Place on cookie sheet and bake at 350 degrees for 15 minutes, or until heated through. (Canapés can be frozen before baking. Place on cookie sheets until frozen, then transfer to self-sealing freezer bags. Not necessary to thaw before baking; add a few minutes to baking time.)

ONION PARMESAN SPREAD

16 ounces cream cheese, softened
½ cup (1 stick) butter, softened
6 tablespoons mayonnaise
6 green onions, chopped or ½ cup snipped fresh chives
few dashes Tabasco (optional)
¾ cup freshly shredded Parmesan cheese
paprika to dust on top

CHEDDAR PECAN SPREAD

1½ cups grated Cheddar cheese
¾ cup mayonnaise
½ to 1 teaspoon curry powder
½ cup chopped green onions
1 cup chopped pecans, toasted or 1 cup chopped black olives
5 strips crisp bacon, crumbled
few dashes Tabasco (optional)

MUSHROOM CHIVE SPREAD

¾ pound fresh mushrooms, chopped and sautéed in 2 tablespoons butter
salt and pepper
1 teaspoon Worcestershire sauce
¼ teaspoon garlic powder
⅓ cup snipped fresh chives or minced green onion
12 ounces cream cheese
dash Tabasco

STERLING SILVER SERVING SPOON, BIRD'S NEST PATTERN, DESIGNED 1869, GORHAM MFG. CO., PROVIDENCE, RI, 1991.101.10

Long, uncut chives are wonderful for creating garnishes. Use them to tie bows around bundles of green beans or julienned vegetables. Form them into a variety of shapes such as circles or triangles, securing the shape by inserting the tip into the cut end. If chives seem too stiff, blanch them in boiling water for 10 seconds to make them more flexible.

Picadillo Sarita

PERFECT FOR A SUPER BOWL
PARTY. SERVES 20

2 pounds ground round (can use half ground pork)
1 cup chopped onion
2 teaspoons minced garlic
2 teaspoons Cajun seasoning
2 teaspoons garlic pepper
1 can (10-ounce) Rotel tomatoes with chilies, undrained
1 cup raisins
1 cup sliced mushrooms
1 cup sliced black olives
1 cup chopped roasted red peppers
1 apple, chopped
¾ pound Mexican-style Velveeta cheese, diced
2 teaspoons cinnamon
2 teaspoons sugar
2 teaspoons ground coriander
2 teaspoons chili powder
2 teaspoons ground cumin
1 cup slivered almonds, toasted

Brown meat with onion, garlic, Cajun seasoning and pepper. Line a colander with paper towels and pour meat mixture in to drain off excess grease. Combine tomatoes, raisins, mushrooms, olives, roasted red peppers, apple and cheese, blending well. Add to meat. Combine cinnamon, sugar, coriander, chili powder and cumin; add to meat mixture. Stir to blend completely.

Pour mixture into large casserole. Bake, uncovered, at 250 degrees for 2 hours. Stir twice during baking. Remove from oven and stir in almonds. Serve with sturdy tortilla chips or soft flour tortillas.

TO MAKE **PICANTE SAUCE** FOR SOUTHWESTERN APPETIZERS, COMBINE 5 LARGE, COARSELY CHOPPED ONIONS, 3 CANS (14 1/2-OUNCE) TOMATOES, 3 CANS (14 1/2-OUNCE) STEWED TOMATOES AND 5 OR 6 CHOPPED JALAPEÑOS. PURÉE IN A FOOD PROCESSOR IN SMALL BATCHES USING A PULSING ACTION (MIXTURE SHOULD NOT BE SMOOTH).

POUR INTO A LARGE POT AND ADD 1/2 TEASPOON CAYENNE, 4 TO 5 TABLESPOONS SALT, 1 TEASPOON GARLIC SALT, 1 1/4 CUPS VINEGAR, 3 TABLESPOONS CORNSTARCH DISSOLVED IN A SMALL AMOUNT OF WATER, AND 1 CAN STEWED TOMATOES (NOT PURÉED).

BRING TO A BOIL OVER MEDIUM HEAT, STIRRING FREQUENTLY. REDUCE HEAT AND SIMMER 10 MINUTES. REMOVE FROM HEAT AND LADLE INTO HOT STERILIZED JARS. PUT LIDS ON LOOSELY AND ALLOW TO COOL. TIGHTEN LIDS BEFORE STORING IN THE REFRIGERATOR. KEEPS SEVERAL MONTHS. YIELDS 5 QUARTS.

BLACK BEAN SALSA

YIELDS 8 CUPS

3 cans (16-ounce) black beans, rinsed and drained
1 can (8-ounce) white shoepeg corn, drained
1 can (8-ounce) yellow corn, drained
1 red bell pepper, diced
1 green or yellow bell pepper, diced
2 large tomatoes, seeded and chopped
3 cans (10-ounce) Rotel tomatoes with green chilies, drained
1 cup jalapeños, seeded and chopped
1/2 red onion, finely chopped
1/2 large bunch cilantro, chopped
1/4 cup red wine vinegar
juice of 1 lemon
2 large cloves garlic, finely chopped
1/8 teaspoon cayenne pepper, or to taste
1/8 teaspoon chili powder, or to taste
1/8 teaspoon cumin, or to taste
1/4 teaspoon salt, or to taste

Combine all ingredients and refrigerate in non-metallic container. This will keep several weeks; however, if you are planning to keep this more than 3 days, it would be best to add the tomatoes the day of serving. Serve with tortilla chips, as a salad, or as a relish to accompany pork or beef.

SILVER AND IVORY TEA SET, CA. 1960, ANTONIO PINEDA, TAXCO, MEXICO, 1994.229.1-3

PINEDA'S TEA SET, REMINISCENT OF THE WORKS OF THE ITALIAN FUTURIST SCULPTOR UMBERTO BOCCIONI, IS DESIGNED TO STAND ON ITS END OR FRONT IN ORDER TO BE TALL OR LOW ACCORDING TO THE WISH OF ITS OWNER.

SOUTHWESTERN PIZZA

YIELDS ONE 12- TO 14-INCH PIZZA
(CUT INTO 2½-INCH SQUARES
FOR APPETIZER)

CRUST
3 to 3½ cups flour (divided use)
¾ teaspoon salt
1 tablespoon dried yeast
2 tablespoons sugar
1 cup hot water
1 tablespoon olive oil
cornmeal for dusting

TOPPINGS
1 cup Texas Black Beans (page 172)
1 cup shredded Monterey Jack cheese
1 avocado, sliced
½ pound Chorizo sausage, cooked and drained
  (optional)
salsa to taste

Oil a 2-quart bowl liberally with olive oil and set aside. Place 2 cups flour, salt, yeast and sugar in food processor and mix until combined. With motor running, add hot water (will not kill yeast) and process just until dough forms. (Dough will be very gooey at this point.) Keep motor running and add 1 cup flour. Scrape sides and add olive oil. Add more flour if dough is too sticky to handle easily (must not be dry though). Place dough in prepared bowl and set aside to rise in warm place, about 1 hour, until doubled in bulk.

When dough has risen, punch down and push against sides of bowl letting it hang over rim. (This will do most of shaping.) Gently remove dough and place on cornmeal-dusted pizza pan or pizza peel.

Finish with desired toppings. Spread beans over dough, sprinkle with cheese, and top with avocado. After baking, drizzle with salsa.

Bake 10 minutes at 425 degrees or until lightly browned. If using pizza stone, preheat stone for 30 minutes at 425 degrees. Slide pizza off peel onto hot stone and bake 10 minutes. (Be sure cornmeal coating is heavy enough to allow pizza to slide onto stone.)

THE DOUGH FOR SOUTHWESTERN PIZZA CRUST MAKES A DELICIOUS BREAD. BRUSH DOUGH WITH ROSEMARY-FLAVORED OLIVE OIL AND SPRINKLE WITH SHREDDED PARMESAN BEFORE BAKING. SERVE AS A BREAD WITH SOUP OR SALAD.

ALTERNATIVE TOPPINGS:
~SMOKED CHICKEN, GOAT CHEESE, SUN-DRIED TOMATOES AND MOZZARELLA.
~GRILLED EGGPLANT, RED BELL PEPPER, GARLIC AND FETA CHEESE.
~MOZZARELLA, SUN-DRIED TOMATOES, CALAMATA OLIVES AND MUSHROOMS. DRIZZLE WITH BASIL PESTO.
~ARTICHOKE HEARTS, GOAT CHEESE AND COOKED SWEET ITALIAN SAUSAGE.
~SPINACH, GORGONZOLA, MOZZARELLA AND PINE NUTS.

Soups, Chilis and Stocks

Mushroom Leek Soup with Port Wine

Serves 6

4 tablespoons butter
2 pounds mushrooms, sliced
2 cups chopped leeks
4 cups chicken stock
1 medium potato, peeled and diced
¼ cup port wine
salt and pepper to taste
½ to 1 cup heavy cream (optional)

Melt butter in large saucepan and sauté mushrooms and leeks until leeks are translucent. Remove one-fourth of mixture and set aside to add to soup later. Add stock and potatoes to mushroom mixture in saucepan and bring to a boil. Reduce heat and simmer until potatoes are tender. Cool slightly, then purée in food processor until smooth.

Return purée to pan, cooking over low heat. Add port, reserved mushroom mixture, and season with salt and pepper. If desired, add cream at this point. If soup seems too thick, it can be thinned with additional chicken stock.

Vodka Fire and Ice Soup

A perfect opener to any brunch. Serves 6

6 medium tomatoes, peeled, seeded and chopped
1 small green chile, roasted, peeled and minced
½ cucumber, peeled, seeded and chopped
1 tablespoon red wine vinegar
1 tablespoon fresh marjoram
 (or ½ teaspoon dried)
juice of ½ lemon
1 cup sour cream
¼ cup vodka
salt and freshly ground pepper to taste

Combine tomatoes, green chile, cucumber, vinegar, marjoram and lemon juice in blender or food processor and purée until smooth. Stir in sour cream, vodka, salt and pepper. Chill thoroughly before serving.

SOUR CREAM CAN BE REPLACED WITH REDUCED-FAT SOUR CREAM OR YOGURT. DILL WEED AND GARLIC CAN BE USED IN PLACE OF MARJORAM.

STERLING SILVER
NUT SPOON, *LOTUS*
PATTERN, CA. 1865,
GORHAM MFG. CO.,
PROVIDENCE, RI,
1991.101.18
GLASS GOBLET,
WINE GLASS AND
SHERRY, *EMBASSY*
PATTERN, DESIGNED
1939 BY WALTER D.
TEAGUE AND
EDWIN W. FUERST,
LIBBEY GLASS CO.,
1989.18.1-3

CHICKEN DIJON BISQUE WITH TARRAGON AND LEMON

SERVES 8

1½ medium potatoes, peeled and chopped
2 cups chicken stock
½ cup (1 stick) butter or margarine (divided use)
1½ leeks (white part only), cleaned and chopped
2 green onions, chopped
2 stalks celery, chopped
¾ pound boneless chicken, cut into 1-inch cubes
5 tablespoons flour
2 cups half and half
3 cups milk
¾ cup white wine
¼ cup chopped fresh parsley
2 teaspoons fresh tarragon
   (or 1 teaspoon dried)
2 tablespoons Dijon mustard
1 tablespoon lemon juice
salt and pepper to taste

Place potatoes and stock in large stockpot and boil until potatoes are tender. In separate pan, combine 1½ tablespoons butter, leeks, green onions and celery. Sauté until tender and add to potatoes. Add 1½ tablespoons butter to same pan and sauté chicken about 5 minutes, or until cooked. Add to potato mixture.

Combine flour and remaining 5 tablespoons butter in saucepan. Cook, stirring frequently, about 5 minutes to form a roux (a base of fat and flour used to thicken sauces). When done, mixture will resemble coarse, wet sand.

Slowly add half and half, stirring constantly and allowing mixture to thicken before each addition. Add milk using same process.

Slowly add milk mixture and wine to stockpot. Season with parsley, tarragon, mustard, lemon juice, salt and pepper. Simmer about 10 minutes.

CURRIED ZUCCHINI SOUP WITH PARMESAN

SERVES 6 TO 8

5 cups chicken stock
3 pounds zucchini, chopped
1 large carrot, peeled and diced
1 large onion, chopped
4 slices bacon, chopped
1 teaspoon salt
freshly ground pepper to taste
1 teaspoon dried basil
1 teaspoon curry powder, or to taste
chopped fresh parsley (garnish)
freshly shredded Parmesan cheese (garnish)

Bring chicken stock to boil in stockpot. Add zucchini, carrot, onion, bacon, salt, pepper, basil and curry. Simmer for 30 minutes, or until vegetables are tender. Allow to cool slightly, then blend to coarse purée in food processor. (Soup can be prepared to this point and refrigerated several days or frozen.) Reheat to serve. Garnish with parsley and Parmesan cheese.

SOUTHWESTERN CORN CHOWDER WITH ROASTED POBLANOS

SERVES 4 TO 6

2 tablespoons butter
1 large onion, chopped
2 to 3 cloves garlic, minced
2 tablespoons flour
1 can (15-ounce) whole kernel corn, undrained
1⅓ cups chicken stock
¼ cup chopped fresh parsley
1 can (15-ounce) creamed corn
2 cups half and half
1 teaspoon salt
½ teaspoon freshly ground pepper
¼ teaspoon dried oregano
2 poblano peppers, roasted (see note) and finely chopped
1 jalapeño pepper, roasted and finely chopped (optional)

CONDIMENTS
½ cup shredded Cheddar cheese
½ cup shredded Jack cheese
1 cup peeled, seeded and diced tomatoes
1 avocado, diced
1 cooked chicken breast, cut in julienne strips
6 slices cooked bacon, crumbled
fried tortilla strips

Melt butter in large saucepan and sauté onions and garlic until soft, 3 to 5 minutes. Blend in flour; cook until bubbly, stirring frequently, about 2 minutes. Remove from heat. Mix in whole kernel corn, stock and parsley. Pour mixture into blender or food processor and process until just blended (mixture should not be smooth). Return mixture to pan. Add creamed corn, half and half, salt, pepper and oregano. Stir to combine and simmer for 5 minutes. Add peppers and continue simmering over low heat an additional 5 minutes. Ladle into bowls and top with condiments of choice.

NOTE: TO ROAST PEPPERS, SPEAR THEM ON A LONG-HANDLED FORK AND CHAR OVER AN OPEN FLAME, TURNING PEPPERS FOR 2 TO 3 MINUTES UNTIL SKINS ARE BLACKENED. AN ALTERNATE METHOD IS TO HALVE PEPPERS LENGTHWISE, REMOVING SEEDS AND RIBS, AND PLACE THEM SKIN SIDE UP ON A BROILER PAN. PLACE PAN 3 TO 4 INCHES FROM HEAT AND BROIL UNTIL SKINS ARE BLACKENED. TRANSFER PEPPERS TO A PLASTIC BAG, SEAL TIGHTLY, AND LET THEM STEAM FOR ABOUT 15 MINUTES, OR UNTIL THEY ARE COOL ENOUGH TO HANDLE. REMOVE FROM BAGS AND SLIP OFF CHARRED SKINS. ROASTED PEPPERS CAN BE PLACED IN A CONTAINER, COVERED WITH OLIVE OIL, AND STORED IN THE REFRIGERATOR FOR 1 WEEK.

BLACK BEAN SOUP WITH SHERRY AND THREE SAUSAGES

SERVES 12 TO 16

2 pounds dried black beans
½ cup olive oil (divided use)
3 cups diced yellow onions
10 cloves garlic, minced
1 meaty ham bone
6 quarts water
1½ tablespoons ground cumin
2 tablespoons dried oregano
3 bay leaves
1 tablespoon coarse salt
1 tablespoon freshly ground pepper
pinch cayenne pepper
8 tablespoons chopped fresh parsley (divided use)
2 pounds hot garlic sausage
6 sweet Italian sausage links, cut in ½-inch slices
1 pound bratwurst, cut in ½-inch slices
2 large red bell peppers, diced
⅓ cup dry sherry
2 tablespoons brown sugar
2 tablespoons lemon juice

Cover beans with water and soak over night. Heat ¼ cup olive oil in large stockpot. Add onions and garlic and sauté 10 minutes, or until very soft. Drain and rinse beans and add to pot along with ham bone and water. Stir in cumin, oregano, bay leaves, salt, pepper, cayenne and 3 tablespoons parsley. Bring to boil; reduce heat and simmer 2 hours. Skim foam and stir occasionally.

Heat 2 tablespoons olive oil in separate pan, add garlic sausage and sauté until browned. Remove from heat and purée in food processor. Set aside. Add remaining 2 tablespoons olive oil to same pan and brown Italian sausage and bratwurst. Add to other sausage.

Remove ham bone from pot. Cut meat from bone, dice, and add to sausage. Purée bean mixture in food processor until smooth. Return to pot and add meat from ham bone, sausages and red pepper. Cook 30 minutes. Stir in sherry, sugar and lemon juice and cook another 30 minutes. Add remaining parsley and serve. Garnish with dollop of sour cream, if desired.

FOR A HEARTY WINTER SUPPER, SERVE BLACK BEAN SOUP OVER RICE, ACCOMPANIED BY A GREEN SALAD AND CRUSTY FRENCH BREAD. ADD TO THE ENJOYMENT WITH A GOOD BOTTLE OF MERLOT.

CHILLED SENEGALESE SOUP

SERVES 6

2 medium onions,
  finely chopped
2 stalks celery, finely
  chopped
2 apples, peeled, cored and
  chopped
2 tablespoons butter
2 tablespoons curry powder
¼ cup flour
4 cups chicken stock
salt and cayenne pepper to taste
¾ cup finely chopped cooked
  chicken breast
2 cups half and half
avocado slices and lime slices (garnish)

Sauté onions, celery and apples in butter until tender, but not brown. Add curry and flour; cook, stirring frequently, for 4 minutes. Gradually stir in stock, cooking until smooth and thickened. Add salt, cayenne and chicken. Cool, then refrigerate until thoroughly chilled. Transfer mixture to food processor and purée coarsely. Stir in half and half and adjust seasonings.

Serve chilled, garnished with avocado and lime slices.

Wild Rice Soup with Asparagus

SERVES 8 TO 10

½ cup wild rice
1½ cups water
4 tablespoons butter
1 medium onion, chopped
1 clove garlic, minced
2 carrots, peeled and finely chopped
6 spears asparagus, finely chopped
½ cup flour
5 cups chicken stock
½ teaspoon thyme
1 bay leaf
¼ teaspoon nutmeg
2 tablespoons minced chives
2 tablespoons minced parsley
salt and pepper to taste
2 cups half and half
2 cups milk

Combine wild rice and water in covered pan and cook until done. Set aside.

Melt butter in saucepan. Add onion and garlic and sauté for 1 minute. Add carrots and asparagus and cook until tender. Blend in flour; cook over low heat, stirring frequently, about 2 minutes. Slowly pour in chicken stock, blending with wire whisk until smooth. Add thyme, bay leaf, nutmeg, chives, parsley, salt and pepper. Simmer 20 minutes, then add cream and milk mixing well. Remove bay leaf and heat through to serve.

Spicy Thai Lobster Soup

SERVES 4 TO 6

1 tablespoon freshly grated ginger
½ teaspoon cayenne pepper
1 tablespoon peanut oil
5 cups chicken broth
1 tablespoon coarsely grated lime rind
⅓ cup long-grain rice, uncooked
1 cup unsweetened coconut milk
6 large fresh mushrooms, sliced
½ cup chopped onion
1 tablespoon chopped fresh cilantro
2 fresh lobster tails, meat removed from shells and sliced
2 tablespoons fresh lime juice
chopped green onion (garnish)
sprigs of cilantro (garnish)

Combine ginger and cayenne with peanut oil in large saucepan and cook 1 minute over medium heat. Add broth and lime rind. Bring to a boil and stir in rice. Cover, reduce heat, and simmer 15 to 20 minutes. Add coconut milk, mushrooms, onion and cilantro. Cook 5 minutes, stirring occasionally. Add lobster and cook 3 to 5 minutes. Remove from heat and stir in lime juice. Serve hot with green onion or cilantro garnish.

TRY THIS SOUP WITH 1 POUND OF CRABMEAT OR SHRIMP IN PLACE OF LOBSTER.

CANTONESE CHICKEN SOUP WITH CELLOPHANE NOODLES

SERVES 8

6 cups chicken stock
¾ pound cooked chicken
1 tablespoon butter
¾ cup chopped green onions
½ cup chopped celery
½ cup chopped green bell pepper
½ cup sliced mushrooms
1 package (4-ounce) cellophane noodles
½ cup bean sprouts
¾ cup spinach, torn into small pieces
½ cup shredded Chinese cabbage
1 can (8-ounce) sliced water chestnuts
1 tablespoon soy sauce
1 tablespoon lemon juice
salt and pepper to taste

GARNISH

wonton skins, cut into strips and fried crisp

Bring chicken stock to boil in large stockpot. Reduce heat to simmer and add chicken.

Heat butter in medium skillet. Add green onions, celery and bell pepper and sauté until just tender. Add mushrooms and sauté 2 more minutes. Transfer vegetables to stockpot.

Break noodles into pieces and add to stockpot along with sprouts, spinach, cabbage and water chestnuts. Season with soy sauce, lemon juice, salt and pepper. Simmer for 5 minutes, or until cabbage is tender. Serve hot soup garnished with wonton strips.

ENAMELED
PORCELAIN
PLATE, *PARASOL
LADIES*
PATTERN,
CA. 1736-38,
CHINA,
1985.R.1080.2

FOR AN UNUSUAL AND DRAMATIC PRESENTATION, TRY SERVING "BLACK AND WHITE CHILI." SIMULTANEOUSLY LADLE EQUAL PARTS OF BLACK BEAN CHILI AND WHITE BEAN CHILI INTO LARGE, FLAT-RIMMED SOUP PLATES, POURING ONE CHILI DOWN ONE SIDE OF THE BOWL AND THE OTHER DOWN THE OPPOSITE SIDE OF THE BOWL. THE CHILIS WILL BE DIVIDED DOWN THE MIDDLE WITHOUT COMBINING. SPRINKLE GARNISHES OVER TOP. THIS "RAINBOW" PRESENTATION CAN BE USED WITH OTHER SOUPS AS WELL. THE SOUPS MUST HAVE COMPLEMENTARY FLAVORS AND BE OF SIMILAR CONSISTENCY SO THEY DON'T MIX IN THE CENTER.

BLACK BEAN CHILI

SERVES 8

⅓ cup olive oil
1½ pounds boneless sirloin, cut into ½-inch cubes
½ pound boneless sirloin, ground
2 cups chopped yellow onion
2 tablespoons minced garlic
2 fresh jalapeños, seeded and minced (or 6 tablespoons minced, bottled jalapeño slices)
⅓ cup masa harina (corn tortilla flour mix)
2 tablespoons chili powder
½ teaspoon cayenne pepper
½ teaspoon ground cumin
½ teaspoon freshly ground pepper
salt to taste
2 cans (14½-ounce) beef broth
3 cans (15-ounce) black beans, rinsed and drained
mild Cheddar cheese, grated (garnish)
red onion, minced (garnish)

Heat oil in heavy kettle over moderately high heat until very hot, but not smoking. Add cubed sirloin and brown; remove to a bowl with a slotted spoon. Repeat process with ground sirloin.

Add onion, garlic and jalapeños to kettle. Cook over moderate heat, stirring, until onion is softened. Add masa harina, chili powder, cayenne, cumin, pepper and salt. Cook mixture, stirring, for 5 minutes.

Add broth and reserved sirloin. Simmer, uncovered, for 45 minutes, stirring occasionally, until meat is tender. Stir in beans and simmer for 15 minutes. Serve chili garnished with cheese and red onion.

WHITE BEAN CHILI

SERVES 8 TO 10

¼ cup olive oil

1 cup chopped onion

2 tablespoons minced garlic

1 tablespoon ground cumin

1 pound ground turkey

2 pounds skinless boneless turkey breast, cut
   into ½-inch cubes

1 cup pearl barley

2 cans (16-ounce) chick-peas, drained and rinsed

2 to 3 tablespoons minced bottled jalapeño slices
   (see note)

8 cups chicken broth

1 teaspoon dried marjoram

½ teaspoon dried savory, crumbled

⅓ cup masa harina (corn tortilla flour mix)

salt to taste

½ teaspoon pepper

3 cups (¾ pound) coarsely grated
   Monterey Jack cheese

½ cup thinly sliced green onions

Heat oil in large kettle over moderately low heat. Sauté onion and garlic until soft. Add cumin and cook for 5 minutes while stirring. Raise heat to moderate; add ground and cubed turkey. Cook, continuing to stir, until turkey is no longer pink.

Add barley, chick peas, jalapeños, broth, marjoram and savory. Simmer, covered, for 45 minutes, stirring occasionally. Add masa harina and simmer, uncovered, for 15 minutes, stirring frequently. Season with salt and pepper.

To serve, ladle into heated bowls, and top with cheese and green onions.

NOTE: IF YOU ARE PLANNING TO SERVE WHITE BEAN CHILI ALONE (NOT AS A "RAINBOW" PRESENTATION WITH THE BLACK BEAN CHILI), YOU MAY WANT TO INCREASE THE AMOUNT OF JALAPEÑOS. THIS CHILI MAY BE MILD ON ITS OWN, BUT IT IS THE PERFECT COMPLEMENT TO THE SPICIER BLACK BEAN CHILI WHEN THE TWO ARE SERVED TOGETHER.

CASCADILLA

SERVES 4 TO 6

1 clove garlic, minced

1 cucumber, peeled, seeded and finely chopped

1 green onion, minced

½ teaspoon dried dill

4 cups tomato juice

1 cup plain yogurt

1 small green bell pepper, minced

salt and pepper to taste

Thoroughly combine all ingredients and chill several hours. Serve as first course for a light summer luncheon or supper.

CASCADILLA IS A DELICIOUS LOW-CALORIE SOUP TO KEEP IN THE REFRIGERATOR.

ALEXANDER CALDER'S FAVORITE SOUPE AU PISTOU

ALEXANDER CALDER OFTEN PREPARED THIS SOUP FOR FRIENDS WHEN HE LIVED IN FRANCE.

SERVES 12 TO 16

SOUP
2 cups diced carrots
2 cups diced potatoes
2 cups diced leeks or onions
3 quarts water
2 teaspoons salt
2 cups diced green beans (can use frozen)
2 cups canned navy beans or white beans
⅓ cup broken spaghetti
1 slice stale white bread, torn into pieces
1 teaspoon freshly ground pepper
1 pinch saffron

PISTOU
8 cloves garlic
12 tablespoons tomato paste
½ cup fresh basil, packed
1 cup grated Parmesan cheese
6 tablespoons olive oil

Combine carrots, potatoes, leeks, water and salt in large pot and bring to boil. Reduce heat and simmer for 40 minutes. Add beans, spaghetti, bread, pepper and saffron; simmer 20 minutes.

To prepare pistou, combine garlic, tomato paste, basil and Parmesan in food processor. With motor running, slowly add oil and process until a smooth paste is formed.

Immediately before serving, stir pistou into soup.

SHERRIED BRIE SOUP

SERVES 4

1 bunch green onions, chopped
4 tablespoons minced shallots
1½ cups sliced fresh mushrooms
2 tablespoons butter
6 tablespoons sherry (divided use)
3 cups chicken stock
2 tablespoons corn starch
2 cups (1 pint) heavy cream
8 ounces Brie cheese (divided use)
salt and pepper to taste
4 large croutons (½-inch thick slices of French baguette)

Combine onions, shallots, mushrooms and butter in saucepan and sauté until tender. Add 3 tablespoons sherry and stock; simmer 10 minutes. Dissolve cornstarch in remaining 3 tablespoons sherry and add to stock mixture along with heavy cream. Simmer until thickened. Add 4 ounces Brie and stir until melted. Season with salt and pepper.

Place remaining 4 ounces Brie on croutons and melt under broiler. To serve, ladle hot soup into bowls and top each with Brie crouton.

VEAL STOCK

YIELDS 6 QUARTS

4 to 5 pounds veal bones
4 medium onions, coarsely chopped
3 carrots, chopped
6 quarts water
2 tablespoons cracked pepper
1 handful fresh parsley
1 teaspoon dried thyme
2 bay leaves
3 to 4 whole cloves
1 handful celery leaves
4 cloves garlic
12 ounces tomato paste
½ cup (1 stick) butter
½ cup flour
1½ tablespoons salt

Place veal bones in roasting pan and layer onions and carrots on top. Roast uncovered, stirring occasionally, in 350-degree oven for 1 hour, or until bones are browned.

Transfer bones and vegetables to 10-quart stock pot, leaving any rendered fat in roasting pan. Add water and season with pepper and a bouquet garni made of parsley, thyme, bay leaves, cloves, celery leaves and garlic (see note). Stir in tomato paste.

Bring to a boil; reduce heat and simmer, uncovered, all day. Add hot water periodically to maintain original water level. Allow to cool, then refrigerate overnight.

Skim off fat and return stock to a boil. Keep stock simmering on stove.

Make a roux in another large pan by melting butter and blending in flour. Cook slowly for 10 to 15 minutes, or until mixture is well browned. Strain hot stock into roux and season with salt. Cook and stir until mixture is thoroughly blended, about 10 minutes. Cool, then freeze in 1 cup containers to be used as needed.

NOTE: TO MAKE A BOUQUET GARNI, PLACE SEASONINGS ON A SMALL SQUARE OF DOUBLE-LAYERED CHEESECLOTH. PULL EDGES TOGETHER TO FORM A SACK AND TIE TIGHTLY WITH STRING. WHEN COOKING IS COMPLETED, IT CAN EASILY BE LIFTED OUT OF THE POT. YOU CAN USE ANY BLEND OF SPICES OR HERBS, FRESH OR DRIED, TO CREATE YOUR OWN BOUQUET GARNI.

STERLING SILVER AND SILVER GILT SALAD SERVING SPOON, CA. 1866-73, ATTRIBUTED TO J. R. WENDT & CO., NY, 1992.7.11.2

STERLING
SILVER,
SILVERGILT,
AND WOOD
SALAD
SERVING
SPOON, CA.
1880-85,
WHITING
MGF. CO., NY,
1990.148.B.

VEGETABLE STOCK

YIELDS 1 ½ QUARTS

2 leeks (white part only), chopped
3 celery ribs, chopped
4 carrots, peeled and chopped
2 onions, peeled and chopped
1 to 2 bulbs fennel, chopped
1 to 2 bulbs celery root, peeled and chopped
2 turnips, peeled and chopped
2 parsnips, peeled and chopped
2 rutabagas, peeled and chopped
3 tomatoes, quartered
1 white potato, quartered
4 quarts water
2 bay leaves
1 bunch parsley, stems only
½ bunch fresh thyme
1 tablespoon black peppercorns
2 tablespoons whole coriander seeds

Place vegetables in a stockpot. Cover with water and bring to a boil. Reduce heat to a simmer and skim off any foam that rises to the top. Add herbs and spices; simmer, uncovered, for 1½ hours until reduced by half.

Strain through a double thickness of dampened cheesecloth, pressing lightly on the vegetables with the back of a spoon.

KEEP THIS SALT-FREE AND MEATLESS BASE ON HAND FOR QUICK AND FLAVORFUL SOUPS, STEWS AND SAUCES.

TORTILLA SOUP WITH GRILLED CHICKEN

SERVES 6 TO 8

SOUP

6 corn tortillas, cut in strips
6 tablespoons oil (divided use)
2 onions, chopped
6 cloves garlic, minced
1 can (10-ounce) Rotel tomatoes
1 can (4-ounce) chopped green chilies
2 quarts chicken broth
2 bay leaves
1 tablespoon ground cumin
1 tablespoon chili powder
1 teaspoon white pepper
1 teaspoon salt
½ teaspoon cayenne pepper
½ teaspoon oregano

CONDIMENTS

6 corn tortillas, cut in strips and fried
grilled chicken
grated Cheddar cheese
chopped tomatoes
sliced avocado

Fry tortilla strips in 4 tablespoons oil. (Fry tortilla strips for both soup and condiments at same time, reserving 6 tortillas for condiments.)

In remaining 2 tablespoons oil, sauté onions and garlic until tender. Add tomatoes, chilies, broth, half the fried tortilla strips and all seasonings. Simmer to blend flavors.

To serve, ladle into individual bowls and sprinkle condiments on top.

ACORN SQUASH BISQUE

SERVES 4 TO 6

1 cup diced onions
¼ cup diced carrots
3 tablespoons butter
2 medium potatoes, peeled and cubed
2 acorn squash, peeled, seeds and pith removed, and cubed
4 cups chicken broth
½ cup milk
½ cup heavy cream
cayenne pepper to taste
salt and pepper to taste

Sauté onions and carrots in butter until onions are tender. Add potatoes, squash and broth, simmering until tender. Cool slightly, then purée in food processor until smooth. Return to pan and add milk, cream, cayenne, salt and pepper. Reheat to serve.

FOR **PUMPKIN BISQUE,** USE 2 CUPS FRESH PUMPKIN (OR ONE 16-OUNCE CAN) INSTEAD OF SQUASH, DELETE CAYENNE AND ADD ½ TEASPOON CURRY AND ¼ TEASPOON NUTMEG.

SUMMER SQUASH SOUP
WITH BASIL CREAM

SERVES 4

4 tablespoons butter
I cup chopped leeks, white part only
I to 1¼ pounds small yellow squash, sliced
I teaspoon chopped garlic
5 cups chicken stock
I cup loosely packed basil leaves
I cup heavy cream
salt and freshly ground black pepper to taste

Melt butter in saucepan and add leeks, stirring until softened, about 3 or 4 minutes. Add squash slices and cook 1 minute longer. Stir in garlic and chicken stock. Simmer mixture, uncovered, 25 minutes or until vegetables are tender.

Chop basil leaves in food processor. With machine running, pour cream through feed tube. Process about 15 seconds until basil leaves are finely minced. (Be careful not to over process or cream will turn into butter.) Set cream aside in separate dish.

When soup has finished cooking, transfer to food processor and purée. Return soup to pan and whisk in basil cream. Season with salt and pepper.

Some herbs, like basil, lose much of their flavor and aroma when cooked for more than about 15 minutes. Always taste soups at the end of cooking time and, if necessary, stir in 1 or 2 tablespoons chopped fresh herbs before serving.

B R E A D S

WALNUT DATE LOAVES

YIELDS 3 SMALL LOAVES

1 pound walnut or pecan halves
1 pound pitted whole dates
½ pound Brazil nuts
¾ cup flour
½ teaspoon baking powder
½ teaspoon salt
¾ cup sugar
3 eggs, beaten
½ teaspoon vanilla

Combine nuts and dates in large bowl. Sift flour, baking powder and salt together and add to nuts. Add sugar, eggs and vanilla. Mix well with hands. Grease and flour 3 small loaf pans (each 7½ x 3½ inches). Divide batter among pans, packing well to avoid air pockets.

Bake at 325 degrees for 50 minutes (longer if still wet when tested with a toothpick). Cool slightly. Loosen around edges and remove to racks. Wrap in plastic wrap and heavy foil when cool.

WALNUT DATE LOAVES FREEZE WELL. A GIFT OF THESE LOAVES WILL WIN RAVE REVIEWS FROM FRIENDS.

PUMPKIN BREAD WITH RAISINS AND DATES

A DELICIOUS, MOIST BREAD THAT CAN BE MADE IN QUANTITY FOR HOLIDAY GIVING. YIELDS 6 LOAVES

8 eggs
4 cups sugar
2 cups oil
2 cans (16-ounce) pumpkin
1 tablespoon vanilla
4 cups sifted flour
4 teaspoons baking soda
2 tablespoons pumpkin pie spice
1½ teaspoons salt
1½ cups chopped pecans
1½ cups golden raisins
1½ cups chopped dates

CREAM CHEESE ICING (OPTIONAL)
8 ounces cream cheese, softened
1 cup (2 sticks) butter, softened
2 pounds powdered sugar, sifted
1 cup chopped raisins
1 cup chopped pecans
1 cup shredded coconut
2 teaspoons vanilla

Beat eggs and sugar together until slightly thickened. Add oil, pumpkin and vanilla, beating thoroughly. Combine flour, baking soda, spice and salt. Fold into pumpkin mixture. Add nuts, raisins and dates, mixing well. Divide batter into 6 greased and floured 8 x 4-inch loaf pans. Bake at 350 degrees for 50 to 60 minutes, or until center springs back when touched.

To make Cream Cheese Icing, whip cream cheese and butter together until light and fluffy. Add powdered sugar and beat until incorporated. Fold in remaining ingredients. (If using icing, you may want to delete pecans, raisins and dates from batter and bake cakes in two 13 x 9 x 2-inch pans. Reduce baking time to about 40 minutes.)

PUMPKIN BREAD FREEZES BEAUTIFULLY, BUT IF YOU DON'T WANT 6 LOAVES, THE RECIPE HALVES EASILY.

FOR ROUND CAKES, BAKE IN 2 BUNDT PANS AND DUST COOLED CAKES WITH POWDERED SUGAR. TO MAKE TEA SANDWICHES, SPREAD WHIPPED CREAM CHEESE FLAVORED WITH A LITTLE GRATED ORANGE ZEST AND POWDERED SUGAR BETWEEN 2 THIN SLICES OF PUMPKIN BREAD. CUT IN HALF OR INTO 3 TRIANGLES.

FRESH CHERRY NUT BREAD WITH ALMOND GLAZE

A DELICIOUS BREAKFAST BREAD THAT MAKES A WONDERFUL GIFT. YIELDS ONE 9 X 5-INCH LOAF OR TWO 3 X 6-INCH LOAVES

BREAD
2 cups flour
½ cup sugar
½ cup packed brown sugar
1 tablespoon grated orange peel
1½ teaspoons baking powder
¼ cup canola oil
½ cup orange juice
1 egg slightly beaten
2 cups fresh cherries, pitted and halved
½ cup chopped walnuts

GLAZE
2 tablespoons milk
½ teaspoon almond extract
1 cup sifted powdered sugar

Combine flour, sugars, orange peel and baking powder in large bowl. Add oil, juice and egg, mixing well. Fold in cherries and nuts. Spoon into greased loaf pan. Bake at 350 degrees until firm, 1½ hours for a 9 x 5-inch pan or 45 to 50 minutes for 3 x 6-inch pans.

Combine glaze ingredients and stir until smooth. Drizzle glaze over cooled bread, allowing a little to drip down sides.

FROZEN CHERRIES WORK AS WELL AS FRESH.

FOR VARIETY, TRY FRESH OR DRIED BLUEBERRIES OR STRAWBERRIES.

GLASS
ROLLING
PIN, 1850-
1900, U. S.,
1992.338

SOUR CREAM COFFEE CAKE

SERVES 10 TO 12

½ cup (1 stick) butter
1 cup sugar
2 eggs
2 cups cake flour
1 teaspoon baking powder
1 teaspoon baking soda
1 teaspoon vanilla
1 cup sour cream
1 cup brown sugar
½ cup chopped pecans
1¼ teaspoons cinnamon
1 tablespoon flour

Cream butter and sugar until light and fluffy. Beat in eggs one at a time. Sift together cake flour, baking powder and baking soda; alternately add to butter mixture with sour cream and vanilla. Mix well to combine thoroughly.

Combine brown sugar, pecans, cinnamon and flour in small bowl and mix well.

Pour one-third of batter into greased Bundt pan. Sprinkle one-half of brown sugar mixture over. Repeat layers, ending with batter. Bake at 350 degrees for 45 minutes. Cool in pan 5 minutes before turning out on rack to cool.

OATMEAL BERRY MUFFINS

YIELDS 12 MUFFINS

MUFFINS
¾ cup flour
¾ cup whole wheat flour
½ cup quick-cooking oats
½ cup packed brown sugar
2 teaspoons baking powder
1 teaspoon baking soda
1 cup fresh or partially frozen berries
2 eggs
½ cup buttermilk
½ cup (1 stick) butter, melted

CRUNCHY CRUST
3 tablespoons butter
¼ cup packed brown sugar
¼ cup rolled oats
¼ cup flour
1¼ teaspoons cinnamon

Combine flours, oats, sugar, baking powder and baking soda in large bowl. Add berries and toss gently to coat. Whip eggs, buttermilk and butter together. Add to flour mixture, stirring just until blended. Fill greased muffin tins two-thirds full.

To make crust, combine butter, sugar, oats, flour and cinnamon, mixing until crumbly. Sprinkle over muffin batter.

Bake at 400 degrees for 15 to 20 minutes, or until a toothpick inserted in center comes out clean.

TRY USING CRANBERRIES, BLUEBERRIES, RASPBERRIES, PITTED CHERRIES, OR ANY DRIED BERRIES IN THESE BREAKFAST TREATS.

BAKED FRENCH TOAST WITH BROWN SUGAR AND PECANS

THIS IS A SIMPLE AND DELICIOUS "DO AHEAD" BREAKFAST TREAT.

SERVES 6 TO 8

½ loaf of French bread, cut into 1-inch slices
6 large eggs
1½ cups half and half
1 teaspoon vanilla
¼ teaspoon cinnamon
¼ teaspoon nutmeg
¼ cup (½ stick) butter, softened
½ cup firmly packed brown sugar
½ cup chopped pecans, toasted
1 tablespoon light corn syrup
maple syrup

Arrange bread slices, slightly overlapping, to fill bottom of buttered 9 x 13-inch baking dish. Combine eggs, half and half, vanilla, cinnamon and nutmeg in medium bowl and mix well. Pour over bread slices. Cover and refrigerate overnight.

Remove bread slices and place in large greased pan in single layer (do not overlap). Combine butter, sugar, nuts and corn syrup in small bowl. Mix well and spread over bread. Bake 40 minutes at 350 degrees. Serve warm, topped with maple syrup.

BUTTERMILK SCONES

YIELDS 1 DOZEN 2½-INCH SCONES

2 cups flour
4 teaspoons sugar
1 tablespoon baking powder
⅛ teaspoon baking soda
⅔ cup cold butter, cut into pieces
⅔ cup buttermilk
  (plus ¼ cup for brushing tops of scones)

Combine flour, sugar, baking powder and baking soda in mixing bowl. Cut in butter until mixture resembles coarse meal. Make well in center of mixture; add ⅔ cup buttermilk and stir with fork until moistened.

Turn dough out onto lightly floured surface and knead 10 to 12 strokes, or until dough is nearly smooth. Roll out to ½-inch thickness and cut into circles with 2½-inch biscuit cutter. Place on greased baking sheet and brush tops with remaining ¼ cup buttermilk. Bake at 400 degrees for 15 minutes, or until very lightly browned.

TRY ADDING ¼ CUP CHOPPED APRICOTS AND ¼ CUP CHOPPED CRYSTALLIZED GINGER FOR A DELICIOUS SCONE TO ENJOY AT AFTERNOON TEA.

ANOTHER OPTION IS TO ADD ½ CUP DRIED FRUIT SUCH AS BLUEBERRIES, CHERRIES OR CRANBERRIES.

Orange Buttermilk Muffins

YIELDS 2 DOZEN MEDIUM MUFFINS
OR 5 DOZEN MINIATURES

1 cup (2 sticks) butter
1 cup sugar
2 eggs
1 teaspoon baking soda
1 cup buttermilk
2 cups sifted flour
½ teaspoon vanilla
grated rind of 2 oranges
½ cup golden raisins or coarsely chopped pecans
1 cup packed brown sugar
juice of 2 oranges

Cream butter and sugar together. Add eggs, beating well. Dissolve soda in buttermilk and add alternately with flour to butter mixture. (Do not overmix as batter should not be smooth.) Add vanilla, orange rind and raisins, stirring just until incorporated.

Fill well-greased muffin tins two-thirds full. Bake at 400 degrees for 20 to 25 minutes for medium-size muffins or about 12 minutes for miniature muffins.

While muffins are baking, combine orange juice and brown sugar. Drizzle juice mixture over tops and around edges of each muffin. Remove from pans immediately and allow to cool on racks. (Muffins can be made ahead and frozen.)

Multi-Grain Bread

YIELDS TWO 9 X 5-INCH LOAVES

2¼ cups warm water (105 to 115 degrees)
⅝ cup safflower oil
½ cup honey
2½ tablespoons active dry yeast
6½ cups whole wheat flour (divided use)
1½ teaspoons salt
½ cup rolled oats
¼ cup hulled millet
¼ cup sunflower seeds

Prepare a large mixing bowl by filling it with hot water. Let sit 1 minute to warm bowl, then empty.

Measure water, oil and honey into prepared bowl. Stir until honey is dissolved. Sprinkle yeast into mixture, stirring until softened. Set aside to proof. (Mixture will foam if yeast is active.)

After yeast mixture has foamed, add 3¼ cups flour and beat at least 100 strokes. (Batter should develop an elasticity and glossiness.) Cover with a cloth and allow to rise in warm place until doubled, about 20 minutes.

Stir batter down until approximately original size. Add salt, oats, millet and sunflower seeds, blending into dough. Measure out remaining 3¼ cups flour. Add 1 cup at a time, mixing well, until dough becomes too stiff to stir. (Amount of flour used will vary with atmospheric conditions. Dough should be moist, but not sticky; firm, but not dry.)

Turn dough out onto board and knead 10 minutes. (Dough will absorb more flour during kneading process.) Return dough to bowl and lightly oil surface. Cover and let rise in warm place until at least doubled in bulk.

Punch dough down and knead for about 5 minutes. Cut dough in half and shape into 2 loaves. Place in oiled, lightly floured pans. Cover and let rise until slightly more than doubled.

Bake at 350 degrees for 40 minutes, or until hollow sound is made by tapping loaves. Remove from pans and cool on racks. Freezes well.

TRY ADDING ¼ CUP FLAX SEED, CRACKED BULGAR WHEAT SEEDS OR RED WHEAT-BERRIES. (WHEAT GRAINS NEED TO BE SOAKED IN HOT WATER, ½ TO 1 HOUR, TO SOFTEN BEFORE USING.) UP TO 2 CUPS OF VARIOUS COMBINATIONS OF SEEDS CAN BE USED TO ACHIEVE A VARIETY OF TASTES WITHOUT HARMING OVERALL TEXTURE AND APPEAL OF THIS NUTTY, CRUNCHY BREAD.

SWEET POTATO BISCUITS

YIELDS 16 BISCUITS

2 to 3 medium sweet potatoes, peeled,
  cut into 1-inch cubes
½ cup butter
½ cup sugar
1 teaspoon salt
½ teaspoon cinnamon
3½ to 4 cups flour
4½ teaspoons baking powder

Boil potatoes until tender; drain and mash. While still hot, measure 1½ cups potatoes into large bowl. Add butter, sugar and salt, mixing well.

Sift together cinnamon, 3½ cups flour and baking powder. Add to potato mixture. Knead to make a soft dough, adding remaining ½ cup flour if needed.

Chill dough at least 30 minutes. Roll out to ½-inch thickness and cut into circles using 2½-inch biscuit cutter. Bake on greased baking sheet at 350 degrees for 15 minutes, or until biscuits begin to brown. (Can be made ahead and frozen.)

FOR A COCKTAIL BUFFET, SERVE HAM OR SMOKED TURKEY ON SWEET POTATO BISCUITS. ACCOMPANY WITH CRANBERRY APPLE CHUTNEY (PAGE 130).

SILVER AND SILVERGILT TEA SET, 1880, FREDERICK ELKINGTON & CO., AND MARTIN HALL & CO., LONDON AND SHEFFIELD, ENGLAND, 1989.22.1-2

CHEDDAR BISCUITS

YIELDS 12 TO 16 BISCUITS

2 cups flour

2½ teaspoons baking powder

1 teaspoon salt

2 teaspoons sugar

5 tablespoons butter or solid vegetable
  shortening, cold

⅓ cup grated Cheddar cheese

¾ cup milk

Sift flour and baking powder into a bowl. Add salt and sugar. Cut butter and cheese into flour mixture until texture resembles coarse meal. Stir in enough milk to make a smooth, soft dough. (Don't add milk all at once or dough may become too sticky to handle.)

Turn dough out on floured surface and knead gently for 1 minute. Roll out to ½-inch thickness and cut into rounds with a 2-inch cutter or a glass. Place on buttered baking sheet and bake at 450 degrees for 12 to 15 minutes, or until lightly browned.

FLAVOR BISCUITS WITH FINELY MINCED HAM, BACON, GREEN ONIONS OR CARAMELIZED ONIONS. TO CARAMELIZE, BROWN 1 CHOPPED ONION IN 2 TEASPOONS BUTTER UNTIL VERY SOFT.

DELETE CHEDDAR TO MAKE ANY OF THE FOLLOWING OPTIONS. TO MAKE **SHORTCAKE,** INCREASE SUGAR TO 5 TABLESPOONS AND USE HEAVY CREAM INSTEAD OF MILK. FORM 2 LARGE ROUNDS, ONE SLIGHTLY SMALLER THAN THE OTHER. BUTTER THE TOP OF THE LARGER ONE AND PLACE THE SMALLER ONE ON TOP. BAKE 15 TO 20 MINUTES AT 450 DEGREES, OR UNTIL LIGHTLY BROWNED. TO USE FOR STRAWBERRY (OR OTHER FRUIT) SHORTCAKE, SPLIT THE SHORTCAKE HORIZONTALLY. SPOON SLICED, SWEETENED BERRIES OVER BOTTOM LAYER. PUT TOP LAYER ON AND SPOON A FEW BERRIES OVER THAT. SERVE TOPPED WITH A LARGE DOLLOP OF WHIPPED CREAM.

MAKE **HERBED BISCUITS** BY ADDING 3 TABLESPOONS CHOPPED FRESH PARSLEY, DILL OR OTHER FRESH HERB. YOU CAN ALSO USE 1 TEASPOON DRIED HERBS.

MAKE **DUMPLINGS** BY CUTTING DOUGH INTO DIAMOND SHAPES AND DROPPING THEM INTO CHICKEN BROTH TO POACH. ANOTHER WAY IS TO ADD AN ADDITIONAL ¼ CUP MILK TO THE DOUGH AND DROP SPOONFULS INTO BROTH.

BOLILLOS

YIELDS 12 TO 14 ROLLS

1 package (2¼ teaspoons) active dry yeast
¼ cup warm water (105 to 115 degrees)
1 teaspoon sugar
3 to 3½ cups white bread flour
1 teaspoon salt
1 cup water, room temperature
2 tablespoons butter, melted (optional glaze)
1 egg white beaten with 2 tablespoons water and
   pinch of cornstarch (optional glaze)

Dissolve yeast in water; add sugar and set aside to proof. (Mixture will foam if yeast is active.) Combine 3 cups flour and salt in large mixing bowl. Form a well in center and pour in yeast mixture and room-temperature water. Stir to blend completely.

Gather dough into a ball and turn out onto lightly floured board. Knead about 10 minutes, or until dough is firm and satiny and a depression made in dough will rise, not bounce, back to original shape. (If depression stays, knead some more!) Add additional flour if dough seems sticky during kneading. If dough is dry, moisten hands and knead until extra flour is incorporated.

Place dough in an oiled bowl, turning to coat evenly. Cover with towel or plastic wrap and place bowl in warm, draft-free place to rise.

When dough has doubled in bulk, punch down and gently mold into long roll, about 18 to 24 inches. Try to close up creases in dough and remove air bubbles as you shape it. Cut into 12 to 14 pieces and mold each into oval shape. Place on greased cookie sheet about 1 inch apart. Cover with towel and let rise 15 to 30 minutes.

Prepare selected glaze while ovals are rising. For chewier crust, use egg white glaze; for nuttier taste and slightly softer crust, use butter glaze.

Make ¼-inch deep lengthwise cut in top of rolls using sharp knife. Bake in center of oven at 400 degrees for 20 to 25 minutes. For enhancement of appearance and crust, take bread out after 10 minutes of baking and reglaze. Put back in oven on higher shelf to finish baking.

WHOLE WHEAT WALNUT BREAD WITH MOLASSES

YIELDS 2 LOAVES

3 cups unbleached flour
2 cups whole wheat flour
1 tablespoon salt
1 tablespoon active dry yeast
1½ cups chopped walnuts, toasted
2 tablespoons olive oil
2 tablespoons molasses
1½ cups warm water

Combine flours, salt, yeast and walnuts in large bowl. Stir olive oil and molasses into water and add to flour mixture. Mix thoroughly until dry ingredients are well incorporated and dough is formed. Knead about 15 minutes (or use kneading blade of food processor). Place in greased bowl and let dough rise until doubled in volume. Punch down and form into 2 loaves. Place on baking sheet and let rise again until doubled in bulk.

Bake 10 minutes at 450 degrees, then reduce oven temperature to 375 degrees and bake 30 to 40 minutes.

PARMESAN PUFFS

MAKE THESE DELICIOUS MORSELS IN QUANTITY AND STORE THEM IN THE FREEZER. THEY'RE WONDERFUL TO HAVE ON HAND TO BAKE AS NEEDED. YIELDS 9 TO 12 PUFFS

1 egg
½ cup milk
9 slices firm white bread, crusts removed
½ cup (1 stick) butter, melted
1½ cups grated Parmesan cheese

Beat egg and milk together in small dish. Soak 3 slices of bread in milk mixture, then place each between 2 slices of fresh bread. (This creates 3 "sandwiches" with the soaked bread in the center of each.) Press gently on top of each sandwich to be sure slices stick together.

Cut each sandwich into 3 or 4 pieces. Roll each piece in melted butter, then in Parmesan cheese. Place on cookie sheet and chill at least 4 hours. (Can be frozen at this point. Leave on cookie sheet until frozen, then store in plastic bags.)

Bake at 350 degrees for 10 to 15 minutes, or until very lightly browned. Add 5 minutes to cooking time if frozen. Serve as an appetizer or as an accompaniment to soup or salad.

CORN MUFFINS WITH ROASTED RED PEPPER

YIELDS 12 MUFFINS

1¼ cups yellow corn meal
½ cup flour
1 tablespoon sugar
1½ teaspoons baking powder
1 teaspoon baking soda
1 teaspoon salt
1 cup grated extra-sharp Cheddar cheese
   (about 4 ounces)
¾ cup buttermilk
1 large egg
¼ cup (½ stick) unsalted butter, melted
   and cooled
2 tablespoons minced, seeded, pickled jalapeños
1 jar (7-ounce) roasted red peppers, drained,
   rinsed, patted dry between paper towels, and
   finely chopped

Combine cornmeal, flour, sugar, baking powder, baking soda, salt and cheese in large bowl. Whisk together buttermilk, egg, butter and jalapeños. Add to cornmeal mixture, stirring until just combined. Stir in peppers, being careful not to overmix.

Divide batter evenly among greased muffin tins. Bake in middle of oven at 425 degrees for 15 to 20 minutes, or until a toothpick inserted in center comes out clean. Serve immediately.

GRILLED GARLIC BREAD WITH FRESH HERBS

SERVES 8

½ cup (1 stick) butter
1 teaspoon Chinese chili sauce (hot!)
½ teaspoon freshly ground pepper
8 cloves garlic, minced
1 bunch chives, minced
⅓ cup minced cilantro
1-foot loaf French bread
½ cup freshly grated Parmesan cheese

Place butter, chili sauce, pepper and garlic in saucepan. Melt over low heat until just beginning to bubble. Remove from heat and stir in chives and cilantro.

Split bread in half lengthwise. Brush each half with thin layer of butter sauce and top with generous sprinkling of cheese. Shake to distribute cheese evenly. Toast bread under broiler until golden. Cut into slices to serve.

Because low-calorie cheeses contain less fat, they don't melt as well as regular cheese.

STERLING SILVER, SILVERGILT, AND IVORY JELLY SERVER, *IVORY* PATTERN, DESIGNED 1890, WHITING MFG. CO., NY, 1993.53

Cheese Bread with Parsley and Poppy Seeds

Yields 1 loaf

1 round loaf sourdough bread
½ cup (1 stick) butter, melted
1 tablespoon chopped parsley
1 teaspoon poppy seeds
½ pound Monterey Jack cheese, sliced

Cut loaf into 1½-inch squares, leaving bottom crust intact. Combine butter, parsley and poppy seeds and drizzle into openings of bread. Insert cheese slice into each opening. Wrap in foil. (Can be prepared to this point several hours in advance.)

Place on baking sheet and bake 15 minutes at 350 degrees. Loosen foil to expose top and bake another 15 minutes to lightly brown. Serve hot.

Crostini with Romano and Basil

Serves 10 to 12

⅓ cup mayonnaise
½ cup freshly grated Romano (divided use)
4 tablespoons basil pesto
  (purchase or see page 147)
1 baguette French bread, halved lengthwise

Combine mayonnaise, ⅓ cup Romano and pesto in small bowl, mixing well. (This can be prepared 1 day in advance. Cover tightly and refrigerate until ready to use.)

Place bread under preheated broiler until just beginning to brown. Spread each half generously with mayonnaise mixture and sprinkle with remaining cheese. Broil until bubbling and beginning to brown. (Watch carefully!)

Cut crosswise into 1½-inch pieces.

Crostini (Italian for "little crusts") make great soup or salad accompaniments. Crostini can also be topped with pâté, cheese, olive or other spread for a quick and tasty appetizer.

SALADS

Baja Salad with Cumin Lime Dressing

SERVES 8

SALAD

1 pound dried black beans, picked over, soaked overnight in cold water to cover and drained
1 red bell pepper, diced
1 green bell pepper, diced
⅓ cup chopped green onions
1 package (10-ounce) frozen corn, thawed
⅓ cup chopped cilantro
8 skinless boneless chicken breast halves, grilled

CUMIN LIME DRESSING

½ cup fresh lime or lemon juice
1 tablespoon Dijon mustard
2 tablespoons ground cumin
1 teaspoon minced garlic
1 teaspoon pepper
½ teaspoon salt
¾ cup olive oil
¾ cup vegetable oil

GARNISH

1 to 2 avocados, sliced
1 cup salsa
½ cup sour cream
chopped cilantro

In large saucepan, combine black beans and enough cold water to cover by 2 inches. Bring water to a boil and simmer for 45 minutes to 1 hour, or until tender, but not too soft.

Combine dressing ingredients, mixing well, and let stand at least 1 hour. (Can be done 1 day ahead.)

Drain black beans and mix together in large bowl with peppers, onion, corn and cilantro. Toss with dressing. Cut chicken into strips.

To serve, place vegetables with dressing on large platter. Arrange chicken strips and avocado slices on top. Drizzle with salsa and scatter cilantro over all. Pass sour cream and extra salsa.

IN A HURRY? USE 4 CANS (16-OUNCE) BLACK BEANS, RINSED AND DRAINED, INSTEAD OF COOKING DRIED BEANS.

YOU MAY ALSO SUBSTITUTE GRILLED SHRIMP FOR CHICKEN.

Toasting nuts before using intensifies their flavor. Toasted nuts are less likely to sink in cakes and breads and they give a special crunch to salads. Toast nuts or seeds in an unbuttered skillet over medium heat, stirring frequently, until golden. Or toast in a 350-degree oven, stirring occasionally, for 10 to15 minutes.

ROMAINE, ARTICHOKE AND HEART OF PALM SALAD

SERVES 8

CIDER VINAIGRETTE

¼ small onion, chopped

3 tablespoons cider vinegar

2 teaspoons spicy brown mustard

½ teaspoon sugar

½ teaspoon salt

¼ teaspoon freshly ground pepper

¾ cup olive oil

SALAD

2 heads romaine, washed, dried and torn into small pieces

1 can (14-ounce) hearts of palm, drained and sliced

1 can (13¾-ounce) artichoke hearts, drained and quartered

4 ounces blue cheese, crumbled

½ pound bacon, cooked crisp, drained and crumbled

Purée onion with vinegar in blender. Transfer to bowl and add mustard, sugar, salt and pepper, mixing well. Gradually add oil, whisking constantly, until well mixed and slightly thickened. (Can be made 1 day ahead.)

Combine romaine, hearts of palm, artichokes and cheese in large bowl. Toss with dressing to coat, sprinkle with bacon, and serve immediately.

TRY ADDING SLICED AVOCADO, SHREDDED CHICKEN OR CHOPPED, TOASTED ALMONDS.

VINTNER'S SALAD

SERVES 8

2 heads bibb lettuce

½ head romaine lettuce

1 bunch watercress

½ cup walnut halves

½ cup grated Gruyère cheese

RED WINE VINAIGRETTE

½ cup olive oil

2 tablespoons red wine

1½ tablespoons red wine vinegar

1 tablespoon Dijon mustard

1 teaspoon salt

¾ teaspoon freshly ground pepper

Chill washed and dried greens, walnuts and Gruyère in large bowl until serving time.

Combine dressing ingredients in jar with tight-fitting lid and shake well. Just before serving, pour dressing over salad and toss gently.

SAUTÉ A SLICED RED ONION IN A LITTLE BUTTER AND ADD TO THE SALAD WHILE STILL WARM.

CONSIDER ADDING THE SEASONAL COLOR AND FLAVOR OF A THINLY SLICED APPLE OR PEAR.

FRESH PEAR SALAD WITH RASPBERRIES AND HAVARTI

SERVES 8

ORANGE VINAIGRETTE

2 tablespoons orange zest
¼ cup raspberry vinegar
¾ cup oil
vanilla to taste

SALAD

4 pears, halved and cored (peeling optional)
juice of 1 lemon
1 to 2 heads bibb lettuce
8 ounces Havarti or other semisoft mild cheese
2 cups raspberries
8 leaves watercress

To make dressing, combine orange zest with vinegar and oil, mixing well. Add vanilla to taste.

Sprinkle pear halves with lemon juice. Arrange lettuce leaves on 8 plates and top each with pear half. Shred cheese and sprinkle over pears. Garnish with raspberries and watercress leaves. Drizzle about 2 tablespoons dressing over each.

MIXED GREENS WITH APPLES, PEARS AND BLUE CHEESE

SERVES 4

SHERRY WALNUT OIL VINAIGRETTE

4 tablespoons sherry wine vinegar
I tablespoon Dijon mustard
¼ cup walnut oil
¼ cup olive oil
salt and pepper to taste

SALAD

½ yellow onion, thinly sliced
I tablespoon butter
½ cup white wine
I red Bartlett pear
I Granny Smith apple
4 cups mixed greens
⅔ cup blue cheese, crumbled
¼ cup walnut halves, toasted

To prepare dressing, combine vinegar, mustard, oils, salt and pepper. Mix well.

Sauté onion in butter until golden. Add wine and simmer until wine has evaporated. Core and slice pear and apple (but do not peel) and toss with vinaigrette.

To serve salad, toss greens with onion, fruit and vinaigrette. Top with blue cheese and walnuts.

CANTALOUPE, TOMATO AND RED ONION WITH MINT VINAIGRETTE

SERVES 8 TO 10

SALAD

4 large tomatoes, halved lengthwise
    and sliced ¼-inch thick
½ red onion, thinly sliced in rings
I cantaloupe, thinly sliced

MINT VINAIGRETTE

juice of I lemon
3 tablespoons white wine vinegar or cider
    vinegar
I tablespoon chopped fresh parsley
I tablespoon chopped fresh basil
I½ teaspoons minced fresh mint
I teaspoon salt
½ teaspoon pepper
¾ teaspoon dry mustard
8 to 10 tablespoons oil

Arrange tomato slices in bottom of clear glass dish. Spread onion rings over tomatoes and cantaloupe over onions.

Mix lemon juice, vinegar, parsley, basil, mint, salt, pepper and mustard in food processor. With motor running, slowly add oil, processing until well blended.

Pour dressing over salad and chill at least 3 hours or overnight. Remove from refrigerator about ½ hour before serving.

Warm Cabbage Salad with Roquefort and Bacon

Serves 6

6 ounces peppered bacon, diced
1 shallot, minced
1 cup white wine
freshly ground pepper
1½ cups heavy cream
1 tablespoon Dijon mustard
1 medium head green cabbage, cored and finely sliced
1 tablespoon white vinegar
4 ounces Roquefort cheese, crumbled

Cook bacon until crisp. Drain bacon and reserve grease. Combine shallot, wine and pepper and cook over medium heat until most of wine has evaporated. Add cream and mustard, continuing to cook until thickened. Heat bacon grease in skillet; add cabbage and toss for 1 minute. Add vinegar and toss 1 minute more. Add cream mixture and Roquefort, tossing to combine well. Serve immediately topped with bacon.

Spicy Mustard Caesar Salad

Serves 4 to 6

2 to 3 cloves garlic
½ cup oil
¾ teaspoon Worcestershire sauce
¾ lemon (divided use)
2½ tablespoons pasteurized egg substitute
½ teaspoon spicy brown mustard
¾ teaspoon cider vinegar
1 inch anchovy paste (optional)
½ teaspoon water
1 head romaine, torn or cut into pieces
⅓ cup shredded Parmesan cheese
⅓ cup croutons

Crush garlic with knife and combine with oil in blender. Purée for about 25 seconds. Let stand for 1 hour. Add Worcestershire, juice of ½ lemon, egg substitute, mustard, vinegar, anchovy paste and water. Purée until thick and creamy. (Dressing can be thinned with water if desired).

Place romaine in large salad bowl and squeeze remaining ¼ lemon on top. Add dressing and toss well. Top with cheese and croutons and toss again.

ADD COOKED SHRIMP OR GRILLED CHICKEN FOR A HEARTIER SALAD.

FIELD GREENS WITH BLUEBERRIES, STILTON AND RASPBERRY VINAIGRETTE

SERVES 8

¼ cup raspberry vinegar
¾ cup oil
1 teaspoon sugar
salt and pepper to taste
8 cups mixed field greens
1 cup fresh blueberries
6 ounces Stilton cheese, crumbled
¾ cup pecans, toasted and chopped

Combine vinegar, oil, sugar, salt and pepper. Mix well. Place torn greens in large bowl. Add blueberries, cheese and pecans. Toss with enough dressing to coat.

GLAZED EARTHENWARE BOWL, 1949, GERTRUD AND OTTO NATZLER, LOS ANGELES, 1949.29 GETRUD AND OTTO NATZLER WERE BORN, MET AND MARRIED IN VIENNA. IN 1938 THEY CAME TO THE UNITED STATES WHERE GERTRUD BECAME KNOWN FOR HER FINE-WALLED BOWLS, WHILE OTTO BECAME KNOWN FOR THE BEAUTIFUL GLAZES HE DEVELOPED.

Spinach Apple Salad with Oriental Dressing

SERVES 6

⅓ cup cider vinegar
⅓ cup water
1 tablespoon soy sauce
1 teaspoon sesame oil
¼ cup natural peanut butter, smooth or crunchy (see note at right)
3 tablespoons brown sugar
7 cups spinach leaves, washed, dried, stemmed and chopped
1 Red Delicious apple, cored and thinly sliced
½ cup chopped peanuts (garnish)

Combine vinegar, water, soy sauce, oil, peanut butter and sugar in food processor or blender and purée until smooth.

Combine spinach and apples in large bowl. To serve, add dressing to coat and toss well. Garnish with peanuts.

ENAMELED PORCELAIN PLATE, *MILLENNIUM PATTERN*, CA. 1983, DESIGNED BY HELENA UGLAV, MIKASA CHINA, JAPAN, 11.1991

NOTE: THE KEY INGREDIENT IN THIS DRESSING IS THE NATURAL PEANUT BUTTER. PROCESSED PEANUT BUTTER WILL NOT PRODUCE THE SAME RESULT.

TRY THIS DRESSING ON THAI GRILLED PORK SALAD (PAGE 75).

CALIFORNIA SALAD WITH PAPAYA AND RICE STICKS

EXOTIC PRESENTATION WITH AN ASIAN INFLUENCE. SERVES 4

BALSAMIC ORANGE VINAIGRETTE

1 teaspoon grated orange zest
¼ cup fresh orange juice
¼ cup balsamic vinegar
⅓ cup olive oil
1 tablespoon soy sauce
½ teaspoon Asian chili sauce
2 tablespoons finely minced fresh ginger
⅓ cup chopped basil leaves

SALAD

2 ounces rice sticks (see note)
3 cups cooking oil
1 large ripe avocado, cut into ½-inch cubes
juice from ½ lemon
4 cups torn mixed greens
1 firm papaya, cut into ½-inch cubes
1 cup pecans, toasted

To prepare dressing, combine orange zest, juice, vinegar, oil, soy sauce, chili sauce, ginger and basil. Mix well. (Do not prepare dressing more than 8 hours ahead.)

Heat oil in deep skillet over medium-high heat (375 degrees). Test cook a strand of rice stick; it will puff up immediately when oil is ready. Add small amount of rice sticks at a time, pushing apart. As soon as they expand (about 5 seconds), turn rice sticks over and push back into oil to cook 5 more seconds. Remove when done and drain on paper towels. Repeat with remaining rice sticks.

Sprinkle avocado with lemon juice. Combine greens, avocado, papaya and pecans in large bowl.

To serve, crumble rice sticks slightly (use hands) and arrange on 4 salad plates. Toss salad with dressing to coat. Place atop bed of rice sticks and serve immediately.

ADD BOILED OR GRILLED SHRIMP TO CREATE A MAIN DISH SALAD.

NOTE: RICE STICKS ARE LONG, THIN, DRIED, RICE FLOUR VERMICELLI THAT ARE AN ESSENTIAL INGREDIENT TO MANY CHINESE SALADS AND STIR-FRIED DISHES. WHEN COOKED IN HOT OIL, THEY INSTANTLY PUFF UP MANY TIMES THEIR ORIGINAL SIZE. RICE STICKS ARE AVAILABLE AT ASIAN MARKETS AND MOST SUPERMARKETS.

COUNTRY-FRIED CHICKEN SALAD

SERVES 4 TO 6

CHICKEN

4 skinless boneless chicken breast halves

1 cup milk

½ cup flour (divided use)

½ cup cornmeal

1 tablespoon finely chopped fresh parsley

1 teaspoon mild paprika

½ teaspoon salt

¼ teaspoon pepper

2 eggs, beaten

oil for frying

HONEY MUSTARD VINAIGRETTE

3 tablespoons cider vinegar

2 tablespoons honey, room temperature

1 tablespoon fresh lemon juice

1 tablespoon coarse-grained mustard

½ teaspoon salt

¼ teaspoon white pepper

¼ cup walnut oil

½ cup olive oil

SALAD

2 tart apples, peeled, cored and
  cut into ¾-inch dice

juice of ½ lemon

3 cups torn romaine

3 cups torn leaf lettuce

3 cups torn bibb lettuce

3 cups torn curly endive

½ pound blue cheese, crumbled

1 cup pecan halves, toasted

2 tablespoons snipped fresh chives

To prepare chicken, place breasts between 2 sheets waxed paper and pound to uniform ½-inch thickness. Soak in milk for 30 minutes; drain. Dredge chicken in ¼ cup flour to coat. Combine remaining flour, cornmeal, parsley, paprika, salt and pepper in shallow bowl. Dredge chicken in egg, then immediately in cornmeal mixture to coat evenly. Gently tap each breast several times with dull edge of large knife to secure coating. Repeat dredging in egg and cornmeal and tap once more. Set aside 30 minutes for coating to set.

Fry chicken in ½ inch oil in heavy skillet over medium-high heat. Cook 4 to 5 minutes per side, until golden brown and cooked through. Drain on paper towels. Cut chicken crosswise into ½-inch strips.

Prepare dressing by combining vinegar, honey, lemon juice, mustard, salt and pepper. Gradually whisk in oils until well blended.

Toss apples with lemon juice. Combine greens in large bowl and toss with just enough dressing to coat. Divide among individual plates and scatter apples, cheese and pecans over top. Arrange chicken strips on top of salads, drizzle with remaining dressing, and garnish with chives.

TO TAKE THIS SALAD ON A PICNIC, PACK THE FRIED CHICKEN STRIPS, DRESSING, AND OTHER SALAD INGREDIENTS IN SEPARATE CONTAINERS. BRING ALONG A LARGE BOWL SO YOU CAN DRESS AND TOSS SALAD JUST BEFORE SERVING.

IF TIME IS SHORT, BUY THE CHICKEN ALREADY FRIED. CUT INTO STRIPS AND ADD TO SALAD.

THAI GRILLED PORK SALAD WITH LIME MINT VINAIGRETTE

SERVES 4

1 pound pork tenderloin

HONEY SESAME MARINADE
2 tablespoons soy sauce
2 tablespoons lime juice
1 tablespoon honey
2 tablespoons sesame oil
1 clove garlic, finely chopped
1 jalapeño, thinly sliced

LIME MINT VINAIGRETTE
3 tablespoons lime juice
2 tablespoons finely chopped fresh mint
1 tablespoon rice wine vinegar
½ tablespoon soy sauce
½ cup olive oil
2 tablespoons sesame oil

SALAD
8 cups tender spinach leaves
⅓ medium red onion, thinly sliced
½ cup coarsely chopped peanuts
2 tablespoons finely chopped cilantro

Place pork in shallow dish. Stir together soy sauce, lime juice, honey, sesame oil, garlic and jalapeño. Pour over pork, turning to coat. Cover and marinate in refrigerator 1 to 2 hours.

To prepare dressing, combine lime juice, mint, vinegar, soy sauce and oils. Mix well.

Grill pork until well seared and cooked through. Slice into julienne strips and set aside.

To serve salad, toss spinach, onion, and peanuts with enough dressing to coat. Arrange on individual plates and top with pork. Drizzle lightly with additional dressing. Garnish with cilantro.

TANGY GREEN BEAN AND CELERY ROOT SALAD

SERVES 4

DRESSING
5 tablespoons fresh lemon juice
2 tablespoons coarse-grained mustard
1 teaspoon salt
¾ cup olive oil

SALAD
1¼ pounds celery root, peeled and halved lengthwise
1 pound *haricots verts* (thin green beans), trimmed and cut into 2-inch lengths
salt and pepper to taste

For dressing, whisk together lemon juice, mustard and salt. Slowly add oil, whisking constantly, until well incorporated.

Cut celery root halves crosswise into ⅛-inch slices. Cut slices into ⅛-inch strips. Add to dressing.

Boil beans until crisp tender, 3 to 4 minutes. Refresh in cold water and add to celery root mixture. Season with salt and pepper and toss well. (Salad can be made early in day and refrigerated until serving.)

FIVE SPICE SESAME DRESSING

½ cup white wine vinegar

6 tablespoons sugar

3 tablespoons salad oil

3 tablespoons sesame oil

½ teaspoon five spice powder (see note)

salt and pepper to taste

SALAD

½ pound fresh bean sprouts

¼ pound fresh mushrooms, sliced

1 head romaine, cut into ½-inch strips

¼ cup green onions, cut in 2-inch lengths

3 tablespoons cilantro leaves

Quickly fry 8 to 10 won ton strips at a time in hot oil. Turn strips once and fry until golden. Drain on paper towels. When cool, store at room temperature in self-sealing plastic bags until serving time. (To ensure crispness, fry the day of serving.)

To make salad dressing, combine vinegar, sugar, oils, five spice powder, salt and pepper, mixing well.

Combine bean sprouts, mushrooms, romaine, green onions and cilantro in large bowl.

To serve, toss salad with dressing to coat. Add won tons to salad at last minute or serve on side.

NOTE: FIVE SPICE POWDER IS A BLEND OF SPICES INCLUDING ANISE, FENNEL, CINNAMON, SICHUAN PEPPER AND CLOVES. IT IS A GREAT FAVORITE OF THE CANTONESE FOR MARINADES, POULTRY AND FISH.

WON TON SALAD WITH FIVE SPICE SESAME DRESSING

SERVES 8

WON TONS

2 cups oil

½ package won ton skins, cut in ¼-inch strips

GRILLED CHICKEN AND EGGPLANT SALAD WITH GOAT CHEESE

SERVES 4

CHICKEN AND EGGPLANT

4 skinless boneless chicken breast halves

1 Japanese eggplant, cut crosswise into ½-inch thick slices

HERB MARINADE

6 tablespoons olive oil

2 tablespoons fresh lemon juice

2 tablespoons finely minced garlic

2 teaspoons minced fresh thyme

2 teaspoons minced fresh oregano

salt and pepper to taste

SALAD

2 tablespoon fresh lemon juice

2 teaspoons Dijon mustard

salt and pepper to taste

6 tablespoons olive oil

8 cups assorted salad greens

6 ounces fresh goat cheese

1 yellow bell pepper, diced

2 green onions, minced

Arrange chicken and eggplant in one layer in a shallow dish. Whisk together olive oil, lemon juice, garlic, thyme, oregano, salt and pepper. Pour marinade over chicken and eggplant and cover dish. Marinate, turning once, for 2 hours. Grill chicken and eggplant for 5 minutes on each side. Transfer to warm platter and allow to sit for 5 minutes.

Whisk together lemon juice, mustard, salt and pepper. Add oil slowly, whisking until emulsified.

Place greens, cheese, bell pepper and onions in large bowl. Toss with dressing.

To serve, divide salad among 4 plates. Cut chicken into thin strips and arrange with eggplant over salad. Spoon juices from platter over top.

ENAMELED
AND GILT
PORCELAIN
PLATE,
CA. 1730-40,
CHINA,
1985.R.1043

PRESSED GLASS
PLACE SETTING,
RUBA ROMBIC
PATTERN, 1928,
DESIGNED BY
REUBEN HALEY,
CONSOLIDATED
LAMP & GLASS
CO.,
CORAOPOLIS, PA,
1992.522.1-3

FRESH FRUIT SALAD WITH TEQUILA AND ORANGE JUICE

SERVES 12 TO 14

1 small watermelon, seeded and cubed
1 large cantaloupe, cut into small cubes
1 pineapple, cored and cut into small cubes
½ cup tequila
½ cup orange juice
½ cup powdered sugar
1 pint blueberries, rinsed and drained
grated zest of one lime

Combine watermelon, cantaloupe and pineapple in large glass bowl or any non-metallic container. Mix together tequila, orange juice and sugar. Pour over fruit and gently mix. Cover; refrigerate up to 12 hours. To serve, drain fruit and fold in blueberries and lime zest.

WARM MARZIPAN APRICOTS AND PEARS

SERVES 6 TO 8

I can (I-pound) apricot halves
I can (I-pound) pear halves
I cup orange sections
I tablespoon sugar
I can (8-ounce) almond paste
¼ cup sliced almonds, toasted
I tablespoon grated orange peel
I tablespoon cornstarch
I tablespoon Cointreau liqueur
½ teaspoon cinnamon

Drain apricots and pears, reserving liquid. Slice pear sections in half. Arrange apricots, pears and oranges in shallow baking dish.

Mix sugar into almond paste and blend until it resembles coarse meal. Sprinkle mixture over fruit and top with almonds. (Can be prepared to this point 1 day in advance.) Bake 25 minutes at 325 degrees, or until topping is lightly browned.

Combine reserved liquid from fruit, orange peel and cornstarch in saucepan. Heat to boiling over medium heat, stirring constantly. Reduce heat and simmer for 2 minutes, stirring. Add Cointreau and cinnamon mixing well. Pour over hot fruit and serve.

THIS RECIPE CAN EASILY BE DONE IN LARGE QUANTITIES FOR A BRUNCH BUFFET. THE FRUIT CAN BE BAKED SEVERAL HOURS AHEAD, WRAPPED TIGHTLY IN FOIL AND HELD AT ROOM TEMPERATURE. POURING THE BOILING SYRUP OVER THE FRUIT JUST BEFORE SERVING IS SUFFICIENT TO REHEAT.

VIETNAMESE CHICKEN SALAD WITH RICE WINE VINAIGRETTE

A MAIN DISH SALAD WITH ORIENTAL FLAIR. SERVES 4

RICE WINE VINAIGRETTE
2 jalapeños, seeded and minced
2 cloves garlic, minced
2 tablespoons sugar
I tablespoon rice wine vinegar
I medium onion, thinly sliced
3 tablespoons fresh lime juice
3 tablespoons sesame oil
freshly ground pepper to taste
3 tablespoons Vietnamese fish sauce (optional) or salt to taste

SALAD
2 cups shredded cooked chicken
4 cups finely shredded Napa cabbage
I cup shredded carrot
½ cup chopped mint
½ cup chopped cilantro plus extra for garnish
⅔ cup chopped, dry roasted peanuts

Combine jalapeños, garlic, sugar, vinegar, onion, lime juice, oil, pepper and fish sauce. Mix well and let stand 30 minutes.

Place chicken, cabbage, carrot, mint and cilantro in large bowl. Sprinkle with dressing and toss well. Garnish with additional cilantro and peanuts to serve.

GRILLED PORTABELLA SALAD WITH SPINACH AND FENNEL

FENNEL IMPARTS TANTALIZING FLAVOR AND CRUNCH. SERVES 8

6 to 8 portabella mushrooms
¼ cup white wine vinegar
1 tablespoon balsamic vinegar
1 tablespoon Dijon mustard
1 teaspoon sugar
1 teaspoon salt
½ teaspoon freshly ground pepper
1 tablespoon lemon juice
1 cup olive oil
1 bunch tender spinach leaves, stemmed
1 head red leaf lettuce
1 bulb fennel, cut into thin strips
6 ounces fresh goat cheese, cubed
½ cup pine nuts, toasted

Clean mushrooms and lay in shallow baking dish. Combine vinegars, mustard, sugar, salt, pepper and lemon juice. Gradually whisk in oil, adding in thin, steady stream. Pour dressing over mushrooms. Cover and marinate in refrigerator up to 24 hours.

Grill mushrooms over medium coals for about 10 minutes, turning once. Slice mushrooms and set aside. Add any accumulated juices to marinade. Reserve to use as dressing for salad.

Wash and dry greens and tear into pieces. Combine greens, fennel, goat cheese and pine nuts in large bowl. Toss with enough dressing to coat. Divide among individual plates and lay portabella slices across top. Serve immediately.

SPINACH SALAD WITH MANGO-GINGER CHUTNEY DRESSING

SERVES 4

MANGO-GINGER CHUTNEY DRESSING
½ cup oil
¼ cup mango-ginger chutney
1 teaspoon curry powder
1 teaspoon dry mustard
½ teaspoon salt
2 tablespoons fresh lemon juice
1 teaspoon sugar

SALAD
2 bunches (about 1½ pounds) small-leaf spinach, stemmed, washed and dried
2 apples, cored, halved crosswise and thinly sliced
1 cup pecans, toasted
½ to ¾ cup raisins
½ cup chopped green onions

Combine oil, chutney, curry, mustard, salt, lemon juice and sugar, blending well. Combine spinach, apples, pecans, raisins and green onions in large bowl. Toss salad with dressing and serve immediately.

SPINACH SALAD WITH MARINATED SHRIMP AND FENNEL

SERVES 6

1 pound uncooked, large, unpeeled shrimp
2½ tablespoons tarragon vinegar
1 tablespoon Dijon mustard
1½ teaspoons fresh tarragon
3 large cloves garlic, pressed
¾ cup olive oil
1 fennel bulb, trimmed, halved lengthwise, cored and cut into ⅛-inch strips
4½ tablespoons snipped fresh chives (divided use)
salt to taste
10 ounces fresh spinach leaves, stems removed
freshly ground pepper to taste

Cook shrimp in large pot of boiling water until just opaque (about 2 minutes). Drain and cool shrimp, then peel and devein. Set aside.

Mix vinegar, mustard, tarragon and garlic in medium bowl. Gradually whisk in oil in thin, steady stream. Add shrimp, fennel and 3 table-spoons chives, tossing until well coated. Season with salt. Cover mixture and allow flavors to develop for 30 minutes at room temperature.

Arrange ring of large spinach leaves on each of 6 plates. Tear remaining spinach leaves into bite-sized pieces and toss with shrimp mixture. Mound salad on plates. Season with freshly ground pepper and sprinkle with chives.

CHILI VINAIGRETTE

YIELDS 1 CUP

1 cup oil
⅓ cup fresh lime juice
3 tablespoons cider vinegar
3 tablespoons packed brown sugar
5 pickled jalapeño peppers, stemmed, seeded and quartered
1 tablespoon chili powder
1½ teaspoons cumin
2 teaspoons salt

Combine all ingredients in food processor and purée until peppers are finely minced. Keeps, covered and refrigerated, for several weeks.

SERVE OVER **SOUTHWEST SALAD**. COMBINE GREENS, RED ONION, FRESH ORANGES, AVOCADO. TOP WITH FRIED TORTILLA STRIPS AND TOASTED PINE NUTS.

TOMATOES WITH FRESH LIME VINAIGRETTE

SERVES 8

6 tomatoes, cut in wedges
1 tablespoon fresh lime juice
1 teaspoon sugar
½ cup white wine vinegar
2 cloves garlic, minced
4 green onions, minced
½ cup olive oil
¼ cup chopped fresh basil
¼ cup chopped fresh parsley
3 ounces feta cheese, crumbled
½ teaspoon coarsely ground pepper
salt to taste

Place tomato wedges in non-metallic bowl. Combine lime juice, sugar, vinegar, garlic, onions, oil, basil and parsley. Mix well and pour over tomatoes. Add feta cheese, salt and pepper. Refrigerate at least 1 hour before serving.

MAKE BRUSCHETTA BY CHOPPING TOMATOES IN THIS RECIPE AND SERVING WITH LIGHTLY TOASTED, GARLIC-RUBBED SLICES OF FRENCH BREAD.

MOZZARELLA AND TOMATOES WITH FRESH BASIL VINAIGRETTE

SERVES 4

FRESH BASIL VINAIGRETTE
½ cup fresh basil leaves
½ cup olive oil
2 tablespoons red wine vinegar
1 clove garlic, chopped
½ teaspoon sugar
½ teaspoon salt
½ teaspoon freshly ground pepper

SALAD
2 ripe tomatoes, sliced ¼-inch thick
½ avocado, sliced ¼-inch thick
8 ounces fresh mozzarella, sliced ¼-inch thick
½ red onion, sliced ¼-inch thick, separated into rings

Place basil, oil, vinegar, garlic, sugar, salt and pepper in food processor and blend until semi-smooth. Chill 30 minutes.

Arrange alternating slices of tomato, avocado and cheese on platter. Top with onion rings. Just before serving, drizzle with dressing.

GLAZED
EARTHENWARE
BOWL, 1960,
GERTRUD AND
OTTO NATZLER,
LOS ANGELES,
1981.196;
STERLING SILVER,
SILVERGILT, AND
WOOD SALAD
SERVERS, CA. 1880-
85, WHITING MFG.
CO, NY,
1990.148.A-B.

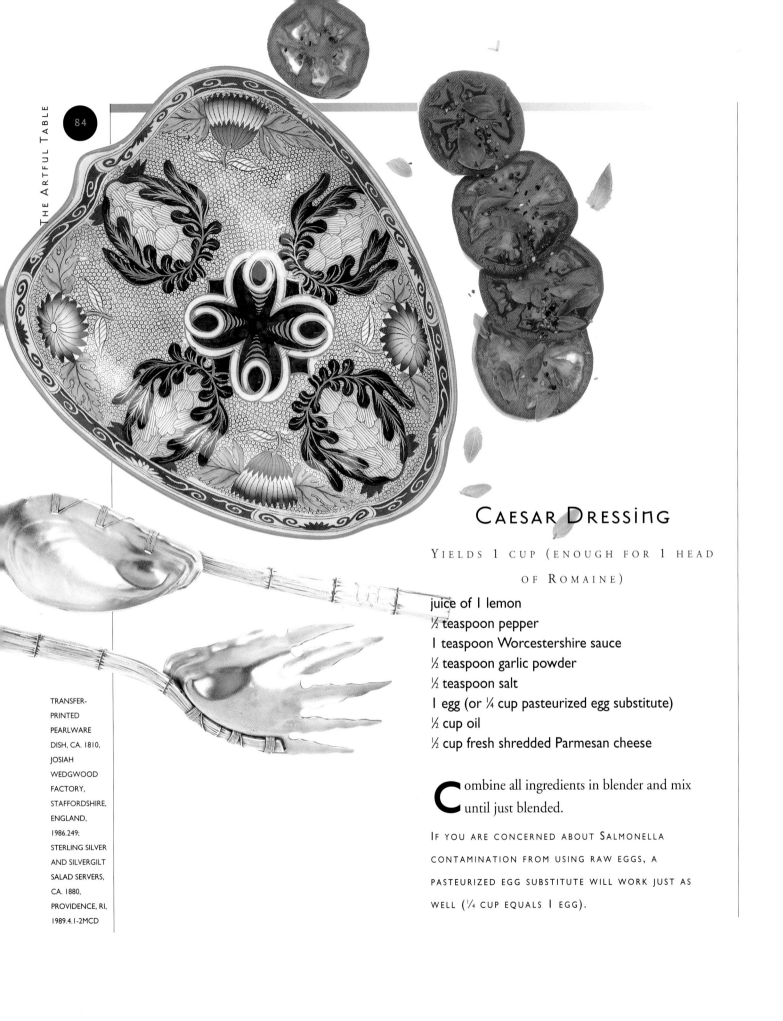

CAESAR DRESSING

YIELDS 1 CUP (ENOUGH FOR 1 HEAD
OF ROMAINE)

juice of 1 lemon

½ teaspoon pepper

1 teaspoon Worcestershire sauce

½ teaspoon garlic powder

½ teaspoon salt

1 egg (or ¼ cup pasteurized egg substitute)

½ cup oil

½ cup fresh shredded Parmesan cheese

Combine all ingredients in blender and mix until just blended.

IF YOU ARE CONCERNED ABOUT SALMONELLA CONTAMINATION FROM USING RAW EGGS, A PASTEURIZED EGG SUBSTITUTE WILL WORK JUST AS WELL (¼ CUP EQUALS 1 EGG).

BALSAMIC DIJON DRESSING

YIELDS 1 ¼ CUPS

1 cup olive oil
¼ cup balsamic vinegar
1 tablespoon grained Dijon mustard
1 teaspoon powdered ranch-style dressing mix
1 tablespoon mayonnaise
1 tablespoon milk

Whisk all ingredients together. Keeps refrigerated at least 1 week.

MUSTARD CIDER VINAIGRETTE

A DELICIOUS DEPARTURE FROM THE USUAL VINAIGRETTE.
YIELDS 3 CUPS

2 cups olive oil
½ cup Maille mustard
½ cup cider vinegar
½ tablespoon minced shallots
½ tablespoon minced garlic
1 tablespoon minced fresh thyme

Whisk all ingredients together. Store in the refrigerator.

RASPBERRY AND GINGER VINAIGRETTE

MAKES A BEAUTIFUL HOLIDAY GIFT FOR FRIENDS. YIELDS ⅔ CUP

RASPBERRY VINEGAR
1 cup raspberries
2 cups white wine vinegar

VINAIGRETTE
⅓ cup oil
⅓ cup raspberry vinegar
1 tablespoon sugar
½ tablespoon freshly grated ginger
⅛ teaspoon salt

To prepare raspberry vinegar, place raspberries in hot, clean glass jar. Heat white wine vinegar and pour into jar. Cover loosely and let stand in a cool dark place for 1 week. Strain to remove seeds and pulp and store vinegar in refrigerator.

To prepare the vinaigrette, combine all ingredients in a screw top jar. Cover tightly and shake well. Store in refrigerator for up to 2 weeks. Shake well before using.

SERVE OVER FRUIT SALAD, GRILLED CHICKEN SALAD OR GRILLED SEAFOOD; THE POSSIBILITIES ARE LIMITLESS. TO USE WITH MIXED GREENS, INCREASE OIL TO 1 CUP.

MEDITERRANEAN ROASTED VEGETABLE SALAD

SERVES 8 TO 12

1 eggplant (1½ pounds), cut lengthwise into 1-inch slices

olive oil

salt and pepper

2 large red onions, cut into 1-inch pieces

2 pounds red-skinned potatoes, cut into 1-inch pieces

9 tablespoons olive oil (divided use)

2 red bell peppers, cut into 1½-inch squares

4 zucchini, halved lengthwise, cut crosswise into 1½-inch pieces

2 tablespoons Dijon mustard

3 tablespoons balsamic vinegar

¾ cup chopped fresh basil

2 heads radicchio, cut into 1½-inch pieces

2 packages (½-ounce) arugula, cut into bite-size pieces

1½ cups shredded Pecorino Romano cheese

Brush eggplant with olive oil and season to taste with salt and pepper. Broil until lightly brown and just cooked through, about 2 minutes per side. Drain on paper towels.

Combine onions and potatoes on large baking sheet. Drizzle with 3 tablespoons oil and toss to coat. Season with salt and pepper. Roast, stirring occasionally, at 425 degrees for about 1 hour, or until tender and golden. Transfer to large bowl.

Place peppers on medium baking sheet. Add 1 tablespoon oil and toss to coat. Season with salt and pepper. Roast, stirring occasionally, until tender and lightly browned, about 35 minutes at 425 degrees. Transfer to bowl with onions and potatoes.

Place zucchini on medium baking sheet and drizzle with 1 tablespoon oil. Toss to coat and season with salt and pepper. Bake until tender crisp, about 20 minutes at 425 degrees. Transfer to bowl with other vegetables. Cut eggplant into 1-inch squares and add to vegetables in bowl.

Combine mustard and vinegar in small bowl. Gradually mix in remaining 4 tablespoons olive oil. Add basil. Pour dressing over vegetables and toss to coat. (Salad can be made 1 day ahead to this point. Cover and chill. Bring to room temperature before continuing.)

Mix radicchio, arugula and cheese into salad. Season with salt and pepper.

MEATS

STUFFED LEG OF LAMB WITH TOMATILLO-MINT SAUCE

PRESENTATION AND SUPERB FLAVOR MAKE THIS A SPECTACULAR DINNER PARTY SELECTION.

SERVES 8

3 to 4 pound leg of lamb, boned, butterflied and flattened for rolling (ask your butcher to do this)
⅓ cup olive oil
2 teaspoons minced fresh thyme
3 cloves garlic, finely chopped
salt and pepper to taste

STUFFING
1 pound ground veal
12 ounces oyster mushrooms, finely chopped
1 medium onion, finely chopped
6 cloves garlic, finely chopped
2 tablespoons olive oil
salt and pepper to taste
2 cups chopped fresh spinach
1 cup chopped fresh mint leaves
⅔ cup chopped macadamia nuts, toasted
½ cup lightly toasted bread crumbs

2 red bell peppers, roasted, peeled, seeded and sliced into thin strips (divided use)
string for tying

TOMATILLO-MINT SAUCE
1 pound fresh tomatillos, quartered
1 jalapeño, seeded and chopped
2 tablespoons finely chopped garlic
3 tablespoons clarified butter
1 cup sherry

¼ cup soy sauce
¼ cup brown sugar
½ cup chopped fresh mint leaves
1 teaspoon ground pepper
edible flowers (garnish)

Rub lamb with olive oil. Sprinkle both sides of lamb with thyme, garlic, salt and pepper. Set aside.

To prepare stuffing, sauté veal, mushrooms, onion and garlic in olive oil until vegetables wilt and veal has browned. Salt and pepper to taste. Stir in spinach, mint, nuts and bread crumbs and heat through. (Stuffing can be prepared early in day; cover and refrigerate until ready to use.)

Place lamb on work surface and open out flat. Evenly distribute stuffing over lamb. Place pepper slices on top of stuffing, reserving some for decoration. Roll up and tie with string to hold during roasting. (Meat can be prepared to this point early in day, then covered and refrigerated.)

Roast at 500 degrees for 15 minutes; lower temperature to 350 degrees and continue to roast 15 minutes per pound for medium rare.

While lamb is roasting, prepare sauce. Sauté tomatillos, jalapeño and garlic in butter until soft. Add sherry, soy sauce, sugar, mint and pepper; cook over low heat for 7 minutes, stirring occasionally. (Can be prepared early in day and reheated.)

When meat is done, remove from oven and allow to rest for 10 minutes. Remove string and carve meat into ½-inch-thick slices. Spoon Tomatillo-Mint Sauce over meat or serve separately. Decorate plates with edible flowers and reserved roasted pepper strips.

SERVE WITH GARLIC MASHED POTATOES (PAGE 179) AND HERBED ASPARAGUS WITH PARMESAN (PAGE 170).

BEEF TENDERLOIN STUFFED WITH SPINACH AND VEAL

SERVES 8

STUFFING

½ cup (1 stick) butter
1 onion, finely chopped
1 clove garlic, minced
½ pound mushrooms, minced
3 shallots, minced
1 tablespoon beef stock base
   (or bouillon powder)
½ pound ground veal
½ pound chicken livers, puréed in food processor
4 slices wheat berry bread, made into crumbs
12 ounces fresh spinach, stemmed and finely
   chopped
salt and pepper to taste
¼ teaspoon lemon juice

1 beef tenderloin (3 to 4-pound), trimmed and
   butterflied
string for tying

SAUCE

pan juices
1 cup red wine
1 cup beef stock
2 tablespoons butter, softened
salt and pepper to taste

Melt butter in large skillet over medium-high heat. Add onion and garlic and sauté until soft. Stir in mushrooms, shallots and beef stock base, cooking about 10 minutes until most of moisture from mushrooms has evaporated. Add veal and chicken liver purée and cook about 4 minutes until brown. Add bread crumbs and spinach and cook another 2 minutes or until moisture has evaporated. Add salt, pepper and lemon juice. Transfer mixture to food processor, in batches if necessary, and purée coarsely.

Stuff pocket of tenderloin with veal mixture; tie at intervals with string. (Meat can be prepared ahead and refrigerated to this point, but should be brought to room temperature before roasting.)

Rub meat with salt and pepper and roast at 450 degrees about 25 to 35 minutes (8 to 10 minutes per pound for rare). Remove from pan, reserving juices for sauce, and let meat rest about 10 minutes.

Skim any excess grease from pan. Add red wine and beef stock and boil until reduced by half, about 5 minutes. Remove from heat and swirl in butter and seasonings.

Remove string from meat, slice, and serve with sauce.

THIS ELEGANT ENTRÉE WOULD BE COMPLEMENTED BY VINTNER'S SALAD (PAGE 67), PORTABELLA AND PORCINI TART (PAGE 20) AND CARROTS WITH PISTACHIOS AND GRAND MARNIER (PAGE 174).

LAMB WITH PESTO AND RADICCHIO

SERVES 8

BASIL HERB PESTO SAUCE
1 cup fresh basil leaves
4 spinach leaves
6 sprigs parsley
3 sprigs marjoram
⅓ cup pine nuts
3 cloves garlic, chopped
⅓ cup grated Parmesan cheese
⅓ cup grated Romano cheese
3 tablespoons olive oil
2 tablespoons butter
¼ teaspoon salt

LAMB
1 leg of lamb (5 to 6 pounds)
1 cup sliced shallots
2 medium heads radicchio, cut into 4 wedges each
1 cup red wine
1 cup beef bouillon
fresh sprigs of basil (garnish)

To make pesto sauce, combine basil, spinach, parsley, marjoram, pine nuts, garlic, cheeses, oil, butter and salt in food processor and purée until well mixed and smooth.

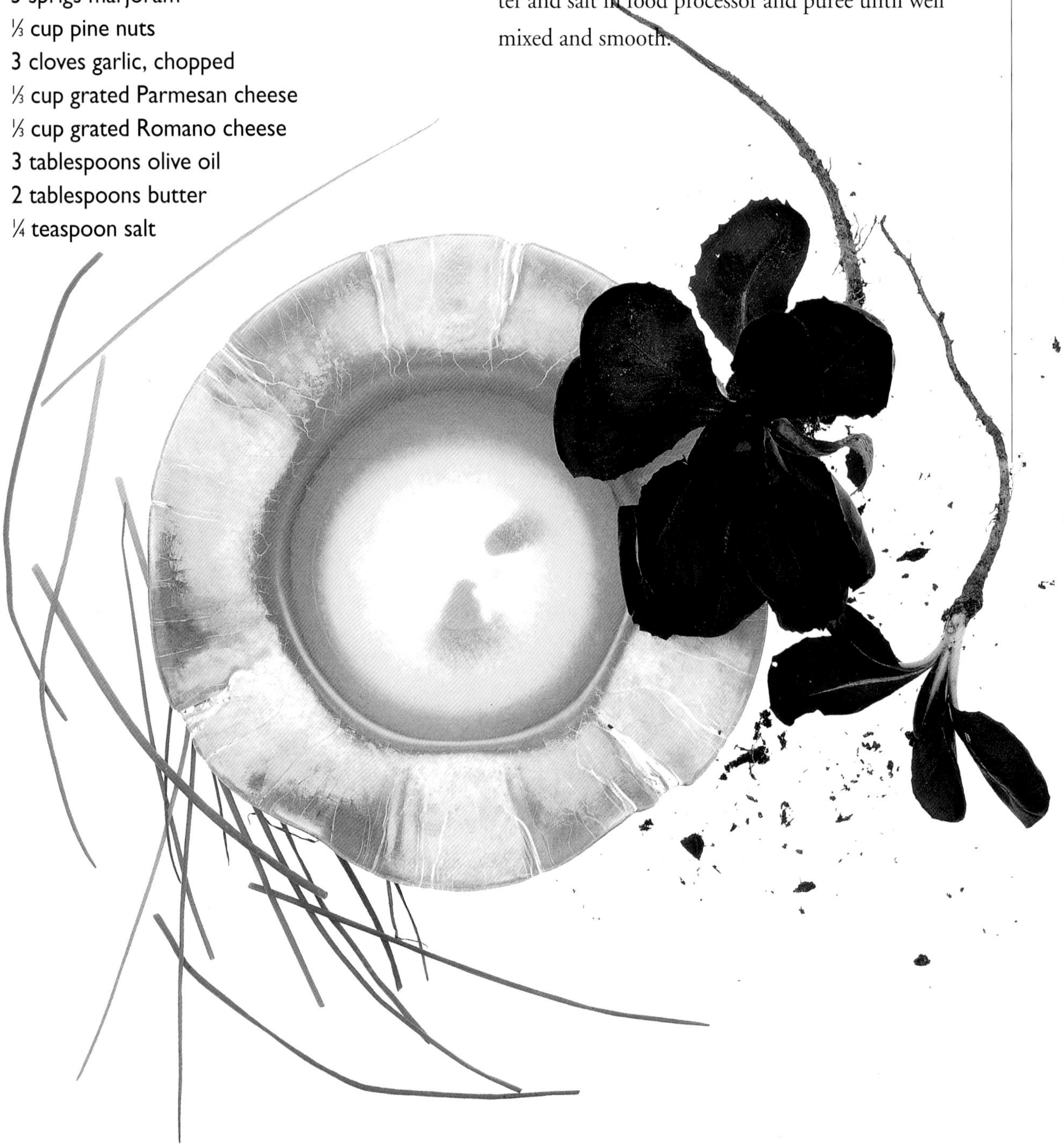

AURENE BOWL,
CA. 1920,
STEUBEN GLASS
WORKS,
CORNING, NY,
1992.494

Trim excess fat from lamb, leaving a thin layer. Place lamb on rack in roasting pan. Make 10 to 12 slits and spoon some pesto sauce into each slit. Rub remaining pesto over top. Cover and let stand for 2 hours at room temperature or refrigerate overnight.

Roast lamb for 30 minutes at 350 degrees. Add shallots, turning to coat in pan juices. Roast 45 minutes. Add radicchio, turning to coat in juices. Continue to roast until thermometer inserted into thickest part of meat registers 140 degrees for medium rare, approximately 45 minutes. Remove from oven and transfer meat to heated platter.

Add wine and bouillon to roasting pan, scraping up any browned drippings from meat. Bring to a boil over high heat and cook until sauce is reduced by half. Sauce can be puréed if desired.

Garnish meat with sprigs of basil. Slice, and serve with sauce.

IF RADICCHIO IS UNAVAILABLE, 4 HEADS OF BELGIAN ENDIVE, HALVED LENGTHWISE, MAY BE SUBSTITUTED.

IF TIME IS LIMITED, SUBSTITUTE PREPARED PESTO SAUCE.

SERVE WITH GARLIC MASHED POTATOES (PAGE 179), GREEN BEANS WITH CAPERS AND WATERCRESS (PAGE 170) AND BROILED TOMATOES.

ASIAN MARINATED LAMB CHOPS

SERVES 4

SOY MARINADE
2 cups soy sauce
1 cup red wine vinegar
¼ cup sugar
¼ cup sesame oil
2 heads (not cloves) garlic, minced
½ cup minced green onions
3 tablespoons crushed red pepper flakes
1 tablespoon Chinese hot bean paste
1 tablespoon Chinese bean paste

LAMB CHOPS
8 loin lamb chops, 1¼ inch thick

Combine ingredients for marinade, stirring well to dissolve sugar. Pour marinade over lamb chops either in a large glass baking dish or in a large self-sealing plastic bag. Coat lamb chops well. Marinate at room temperature for 30 to 45 minutes, no longer or marinade will change color of meat.

Remove chops from marinade and set aside. Pour marinade in saucepan and bring to a boil over high heat. Cook at full boil for 3 to 4 minutes. Set aside.

Grill chops to desired degree of doneness, occasionally basting with reserved marinade.

TRY THIS MARINADE ON SPARE RIBS OR CHICKEN.

CROWN ROAST OF PORK STUFFED WITH WINTER FRUITS

SERVES 8 TO 10

1 crown roast of pork (18 ribs)
salt and pepper

STUFFING
¾ pound ground pork or sausage
1 teaspoon dried thyme
¾ cup chopped dried figs
¾ cup chopped dried peaches
¾ cup chopped dried apricots
¾ cup chopped pitted prunes
¾ cup chopped dried pears
¾ cup chopped dates
¾ cup cored, chopped apples
¾ cup currants
1 large onion, minced
1 lemon, thinly sliced and seeded
2 cups finely crushed biscotti crumbs
1 cup white port

parsley or other fresh herbs (garnish)
crab apples (garnish)

RED WINE SAUCE (OPTIONAL)
1¼ cups beef broth
¾ cup dry red wine

Salt and pepper pork and stand it in shallow roasting pan.

Brown ground pork in a large skillet over medium heat. Drain fat. Add thyme, all fruits, onion, lemon, biscotti crumbs and port. Mix well. (Stuffing can be prepared 1 day in advance. Cover and refrigerate.)

Spoon stuffing into center of roast; cover stuffing with foil. Roast in 350-degree oven for 2½ to 3 hours, or 180 degrees on a meat thermometer.

Carefully remove roast from pan (so as to not lose stuffing) and transfer to platter. Tent with foil to keep warm. Deglaze roasting pan with beef broth and red wine, scraping up any browned bits in bottom of pan. Simmer until sauce is reduced by half.

To serve, arrange parsley and crab apples around roast. Serve wine sauce separately.

BAKED ACORN SQUASH OR SWEET POTATO CUSTARD WITH PECANS (PAGE 180) AND GREEN BEANS WITH CAPERS AND WATERCRESS (PAGE 170) ARE DELICIOUS WITH THIS ELEGANT ENTRÉE.

VEAL CHOPS WITH TOMATOES, PINE NUTS AND CAPERS

SERVES 4

4 veal rib chops (10-ounce), boned and trimmed
salt and pepper
2 tablespoons olive oil (divided use)
4 tomatoes, peeled, seeded, chopped and drained
½ cup pine nuts, toasted (divided use)
2 tablespoons capers, drained
1 tablespoon minced shallot
1 tablespoon minced garlic
1 tablespoon minced fresh basil
1 teaspoon minced fresh oregano
4 tablespoons dry white wine
1 tablespoon fresh lemon juice
2 tablespoons butter

Season veal with salt and pepper. Heat 1 table-spoon oil in skillet and brown veal on both sides. Cook about 5 minutes on each side for medium rare. Transfer veal to platter and tent with foil to keep warm.

Heat remaining olive oil over medium heat in same skillet. Add tomatoes, ⅓ cup pine nuts, capers, shallot, garlic, basil and oregano; sauté 2 minutes. Add wine and lemon juice and continue simmering 4 more minutes. Whisk in butter and keep warm.

Serve veal on individual plates topped with sauce and garnished with remaining pine nuts.

To complete this quick dinner try Microwave Risotto (page 156) or, if you have a little more time, try Wild Mushroom Risotto (page 165). Complete your meal with a green salad dressed with Balsamic Dijon Salad Dressing (page 85).

TIN-GLAZED EARTHENWARE CHARGER, 1691, LAMBETH, ENGLAND, 1992.B.224

RAGOÛT OF VEAL WITH MUSHROOMS

SERVES 6 TO 8

2 pounds veal stew meat cut into 1-inch pieces

3 ounces thick-sliced bacon

1 tablespoon olive oil

1½ cups chopped onions

5 tablespoons flour (divided use)

2 teaspoons paprika

1½ teaspoons ground coriander

salt and pepper to taste

3 cups diced plum tomatoes (divided use)

1 cup chicken broth

1 cup dry white wine

12 large shallots, peeled

4 cloves garlic, minced

3 carrots, sliced 1 inch thick

¼ cup chopped Italian parsley

1 tablespoon dried tarragon leaves

grated zest of 1 orange

8 ounces fresh mushrooms, halved

4 ounces portabello mushrooms, chopped

6 tablespoons butter (divided use)

1 cup heavy cream

HERBED PASTRY (OPTIONAL)

1 cup flour

1 tablespoon chopped fresh herbs (rosemary, parsley)

2 teaspoons sugar

1 teaspoon baking powder

½ teaspoon salt

3 tablespoons butter

⅓ cup heavy cream

Place bacon in large skillet and cook over medium heat until crisp. Drain bacon and set aside. Place veal in same skillet and brown over high heat, about 4 minutes. Remove veal and set aside. Add olive oil and onions to drippings. Reduce heat and sauté about 5 minutes.

Combine veal and onions in oven-proof casserole and sprinkle with mixture of 2 tablespoons flour, paprika, coriander, salt and pepper. Cook over low heat about 5 minutes. Add 2 cups tomatoes, chicken broth, wine, shallots, garlic, carrots, parsley, tarragon, orange zest and reserved bacon. Bring to a boil; cover and place in oven. Bake at 350 degrees until veal is tender, about 1½ hours.

While veal is baking, combine mushrooms and 3 tablespoons butter in skillet and sauté until tender and browned. Set aside.

To prepare pastry, combine flour, herbs, sugar, baking powder and salt. Cut in butter until mixture resembles coarse meal. Add cream, mixing until well blended. Gather dough into a ball and roll out on lightly floured surface to ¼ inch thick. Cut into leaf shapes and refrigerate.

Instead of herbed pastry, puff pastry can be used to make leaves. Roll out 1 or 2 sheets of puff pastry dough and cut out random leaf shapes. Brush with egg wash and bake at 350 degrees for 11 to 15 minutes, or until golden brown.

When stew is done, remove from oven and pour into a strainer placed over a bowl, reserving stew and liquid separately. Melt remaining 3 tablespoons butter in casserole. Sprinkle in remaining 3 tablespoons flour and cook over low heat, whisking constantly, for 3 minutes. Slowly whisk in reserved liquid and simmer for 5 minutes. Add cream and adjust seasonings. (If sauce seems too thick, it can be thinned with a little wine.) Return stew to casserole and stir in remaining 1 cup tomatoes, reserved mushrooms and sauce. Simmer about 5 minutes until heated through.

Place pastry leaves on top of stew to serve. If using herbed pastry dough, place leaves on top in overlapping pattern and bake another 20 minutes, or until leaves have browned. Serve with noodles or rice.

LAMB SIRLOINS WITH CALAMATAS, SUN-DRIED TOMATOES AND CHÈVRE

SERVES 4

¼ cup pitted, chopped Calamata olives
⅓ cup chopped sun-dried tomatoes
⅓ cup crumbled fresh chèvre (goat cheese)
I tablespoon minced garlic
I tablespoon chopped fresh mint
olive oil
4 lamb sirloins

To prepare stuffing, mix olives, tomatoes, chèvre, garlic and mint in a bowl. Set aside for at least 2 hours.

Form a pocket in each sirloin by carefully inserting a knife into side of each piece and working it back and forth to create a large enough space to accommodate stuffing. Fill each pocket with one-fourth of stuffing.

Coat stuffed sirloins with olive oil. Sear in heavy skillet over high heat. When browned on all sides, place sirloins in baking dish and roast at 400 degrees for 20 to 25 minutes.

THE ROASTING PAN CAN BE DEGLAZED WITH A HEARTY PINOT NOIR (PREFERABLY THE ONE SERVED WITH DINNER). POUR I CUP WINE INTO PAN AND BOIL TO REDUCE LIQUID BY HALF. SPOON SAUCE OVER SIRLOINS.

A SIMPLE SIDE DISH TO COMPLEMENT THIS ENTRÉE IS **MINTED ORZO**. COOK ORZO "PILAF-STYLE." SAUTÉ A CHOPPED ONION IN A PAN WITH OLIVE OIL. ADD ORZO AND STIR TO COAT. ADD CHICKEN STOCK (I ½ TIMES THE AMOUNT OF ORZO) AND FRESH CHOPPED MINT TO TASTE. COOK AL DENTE.

IF LAMB SIRLOINS ARE NOT AVAILABLE, DOUBLE LOIN LAMB CHOPS WILL WORK EQUALLY WELL. THEY CAN BE COOKED OR GRILLED, 5 TO 6 MINUTES PER SIDE.

STERLING SILVER SPOON, *LOVE PLAYING WITH TIME*, CA. 1884-85, TIFFANY & CO., NY, 1991.101.1

Keep hot food warm or cold food cool for up to 4 hours by wrapping it in foil and then several layers of newspaper. Place in a styrofoam cooler.

TENDERLOIN OF BEEF STUFFED WITH RED BELL PEPPERS, ONIONS AND SHIITAKE MUSHROOMS

SERVES 6

FILLING

4 tablespoons olive oil

3 large onions, halved and sliced

2 red bell peppers, seeded and thinly sliced

3 large cloves garlic, minced

1 tablespoon fresh rosemary

12 ounces fresh shiitake mushrooms, stemmed and thinly sliced

salt and freshly ground pepper to taste

½ cup chopped fresh parsley

BEEF

1 beef tenderloin (3-pound) trimmed and butterflied

3 tablespoons olive oil (divided use)

1 teaspoon minced fresh rosemary

salt and freshly ground pepper

string for tying

2 cloves garlic, flattened

4 slices bacon, halved crosswise

MUSTARD SAUCE

2 tablespoons butter

2 tablespoons flour

2¼ cups unsalted beef stock

3 tablespoons brandy

1½ tablespoons Dijon mustard

1 teaspoon minced fresh rosemary

6 tablespoons (¾ stick) butter

salt and freshly ground pepper

3 tablespoons minced fresh parsley

sprigs of fresh parsley (garnish)

To prepare filling, heat oil in large skillet over medium heat. Add onions and cook until softened, stirring occasionally, about 10 minutes. Add peppers and cook 4 minutes, or until they begin to soften. Add garlic and rosemary, stirring 1 minute. Add mushrooms, salt and pepper; sauté 5 minutes, or until mushrooms are just tender. Remove from heat and adjust seasoning. When mixture is completely cooled, stir in parsley.

Open tenderloin out flat and place between 2 sheets of waxed paper. Pound meat to even ¾-inch thickness. Rub meat with 1 tablespoon oil, rosemary, salt and pepper. Spread 2 cups of filling down full length of meat on one side. (Reserve remaining filling.) Roll beef into tight cylinder, keeping filling in. Tie string around ends of tenderloin, then around length. Continue tying crosswise at 1-inch intervals. (Dish can be prepared to this point up to 6 hours in advance. Rub outside of meat with olive oil and refrigerate. Bring to room temperature before proceeding.)

Heat remaining 2 tablespoons oil and garlic in large skillet over medium-high heat. Sauté until garlic is brown, about 2 minutes. Discard garlic. Pat meat dry and season with salt and pepper. Brown meat lightly, about 1 minute per side.

Place meat in roasting pan, seam side down, and arrange bacon slices over top. Pour off all but thin film of fat from skillet; set skillet aside. Roast meat at 375 degrees for 35 minutes, or until meat thermometer registers 130 degrees for rare. Transfer roast to platter and tent with foil to keep warm.

To prepare sauce, melt butter in reserved skillet. Add flour and cook, stirring, until lightly browned. Pour ½ cup stock into roasting pan and bring to boil, scraping up any browned bits; add to skillet. Add ½ cup stock to skillet and boil until reduced to thick syrup, scraping up any browned bits, about 8 minutes. Add another ½ cup stock and boil until syrupy, another 3 minutes. Add any drippings accumulated on meat platter, brandy, mustard, rosemary and remaining ¾ cup stock; boil until thickened, about 3 minutes. Reduce heat to medium and whisk in butter, 1 tablespoon at a time. Season with salt and pepper and stir in parsley.

To serve, remove bacon and string from roast. Cut across grain into ½-inch thick slices. Reheat reserved filling and arrange around meat. Spoon sauce over slices and garnish with parsley.

CRACKED PEPPERCORN STEAKS WITH SHALLOTS AND MUSHROOMS
SERVES 4

4 filet mignon steaks (about 5 ounces each),
   cut 1-inch thick
salt
2 teaspoons cracked black peppercorns
2½ tablespoons butter (divided use)
1 tablespoon oil
¼ cup minced shallots
1 pound mushrooms, thickly sliced
½ teaspoon crumbled dried tarragon
⅓ cup dry white wine
2 tablespoons brandy

Season steaks with salt and pat peppercorns firmly into both sides. Melt 1 tablespoon butter with the oil in a large skillet. Sauté steaks over high heat until brown and cooked to desired doneness (about 4 minutes per side for medium rare). Transfer steaks to platter.

Melt remaining 1½ tablespoons butter in same skillet over medium-high heat. Add shallots and stir to coat with butter. Add mushrooms and tarragon and cook until mushrooms are tender (about 10 minutes), stirring frequently. Add wine and brandy to skillet and simmer 1 minute, scraping up browned bits from bottom of pan. Return steaks and any accumulated juices to skillet and cook until steaks are just heated through (about 2 minutes). Place steaks on plates. Arrange mushrooms around steaks and spoon pan juices over.

IF YOU ENJOY A MORE INTENSE, EARTHY FLAVOR, USE A VARIETY OF WILD MUSHROOMS AND REPLACE THE WHITE WINE WITH RED.

SWISS AND PARMESAN ONION PIE (PAGE 177) AND HERBED GREEN BEANS WITH TOMATOES (PAGE 172) ARE SAVORY ACCOMPANIMENTS TO THESE STEAKS.

ROAST PORK WITH WILD MUSHROOMS

SERVES 8

STUFFING

2 cups minced fresh shiitake, oyster or morel mushrooms

2 cups finely chopped leeks

¼ cup butter

¼ cup dry white wine

¾ cup soft bread crumbs

½ cup chopped water chestnuts

½ cup shredded carrots

¼ teaspoon salt

⅛ teaspoon pepper

⅛ teaspoon cayenne pepper

¼ teaspoon thyme

1 teaspoon *fines herbes* (blend of thyme, oregano, sage, rosemary, marjoram and basil)

1 pork loin center rib roast (8 ribs), backbone loosened

MUSHROOM LEEK SAUCE

1 cup sliced leeks

1 cup sliced fresh shiitake, oyster or morel mushrooms

¼ cup dry white wine

1 teaspoon *fines herbes,* crushed

½ cup heavy cream

2 teaspoons lemon juice

1 teaspoon instant chicken bouillon granules

⅛ teaspoon pepper

To prepare stuffing, place mushrooms, leeks and butter in saucepan and cook until tender. Add wine; simmer, uncovered, 5 minutes or until liquid evaporates. Remove from heat. Stir in bread crumbs, water chestnuts, carrots and seasonings.

Position meat with rib side down. On meaty side, cut a pocket above each rib, making a total of 8 pockets. Spoon stuffing into pockets. Place roast, rib side down, in shallow roasting pan and insert meat thermometer. Roast at 325 degrees for 1½ to 2 hours or until thermometer registers 160 degrees. After 1 hour, cover loosely with foil to prevent over browning.

About 30 minutes before roast is done, prepare sauce. Combine leeks, mushrooms, wine and *fines herbes* in saucepan. Bring to boil; reduce heat and simmer, uncovered, 5 minutes or until most of liquid is evaporated. Stir in whipping cream, lemon juice, bouillon granules and pepper. Do not let sauce boil. Keep sauce warm for up to 30 minutes.

Remove roast from oven; let stand 10 minutes before carving. To serve, slice meat between ribs and serve with sauce.

MUSHROOM LEEK SAUCE WOULD BE WONDERFUL ON ANY PORK OR CHICKEN DISH.

PORK TENDERLOIN WITH PRUNES AND CALVADOS

SERVES 4

12 pitted prunes

½ cup Calvados (apple brandy)

2 pork tenderloins

sea salt to taste

freshly ground pepper to taste

3 tablespoons butter

4 shallots, chopped

1 cup hard cider

5 tablespoons chopped Italian parsley
   (divided use)

½ cup crème fraîche

P lace prunes in small bowl and cover with Calvados. Allow to marinate at least 1 hour.

Season pork with salt and pepper. Cut each piece in half to fit into pan more easily. Melt butter in skillet and brown pork on all sides. Stir in shallots, prunes and Calvados, shaking pan. (Calvados will probably flame up for a minute or two.) Add cider and 3 tablespoons of parsley. Reduce heat to low, cover, and simmer for 10 to 15 minutes.

Remove pork and keep warm. Place skillet over high heat and rapidly reduce pan liquid by half, stirring gently. Add crème fraîche and continue cooking on high for 1 or 2 minutes until thickened. Add remaining parsley.

Slice pork into medallions and arrange with prunes on warm dinner plates. Top with sauce.

PORK TENDERLOIN WITH RED ONION CONFIT

SERVES 4

RED ONION CONFIT

2 tablespoons olive oil

4 large red onions, thinly sliced

2 tablespoons sugar

¼ teaspoon salt

¼ cup currants or raisins

¾ cup dry red wine

¼ cup balsamic vinegar

2 tablespoons crème de cassis
   (black currant liqueur)

1½ teaspoons chopped fresh thyme
   (or ½ teaspoon dried)

PORK TENDERLOIN

2-pound pork tenderloin
   (either 1 large or 2 smaller tenderloins)

1 teaspoon salt

½ teaspoon freshly ground pepper

1 tablespoon chopped fresh thyme, or 1
   teaspoon dried thyme

2 tablespoons olive oil

To make confit, heat oil in large nonreactive skillet over medium-low heat. Add onions and cook 5 to 7 minutes, until softened but not browned. Add sugar, salt, currants and wine. Bring to a boil, then reduce heat, and simmer until nearly all liquid is gone, about 20 minutes.

Add vinegar, cassis and thyme and cook about 10 minutes, stirring frequently, until onions have turned a deep golden brown. (This can be prepared several days ahead and stored covered in the refrigerator.) Serve warm or at room temperature.

To prepare meat for grill, trim off fat and silver membrane. Place in baking dish and rub with salt, pepper, thyme and olive oil. Cover with plastic wrap and marinate at room temperature for 30 minutes.

Grill pork tenderloins on oiled grill set 4 to 6 inches from hot coals, turning, until just cooked through, about 15 to 20 minutes. Meat should register 160 degrees on an instant-reading thermometer. Allow meat to rest 5 to 10 minutes before slicing. Serve thin slices on bed of Red Onion Confit.

PORK CAN ALSO BE MARINATED IN INDONESIAN SOY SAUCE (AVAILABLE AT SPECIALTY MARKETS) FOR 2 TO 3 HOURS BEFORE GRILLING. (USE THIS IN LIEU OF SALT, PEPPER, THYME AND OIL USED IN RECIPE.)

PORK TENDERLOIN WITH CHAMPAGNE MUSTARD SAUCE

SERVES 4 TO 6

MARINADE
¼ cup soy sauce
¼ cup bourbon
2 tablespoons brown sugar
3 cloves garlic, crushed

2 pork tenderloins

CHAMPAGNE MUSTARD SAUCE
⅓ cup sour cream
⅓ cup mayonnaise
1 tablespoon champagne mustard
1 tablespoon finely chopped green onion
1½ teaspoons jalapeño-garlic vinegar

To prepare marinade, combine soy sauce, bourbon, brown sugar and garlic. Place pork in shallow, non-metallic pan and pour marinade over. Marinate, covered, at room temperature for 3 hours, turning occasionally.

Remove pork from marinade, reserving liquid. Pour liquid into saucepan and bring to a boil over high heat. Cook at full boil for 3 to 4 minutes.

Place pork in a shallow pan and roast 30 minutes at 425 degrees, or until meat thermometer reads 150 to 160 degrees. Baste pork a few times with reserved marinade during cooking.

While pork is cooking, prepare sauce. Combine sour cream, mayonnaise, mustard, green onion and vinegar in small bowl. Mix well and set aside.

To serve, thinly slice pork on diagonal and top with sauce.

SOME SIDE DISH CHOICES ARE HEAVENLY POTATOES (PAGE 179), BRAISED RED CABBAGE WITH ONIONS AND BACON (PAGE 175) AND GINGERED ASPARAGUS WITH CASHEWS (PAGE 171).

PORK TENDERLOIN CAN ALSO BE COOKED ON THE GRILL INSTEAD OF BAKED IN OVEN. GRILL 15 TO 20 MINUTES OVER HOT COALS.

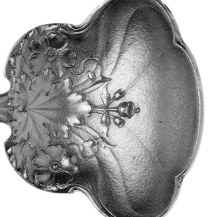

Dark soy sauce is light soy sauce with added molasses or caramel. It adds a richer flavor and color to sauces. One way to tell the difference between dark and light soy is to shake the bottle. Dark soy coats the sides of the bottle.

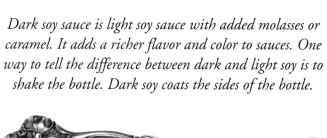

STERLING SILVER AND SILVERGILT SERVING SPOON, CA. 1895-1900, DESIGNED BY WILLIAM C. CODMAN, GOFHAM MFG. CO., PROVIDENCE, RI, 1993.54

THE ARTFUL TABLE

TENDERLOIN STEAKS WITH FENNEL-MARSALA SAUCE

SERVES 4

¼ cup olive oil
4 beef tenderloin steaks, ¾ inch thick
salt and pepper to taste
½ cup dry Marsala wine
½ cup dry red wine
1½ teaspoons minced garlic
1 teaspoon fennel seeds
1 tablespoon tomato paste
1 tablespoon water
¼ teaspoon red pepper flakes
2 tablespoons chopped fresh parsley (garnish)

Heat oil in a large skillet over high heat until a haze forms over oil. Add steaks and cook 3 minutes on each side, or until desired doneness. Transfer steaks to warm platter and season with salt and pepper.

Pour off all but 2 tablespoons of oil from pan. Return pan to high heat and add Marsala and red wine. Boil wine for 30 seconds, scraping pan to incorporate any browned bits. Add garlic, stirring sauce 2 or 3 times. Add fennel, continuing to stir. Combine tomato paste with water and add along with red pepper flakes. Reduce heat; simmer and stir for 1 minute, until sauce is thickened.

Return steaks to pan and coat with sauce. Transfer to a heated platter or individual plates. Garnish with parsley and serve.

FOR ACCOMPANIMENTS, SERVE POTPOURRI OF MUSHROOMS WITH GARLIC AND PARSLEY (PAGE 176), ROASTED POTATOES WITH ROSEMARY (PAGE 178) AND ROASTED RED AND GREEN BELL PEPPERS (PAGE 177).

BROILED LAMB CHOPS WITH CANNELLINI AND SPINACH

SERVES 6

1 cup finely chopped shallots
½ cup olive oil plus 1 tablespoon (divided use)
5 large cloves garlic, minced
1 tablespoon fresh rosemary (or 1 teaspoon dried)
1 or 2 thick lamb loin chops per person
2 cans (15-ounce) cannellini beans (white kidney beans), drained
4 plum tomatoes, chopped
2 packages (10-ounce) fresh spinach, stemmed
salt and pepper to taste

Mix shallots, ½ cup of olive oil, garlic and rosemary in small bowl. Season with salt and pepper.

Lay chops in glass baking dish and spoon shallot mixture over. Turn to coat both sides. Cover and refrigerate 2 hours.

Preheat broiler or grill (best on grill).

Remove lamb chops and transfer shallot mixture to heavy saucepan; bring to simmer. Add beans and chopped tomatoes, stirring to heat through. (May be made ahead to this point.) Season with salt and pepper and keep warm.

Grill or broil chops 5 minutes per side for medium rare.

Meanwhile, heat remaining 1 tablespoon olive oil in heavy skillet over high heat. Add spinach and sauté until just wilted. Season with salt and pepper.

To serve, spoon bean mixture onto plates and top with spinach and chops.

VENISON STEW WITH JUNIPER BERRIES

SERVES 8 TO 10

½ pound thick-cut lean bacon

4 pounds haunch or shoulder of venison, trimmed and cubed

½ cup flour

¼ cup oil

2 cups beef stock, hot

2 cups red wine

2 cloves garlic, chopped

½ teaspoon dried thyme

2 bay leaves

1 teaspoon salt

¼ teaspoon pepper

1 tablespoon crushed juniper berries

3 tablespoons butter

½ medium onion, chopped

½ pound large fresh mushrooms, quartered

beurre manié (2 tablespoons butter blended with 2 tablespoons flour and formed into ½-inch balls)

parsley sprigs (garnish)

Cook bacon over low heat for 10 minutes until brown. Drain, crumble and set aside.

Coat venison lightly with flour, shaking off excess. Heat oil in a large pot and add the meat, in batches, turning to brown on all sides. Add bacon, stock, wine, garlic, thyme, bay leaves, salt, pepper and juniper berries. Cover and bake at 350 degrees for 30 to 60 minutes, or until meat is tender but not falling apart. Check often after 30 minutes. (Tenderness of venison determines cooking time.)

While meat is cooking, melt butter in a heavy frying pan and sauté onions over medium-low heat, until browned. Add mushrooms, and cook a few minutes longer until lightly browned. Set aside.

When meat is done, stir in the onions and mushrooms, and bring to a simmer on top of stove. Begin to stir in *beurre manié* one at a time, incorporating thoroughly before adding the next, until sauce reaches desired thickness.

Serve over noodles, rice or polenta. Garnish with parsley.

ENAMELED PORCELAIN PLATTER, CA. 1760-1780, CHINA, 1954.85

BEEF TENDERLOIN STUFFED WITH PEPPERS, SPINACH AND GOAT CHEESE

SERVES 6

1¼ pounds fresh spinach, stemmed

8 ounces fresh goat cheese, crumbled

1 tablespoon chopped fresh rosemary

1 tablespoon chopped fresh thyme

½ teaspoon salt

½ teaspoon freshly ground pepper

1 beef tenderloin (3-pound) trimmed and butterflied

salt and pepper to taste

3 red bell peppers, roasted, peeled, seeded and quartered

½ pound bacon slices, blanched

string for tying

2 tablespoons olive oil

fresh chives (garnish)

Set aside 8 large spinach leaves. Blanch remaining leaves until just wilted, 1 to 2 minutes. Drain, refresh under cold water, and drain again. Squeeze dry and chop coarsely. Combine spinach with cheese, rosemary, thyme, salt and pepper. Place spinach mixture on waxed paper and form into a 12-inch long roll. Wrap and refrigerate until firm.

Open meat out flat and pound to an even ¾-inch thickness. Season with salt and pepper. Arrange reserved spinach leaves over cut side of beef, leaving a 1-inch border. Layer with peppers, skinned side up. Place spinach log on one side of tenderloin. Roll beef into tight cylinder, keeping filling in. Tie with string at 1-inch intervals (do ends first), then around length of tenderloin. Transfer to roasting rack and arrange bacon slices on top. (Dish can be prepared to this point up to 6 hours ahead. Rub outside of meat with olive oil and refrigerate. Return to room temperature before proceeding.)

Roast at 450 degrees about 25 to 30 minutes for rare, or until meat thermometer registers 130 degrees. Allow to rest 15 minutes before slicing. Discard bacon, and serve slices garnished with chives.

GLAZED EARTHENWARE CHARGER, 1878, JOHN BENNETT, NY, 1990.183.

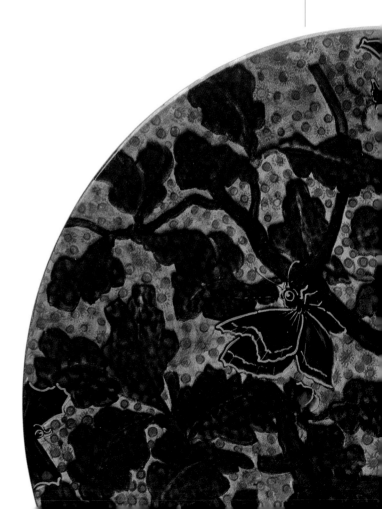

VEAL LOAF FLORENTINE WITH TOMATO CONCASSÉ

SERVES 4

VEAL LOAF
1 pound ground veal
1 small onion, minced
3 cloves garlic, minced
½ teaspoon dried thyme
¾ teaspoon marjoram
½ teaspoon pepper
1 tablespoon soy sauce
1 egg
2 egg whites
1 slice dried, crumbled whole wheat or rye bread
1 package (10-ounce) fresh spinach, stemmed, coarsely chopped, steamed and drained
3 ounces Monterey Jack cheese, cut in thin strips
2 bay leaves

TOMATO CONCASSÉ
2 teaspoons minced garlic
1 tablespoon minced shallots
2 teaspoons olive oil
1 tablespoon dried sweet basil
1 teaspoon freshly ground pepper
1 bay leaf
1 can (18-ounce) whole plum tomatoes, drained and diced

Mix veal with onion, garlic, thyme, marjoram, pepper, soy sauce, egg, egg whites and bread until well combined. Oil bottom of an 8½ x 4½ x 2½-inch loaf pan. Place half veal mixture in pan, patting down to fill corners. Make indentation in middle of meat. Place spinach in indentation and spread cheese over. Top with remaining veal mixture and pat down again. Press bay leaves into top. Place pan in *bain-marie* (larger pan filled halfway with boiling water) and bake at 350 degrees for 1 hour and 10 minutes.

While veal loaf is baking, gently sauté garlic and shallots in oil until softened but not brown. Add basil, pepper, bay leaf and tomatoes. Cover and simmer 5 minutes. Remove cover and simmer 10 to 15 minutes longer, until thick. Remove bay leaf.

Allow meat to stand 5 to 10 minutes before serving for ease in slicing. Serve with Tomato Concassé.

STUFFED FLANK STEAK WITH ROASTED RED PEPPERS AND SPINACH

THIS IS EASIER THAN IT SOUNDS AND MAKES AN IMPRESSIVE PRESENTATION. SERVES 4 TO 6

1 flank steak (1½ to 1¾ pounds), butterflied with the grain (ask your butcher to do this)

MARINADE

1 tablespoon liquid smoke

1 tablespoon steak sauce

¾ cup lemon juice

¾ cup olive oil

¼ cup worcestershire sauce

1 clove garlic, minced

freshly ground pepper

½ teaspoon Tabasco

TRANSFER-
PRINTED
PEARLWARE
CHARGER, CA.
1900, JOSIAH
WEDGWOOD
FACTORY,
STAFFORDSHIRE,
ENGLAND,
1991.412.86

FILLING

1 package (10-ounce) frozen chopped spinach, thawed

1 jar (8-ounce) roasted red peppers, cut into strips

1 cup chopped green onion

2 cans (4-ounce) chopped green chilies

3 cloves garlic, minced

1 to 2 teaspoons ground cumin

1 to 2 teaspoons chili powder

¼ cup grated Monterey Jack cheese

Combine marinade ingredients in a self-sealing plastic bag and add steak. Refrigerate 8 hours or overnight.

Remove meat from marinade and pat dry with paper towels. Open butterflied steak like a book, with horizontal grain along edge of counter. Spread spinach over meat. Layer red peppers and onions over spinach layer. Combine chilies, garlic, cumin and chili powder and sprinkle over meat. Top with cheese. Starting at nearest end, roll steak tightly. Tie string around roll in several places to hold securely.

Bake at 350 degrees for 40 minutes. Allow meat to rest 10 minutes before slicing.

SERVE WITH CORN PIE WITH CHEESE AND GREEN CHILIES (PAGE 175) AND TANGY GREEN BEAN AND CELERY ROOT SALAD (PAGE 75).

GRILLED BUTTERFLIED LEG OF LAMB

SERVES 8

1 cup dry red wine

¾ cup soy sauce

6 large cloves garlic, crushed

½ cup chopped fresh mint

2 teaspoons fresh rosemary, crushed

1 tablespoon coarse cracked pepper

1 butterflied leg of lamb (4 to 5 pounds)

Combine wine, soy sauce, garlic, mint, rosemary and pepper. Place lamb in glass or ceramic dish and pour marinade over. Cover and refrigerate at least 6 hours, turning lamb frequently. Prepare coals for grilling.

Drain meat, reserving marinade. Heat marinade in small pan. Grill lamb 4 inches from coals, basting with hot marinade, about 15 minutes on each side. Check for doneness frequently after 20 minutes. Slice lamb thinly and serve immediately.

SERVE WITH RISOTTO WITH BASIL PESTO (PAGE 154), SPICY MUSTARD-CAESAR SALAD (PAGE 70) AND YOUR FAVORITE RED WINE.

VEAL CHOPS WITH ROSEMARY SAUCE

SERVES 4

ROSEMARY SAUCE
2 tablespoons butter
1 tablespoon finely minced shallots
1½ teaspoons finely minced rosemary
2 tablespoons dry vermouth
½ cup veal stock or beef broth
½ cup whipping cream
salt and pepper

MEAT
4 veal chops (1 inch thick), about 8 ounces each
salt and pepper
¼ cup (½ stick) plus 2 tablespoons butter (divided use)
3 medium zucchini sliced into ¼-inch rounds
1 medium tomato, peeled, seeded and diced
4 fresh sprigs of rosemary

STERLING SILVER SERVING SPOON, *CALLA LILY* PATTERN, CA. 1875, ATTRIBUTED TO WHITING MFG. CO., NY, 1991.101.4.

To make sauce, melt butter in skillet over medium heat. Add shallots and rosemary and cook 3 minutes. Add vermouth and boil until almost no liquid remains (about 2 minutes). Pour in stock and boil until liquid is reduced by half (about 4 minutes). Reduce heat, add cream and cook until slightly thickened. Season to taste with salt and pepper.

Season veal with salt and pepper. Melt ¼ cup butter over medium-high heat. Add veal chops and cook 4 to 5 minutes each side for medium rare. Transfer to platter and tent with foil to keep warm.

Using same skillet, melt 2 tablespoons butter over high heat. Sauté zucchini about 1 minute or until tender crisp.

To assemble, divide zucchini among four plates and top each with veal chop. Pour heated sauce over and sprinkle with chopped tomato. Garnish with rosemary.

SERVE WITH MICROWAVE RISOTTO (PAGE 156) AND CARROTS WITH PISTACHIOS AND GRAND MARNIER (PAGE 174).

TRY PREPARING THE ROSEMARY SAUCE USING CHICKEN OR FISH STOCK AND SERVE WITH GRILLED SWORDFISH OR RED SNAPPER.

YOU CAN SUBSTITUTE PORK CHOPS FOR THE VEAL, COOKING 5 MINUTES PER SIDE OR UNTIL KNIFE INSERTED NEAR BONE REVEALS JUST A HINT OF PINK.

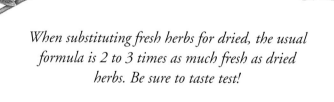

When substituting fresh herbs for dried, the usual formula is 2 to 3 times as much fresh as dried herbs. Be sure to taste test!

BAKED SIRLOIN STEW

SERVES 8

3 to 4 pounds sirloin, trimmed and cut into large
　cubes
3 to 4 cups strong, good quality double bock
　beer, triple stout or ale
¼ to ½ pound thick-sliced smoked bacon
2 tablespoons olive oil
2 onions, sliced
2 cloves garlic, chopped
1 tablespoon dried oregano (divided use)
1 teaspoon dried thyme (divided use)
dash of hot sauce (optional)
salt and cracked pepper to taste
2 tablespoons butter
3 to 4 carrots, peeled and cut into large pieces
2 to 3 potatoes, peeled and cut into large pieces
3 to 4 cups chicken broth
1 can (28-ounce) Italian-style tomatoes, cut into
　pieces
2 to 3 tablespoons flour

Place beef in a glass bowl and pour beer over it;
cover. Refrigerate overnight, or at least 3 to 4
hours.

Heat olive oil in heavy skillet and cook bacon
until crisp. Remove, drain and crumble bacon. Set
aside.

Leave 2 tablespoons fat in skillet, pouring off
excess. Drain beef and reserve marinade. Brown
beef in skillet, searing on all sides. Remove meat to
separate dish.

Sauté onions and garlic in skillet until
caramelized. Season with some of oregano,
thyme, hot sauce, salt and pepper. Set aside.

Add butter to skillet and sauté carrots and
potatoes until slightly cooked. Season with
remaining oregano, thyme, salt and pepper.
Remove to bowl with onion mixture.

Pour broth, reserved beer marinade and liquid
from tomatoes (reserving tomatoes) into a
separate saucepan. Bring to a boil and reduce
liquid by one-third.

Add flour to skillet and make a roux. Add
more olive oil if necessary. (Roux requires equal
parts of oil and flour.) When roux is a golden
color, add reduced liquid from saucepan, stirring
constantly. When well blended, add meat, vegetables, bacon and tomatoes. Bring to a boil.

Cover and bake in 325-degree oven for 3
hours or until tender. Check during baking,
adding more broth if necessary. To intensify flavor, about 30 minutes before stew is finished,
ladle out one-fourth of liquid and heat in small
saucepan. Cook over high heat until liquid is
reduced to a thick, syrupy consistency. Add back
to stew and finish baking.

GRILLED LIME-MARINATED FLANK STEAK WITH CHIPOTLE-HONEY SAUCE

SERVES 4

2½ pounds flank steak

MARINADE
1 canned chipotle, chopped (see note)
2 garlic cloves, minced
1 tablespoon chopped cilantro
¼ cup oil
⅔ cup lime juice (about 5 limes)

CHIPOTLE-HONEY SAUCE
¼ cup honey
2 tablespoons peanut oil
3 canned chipotles, or to taste
2 tablespoons balsamic vinegar
2 tablespoons brown mustard
½ cup lime juice (about 4 limes)
2 cloves garlic
1 teaspoon ground cumin
2 tablespoons chopped cilantro
1 teaspoon salt
Freshly ground pepper to taste

Place steak in a large, non-aluminum pan. Mix all marinade ingredients together and pour over meat. Cover and marinate, refrigerated, for 12 to 24 hours, turning occasionally.

To prepare sauce, combine honey, peanut oil, chipotles, vinegar, mustard, lime juice, garlic and cumin, and purée in blender or food processor. Stir in cilantro, salt and pepper.

Season steak with salt and pepper. Grill over white-hot coals (or highest setting on gas grill) for 2 to 4 minutes per side for medium rare. Remove steak from grill and allow to rest about 5 minutes before carving. Then, using very sharp knife, slice as thinly as possible, against the grain and on a sharp angle.

Serve sliced steak with several tablespoons of sauce.

NOTE: CHIPOTLES (SMOKED JALAPEÑO CHILI PEPPERS) ARE AVAILABLE DRIED OR CANNED. (CANNED ARE PREFERRED IN THIS RECIPE.) IF CHIPOTLES ARE UNAVAILABLE, SUBSTITUTE MIXTURE OF 1 TABLESPOON KETCHUP, ½ TEASPOON LIQUID SMOKE AND 1 FRESH JALAPEÑO PEPPER FOR EACH PEPPER DESIRED.

Lamb Chops with Herbs and Anchovies

THE SUBTLE SALTINESS OF THE ANCHOVIES MAKES THIS DISH A REAL WINNER. SERVES 4

3 cloves garlic, peeled

3 anchovy fillets

2 tablespoons fresh rosemary

¼ cup fresh parsley

½ teaspoon dried thyme

½ teaspoon salt

1 teaspoon freshly ground pepper

3 tablespoons olive oil

2 tablespoons dry red wine

8 thick lamb loin chops, trimmed of fat

8 fresh rosemary sprigs

Place garlic, anchovies, rosemary, parsley, thyme, salt, pepper, oil and wine in food processor fitted with steel blade. Process until smooth.

Using a small, sharp knife, make several shallow incisions in both sides of lamb chops. Rub marinade generously over both sides and press into incisions. Marinate 1 to 2 hours at room temperature.

Prepare charcoal for grilling. For medium rare, grill chops about 4 inches from hot coals, 5 to 6 minutes per side. Serve garnished with fresh rosemary sprigs.

FOR VARIETY ADD A HANDFUL OF FRESH BASIL TO THE MARINADE IN PLACE OF THE THYME. SERVE WITH TOMATO TART WITH OLIVES AND CHEESES (PAGE 25) AND ROASTED CUCUMBERS WITH DILL (PAGE 176).

ENAMELED AND GILDED PORCELAIN PLATE, BENJAMIN HARRISON WHITE HOUSE SERVICE, DESIGNED 1892 BY CAROLINE HARRISON, TRESSEMAN & VOGT, LIMOGES, MAKER, 1994.21

FIRST LADY CAROLINE SCOTT HARRISON, WHOSE HOBBY WAS CHINA PAINTING, DIRECTED A LARGE-SCALE EFFORT TO REMODEL THE WHITE HOUSE, INCLUDING THE INSTALLATION OF A CHINA CLOSET FOR THE PRESENTATION OF PIECES FROM PAST PRESIDENTIAL TABLE SERVICES. THE FIRST LADY ALSO DESIGNED AND ORDERED A 288-PIECE SERVICE.

SOUTHWESTERN VEAL SHANKS

SERVES 4

2 tablespoons olive oil

4 veal shanks (have butcher trim ends; slice shanks 1½ inches thick

6 tablespoons butter

1 large onion, chopped

⅔ cup finely chopped carrot

⅔ cup finely chopped celery

1 teaspoon finely chopped garlic

one 3-inch strip orange peel

one 3-inch strip lemon peel

1 can (14½-ounce) Italian-style tomatoes, drained

1½ cups chicken or beef stock

½ cup dry white wine

2 bay leaves

½ cup chopped fresh basil

1 teaspoon dried thyme

1 tablespoon ground cumin

⅓ cup chipotle peppers in spice sauce (available in 7-ounce cans)

GREMOLADA

1 teaspoon grated lemon peel

½ teaspoon finely chopped garlic

1 tablespoon finely chopped cilantro

Heat olive oil in large skillet over medium-high heat. Sear veal shanks quickly, turning until well browned. Set aside.

Melt butter in oven-proof baking dish large enough to accommodate shanks in one layer. Add onion, carrot, celery and garlic. Sauté, stirring occasionally, until onion is tender, about 15 minutes.

Add seared veal shanks, orange and lemon peels, tomatoes, stock, wine, bay leaves, basil, thyme, cumin and chipotles to baking dish. Bring liquid to a boil. Cover dish with foil and transfer to oven. Roast at 350 degrees for 1½ to 2 hours, or until tender. Turn shanks over every 30 minutes during cooking.

Prepare gremolada by combining lemon peel, garlic and cilantro. Add gremolada to veal shanks during last 5 minutes of cooking.

To serve, transfer shanks to serving platter and tent with foil to keep warm. Skim fat from braising juices in pan and purée in food processor. Thin sauce with additional stock if desired. Spoon sauce over shanks to serve.

SERVE VEAL SHANKS WITH GARLIC MASHED POTATOES (PAGE 179).

POULTRY
AND GAME

CHICKEN WITH ROASTED GARLIC, MUSHROOMS AND SPINACH

SERVES 4

1 large head garlic, cloves separated (unpeeled)
3 tablespoons olive oil (divided use)
4 skinless boneless chicken breast halves
flour to coat chicken
½ pound button or stemmed shiitake
  mushrooms, sliced
1 cup dry white wine
1 pound tomatoes, peeled, seeded and diced
2 cups packed fresh spinach leaves
1 tablespoon chopped fresh rosemary
3 tablespoons butter

Place garlic in small baking pan. Pour 1 tablespoon oil over and toss to coat. Bake at 350 degrees until soft, about 45 minutes. Allow garlic to cool, then press between fingertips to release clove from peel. Transfer to a bowl and set aside. (Can be prepared 1 day ahead. Cover and refrigerate.)

Pound chicken between sheets of plastic wrap to thickness of ½ inch. Coat chicken with flour, shaking off excess.

Heat remaining 2 tablespoons oil in large skillet over medium-high heat. Add chicken and sauté until cooked through, about 3 minutes per side. Transfer chicken to heated platter and tent with foil to keep warm.

Add mushrooms to skillet and sauté 4 minutes. Add wine and boil until liquid is reduced by half, about 4 minutes. Add tomatoes,

spinach, rosemary and roasted garlic and sauté until spinach wilts, about 3 minutes. Add butter and mix just until melted. To serve, divide spinach mixture among 4 plates and top each with chicken breast.

HERB ROASTED CHICKEN

SERVES 4

1 medium roasting hen
½ cup chopped fresh basil, or other fresh herbs
salt and pepper
1 medium orange, quartered
½ cup dry white wine
5 to 8 cloves garlic, peeled
10 shallots

Preheat broiler. Rinse hen and pat dry. Loosen skin over breast and thighs and stuff basil between skin and meat. Rub cavity of hen with salt and pepper. Place hen, breast side down, in roasting pan and brown under broiler. Turn to brown on all sides. Remove from oven and drain grease from pan.

Squeeze juice from orange quarters over hen, then place used orange quarters inside hen. Pour wine over hen and place shallots and garlic around it. Roast uncovered at 350 degrees for 20 minutes per pound, basting frequently. Hen is done when juices run clear when thigh is pierced with a fork.

Transfer hen to serving platter and tent with foil to keep warm. Skim fat from pan juices. Bring to boil and reduce to desired consistency. Slice hen and serve with pan juices.

STUFFED CHICKEN BREASTS WITH CILANTRO PESTO

SERVES 8

CHICKEN BREASTS
8 skinless boneless chicken breast halves
flour
8 teaspoons sun-dried tomato concentrate
5 ounces goat cheese
4 ounces grated Monterey Jack cheese
1 bunch green onions, minced
2 large cloves garlic, minced
1 cup chopped cilantro leaves
3 tablespoons olive oil

CILANTRO PESTO
3 bunches cilantro, stems removed and leaves
   chopped (about 2½ cups)
½ cup freshly shredded Parmesan cheese
½ cup pine nuts
¼ cup chopped elephant garlic
¼ cup fresh lime juice
4 teaspoons chili powder
1 tablespoon ground cumin
1 teaspoon dried crushed red pepper
1½ teaspoons salt
¾ cup olive oil

Place chicken breasts between 2 sheets of plastic wrap and pound to even ½-inch thickness. Dredge in flour, then spread 1 teaspoon tomato concentrate on top of each breast. (Can be prepared to this point early in day and refrigerated.)

To make filling, combine cheeses with onion, garlic and cilantro, mixing well. Place about 2 tablespoons filling on one side of each breast and fold edges in to enclose filling and form a package. Refrigerate to chill thoroughly, or freeze for later use.

Heat olive oil in skillet and brown chicken packets on all sides. Transfer to baking dish. (Can be prepared to this point early in day and refrigerated.)

To prepare pesto, place all ingredients in blender or food processor and purée until smooth. Refrigerate. (Pesto can be made several days in advance. Pour thin film of olive oil over top. Refrigerate for 1 week or freeze.)

Bake chicken at 375 degrees for 20 to 25 minutes. Serve with Cilantro Pesto.

FOR A SIMILAR PRESENTATION BUT DIFFERENT FLAVOR, TRY STUFFING CHICKEN BREASTS WITH BOURSIN CHEESE (TWO 5-OUNCE PACKAGES) AND SERVING WITH BASIL PESTO (PAGE 147).

YOU CAN USE THE CILANTRO PESTO FOR A SIMPLE AND ELEGANT APPETIZER. SPREAD PESTO ON MELBA TOAST OR THINLY SLICED BAGUETTES AND TOP WITH GOAT CHEESE AND A SLIVER OF SUN-DRIED TOMATO. BAKE AT 350 DEGREES FOR 10 TO 15 MINUTES.

CHICKEN WITH SHERRY AND VERMOUTH

SERVES 8

8 skinless boneless chicken breast halves
2 eggs, beaten with 4 tablespoons water
flour for dredging
olive oil for cooking
6 tablespoons butter
salt and pepper to taste
½ cup dry vermouth or white wine
½ cup dry sherry
8 slices mozzarella cheese

Dip each chicken breast in flour, then in eggs. Heat ½ inch of olive oil in heavy skillet over medium-high heat. Add chicken breasts and brown on both sides. Drain on paper towels.

Add butter, salt, pepper, vermouth and sherry to skillet. Cook over medium heat, stirring continuously, until sauce is slightly thickened. Place chicken breasts in pan and top each with a slice of cheese. Cover and cook over moderate heat until chicken is heated through and cheese is melted, about 10 minutes.

To serve, place chicken on heated platter and pour sauce around.

CHICKEN POACHED IN RASPBERRY VINEGAR AND FRESH HERBS

SERVES 4

1 can (14½-ounce) chicken or beef broth
4 skinless boneless chicken breast halves
salt and pepper
2 tablespoons olive oil
4 cloves garlic, minced
½ cup raspberry vinegar
   (purchase or see page 85)
½ cup red wine vinegar
2 plum tomatoes, peeled, seeded and finely
   chopped
1 tablespoon chopped fresh thyme
1 tablespoon chopped fresh rosemary

Boil stock in small saucepan until reduced to 1 cup. Set aside.

Season chicken with salt and pepper. Heat oil in large skillet. Add chicken and garlic; sauté over medium-high heat until lightly browned, about 2 minutes per side. Add raspberry vinegar and ½ cup reduced stock. Cover and simmer 20 minutes, until chicken is cooked through. Remove chicken to warm platter.

Add remaining stock, red wine vinegar, tomatoes, thyme and rosemary to liquid in pan. Bring to a boil and simmer until slightly thickened. Return chicken to pan to heat through, about 1 minute. Serve chicken topped with sauce.

GRILLED
MOROCCAN CHICKEN
BREASTS WITH
MANGO MINT SALSA

SERVES 6

MARINADE

¼ cup olive oil

1 teaspoon sesame oil

1 teaspoon ground coriander

¼ teaspoon ground cinnamon

2 teaspoons ground cumin

¼ teaspoon turmeric

½ teaspoon paprika

pinch of cayenne pepper

1 tablespoon finely chopped ginger

½ teaspoon sea salt

1 tablespoon lemon juice

CHICKEN

6 skinless boneless chicken breast halves

MANGO MINT SALSA

2 mangoes, peeled and diced

½ medium red onion, chopped

1 red bell pepper, seeded and diced

2 small jalapeño peppers, seeded and chopped

1 bunch fresh mint, chopped

juice of 1 lime

1 tablespoon white wine vinegar

Heat oils in a saucepan. Add coriander, cinnamon, cumin, turmeric, paprika and cayenne. Stir over low heat for a minute. Remove from heat and add ginger, salt and lemon juice. Set aside to cool. Place chicken breasts in non-metallic pan and pour marinade over. Cover and refrigerate overnight.

To prepare salsa, combine all ingredients and store in refrigerator. Salsa will keep several weeks.

Wipe off excess marinade and grill chicken breasts over medium heat, 3 to 5 minutes on each side. Serve with Mango Mint Salsa.

MANGO MINT SALSA IS ALSO DELICIOUS WITH GRILLED FISH, ESPECIALLY TUNA OR SWORDFISH, OR GRILLED PORK TENDERS.

GLASS COVERED DISH, CA. 1750-1800, PROBABLY BOHEMIA, 1985.R.322.A-B

CHICKEN WITH PEARS AND STILTON

SERVES 6

6 skinless boneless chicken breast halves
flour for coating
6 tablespoons clarified butter (divided use)
salt and pepper to taste
¾ cup unsalted chicken stock
¾ cup port
1½ cups heavy cream
3 pears, peeled, cored and cut into sixths
4 tablespoons Stilton cheese (divided use)
2 tablespoons minced fresh parsley

Pound chicken breasts to flatten slightly and sprinkle lightly with flour. Heat 4 tablespoons butter in skillet over moderately high heat. When butter begins to color slightly, add chicken. Cook 4 minutes, then turn and continue cooking until chicken is springy to touch. Remove to warm platter. Sprinkle with salt and pepper, tent with foil and set in a 200-degree oven to keep warm.

Add stock and port to same skillet and boil until liquid is reduced by half. Add cream and boil until reduced to a saucelike consistency. Place pears in another skillet and sauté for 5 minutes in the remaining 2 tablespoons butter. Set aside. Add 2 tablespoons Stilton to port sauce and stir until melted.

Place chicken on 6 serving plates and top each with 3 pear slices, some of the sauce, 1 teaspoon crumbled Stilton and 1 teaspoon parsley.

CHICKEN PICCATA WITH MUSHROOMS

SERVES 4

4 skinless boneless chicken breast halves
salt and pepper to taste
1 tablespoon flour
2 tablespoons olive oil
2 tablespoons butter
½ pound mushrooms, sliced
½ cup dry white wine
¼ cup fresh lemon juice
3 tablespoons capers
4 teaspoons grated Parmesan cheese
thin slices of lemon (garnish)

Place chicken breasts between 2 sheets of waxed paper and pound to ¼-inch thickness.

Sprinkle with salt, pepper and flour. Brown on both sides in olive oil. Remove to platter. Add butter to skillet and sauté mushrooms until tender. Remove mushrooms with slotted spoon and set aside.

Add white wine and lemon juice to skillet. Deglaze pan and simmer a few minutes, scraping up any browned bits in pan. Add capers and Parmesan cheese. Return chicken and mushrooms to skillet and simmer 2 minutes. Turn and continue to simmer 1 to 2 minutes more to heat through.

To serve, place chicken on plates and spoon sauce over. Garnish with thin slice of lemon.

SAUTÉED CHICKEN WITH TOMATOES AND CAPERS

SERVES 4

4 skinless boneless chicken breast halves
salt and freshly ground white pepper to taste
I tablespoon olive oil
I tablespoon butter
3 tablespoons minced shallots
I teaspoon minced garlic
2 teaspoons minced fresh tarragon
   (or I teaspoon dried)
4 ripe plum tomatoes, diced
2 tablespoons red wine vinegar
4 tablespoons drained capers
½ cup dry white wine
I tablespoon tomato paste
4 tablespoons chopped fresh parsley

Season chicken with salt and pepper. Heat oil and butter in heavy skillet and add chicken breasts. Sauté over medium-high heat until lightly browned, about 3 minutes per side. Add shallots and garlic, cooking until softened. Add tarragon, tomatoes, vinegar, capers, wine and tomato paste, blending well. Stir to loosen any browned particles in skillet. Bring to a boil. Cover and reduce heat; simmer for 5 minutes. Sprinkle with parsley and serve immediately.

FOR ENTICING MEDITERRANEAN FLAVOR, ADD ½ CUP CRUMBLED FETA CHEESE JUST BEFORE SERVING.

CHICKEN WITH BASIL AND GOAT CHEESE

SERVES 4

4 skinless boneless chicken breast halves
salt and pepper
5 tablespoons butter (divided use)
I cup white wine
½ cup tequila
3½ ounces fresh goat cheese
¼ cup currants
¼ cup golden raisins
½ cup coarsely chopped fresh basil
salt and freshly ground pepper
½ cup pine nuts, toasted
basil leaves (garnish)

Place chicken breasts between 2 sheets of waxed paper and pound lightly to flatten. Sprinkle with salt and pepper. Melt 3 tablespoons butter in a large skillet over medium-high heat. Sauté chicken breasts until golden brown on both sides. Remove pan from heat and pour off any excess butter. Add wine and tequila.

Spoon one-fourth of goat cheese on top of each chicken breast and return pan to heat. Add currants and raisins and continue cooking until chicken is just done and liquid has reduced by half. Transfer chicken to serving platter.

Continue heating sauce to reduce further. Remove from heat and add basil and remaining 3 tablespoons butter. Season to taste with salt and pepper.

To serve, spoon sauce over chicken and sprinkle with pine nuts. Garnish with basil leaves.

ANCHO CHILI-GRILLED CHICKEN BREASTS WITH PICO DE GALLO

USE ANCHO CHILI SAUCE SPARINGLY IF YOU PREFER A MILDER FLAVOR. SERVES 4

ANCHO CHILI SAUCE
1½ cups water
2 dried ancho chilies
2 cloves garlic, peeled
1 teaspoon salt
½ teaspoon dried oregano
1 teaspoon sugar
1 teaspoon olive oil

PICO DE GALLO
1 cup chopped tomatoes
½ cup chopped green onions
¼ cup chopped fresh cilantro
½ jalapeño chili, seeded and minced
1 tablespoon fresh lemon juice
1 clove garlic, minced
1 tablespoon olive oil
salt and pepper to taste

MARINADE
1 tablespoon lime juice
½ teaspoon garlic powder
3 tablespoons olive oil

4 skinless boneless chicken breast halves
salt and pepper to taste
1½ cups (6 ounces) grated Monterey Jack cheese
avocado slices (garnish)

To prepare Ancho Chili sauce, combine water, chilies, garlic, salt and oregano in heavy saucepan and boil until chilies are tender, about 5 minutes. Using slotted spoon, remove chilies and garlic from cooking liquid and reserve liquid. Discard stems and seeds from chilies; chop coarsely. Transfer chilies and garlic to blender and purée until finely chopped. With machine running, gradually add enough reserved liquid (about 1 cup) to form thick sauce. Add sugar and olive oil and blend until sauce is smooth. (Sauce can be prepared 1 day ahead. Cover tightly and refrigerate.)

GLAZED EARTHENWARE PLATE, CUP, AND SAUCER, *HARLEQUIN* PATTERN, DESIGNED 1936 BY FREDRICK RHEAD, HOMER LAUGHLIN POTTERY, EAST LIVERPOOL, OHIO, 1992.526.1-3

LIKE ITS PREDECESSOR BY THE SAME DESIGNER, *FIESTA*, *HARLEQUIN* WAS DESIGNED IN THE ART DECO STYLE AND WAS MEANT TO BE PURCHASED IN MULTI-COLORED SETS. INTENDED TO BE LESS EXPENSIVE THAN *FIESTA*, IT WAS MADE WITH A LIGHTER BODY. IT WAS ORIGINALLY SOLD EXCLUSIVELY THROUGH THE F. W. WOOLWORTH CO. AND WAS NOT REMOVED FROM THE MARKET UNTIL 1964.

To prepare Pico de Gallo, combine tomatoes, onion, cilantro, jalapeños, lemon juice, garlic and olive oil in small bowl. Season to taste with salt and pepper. (Can be prepared 4 hours ahead. Cover and refrigerate.)

Combine lime juice, garlic powder and olive oil. Place chicken in non-metallic pan and pour marinade over. Marinate chicken 1 to 2 hours, covered, in refrigerator.

Season chicken with salt and pepper and grill over medium-high heat until just cooked through, about 5 minutes per side. Brush occasionally with ancho chili sauce during cooking.

Transfer chicken to baking dish; brush with more sauce. Sprinkle with grated cheese and bake at 400 degrees, just until cheese melts, about 3 minutes. Arrange chicken on plates. Top with Pico de Gallo and garnish with avocado slices. Pass remaining Ancho Chili Sauce.

CHICKEN WITH PINE NUTS AND POBLANO SAUCE

SERVES 4

SOUTHWEST SEASONING RUB
2 tablespoons chili powder
2 tablespoons paprika
1 tablespoon ground coriander
1 tablespoon garlic powder
1 tablespoon salt
2 teaspoons ground cumin
1 teaspoon cayenne pepper
1 teaspoon crushed red pepper
1 teaspoon black pepper
1 teaspoon dried leaf oregano

ROASTED POBLANO SAUCE
1 tablespoon olive oil
⅓ cup peeled, seeded and chopped roasted poblanos
½ cup chopped onion
2 teaspoons minced garlic
1 teaspoon Southwest Seasoning Rub
1 teaspoon salt
⅛ teaspoon freshly ground pepper
3 cups chicken stock
3 tablespoons heavy cream

CHICKEN
4 skinless boneless chicken breast halves
1 tablespoon plus 1 teaspoon Southwest Seasoning Rub (divided use)
½ cup flour
1 large egg
¾ cup milk
2 cups finely chopped pine nuts
¼ cup olive oil
¼ cup chopped fresh cilantro

To prepare Southwest Seasoning Rub, thoroughly combine all ingredients. Store in an airtight container.

To prepare Roasted Poblano Sauce, combine oil, poblanos, onion, garlic, seasoning rub, salt and pepper in a medium saucepan over high heat. Cook, stirring occasionally, for about 2 minutes. Stir in stock, bring to a boil and cook over high heat about 18 minutes, reducing to 2 cups. Reduce heat to medium; stir in cream and simmer for 2 minutes. Remove from heat and purée in food processor or blender. (Sauce can be prepared 1 day ahead and refrigerated in airtight container. Reheat over low heat before using.)

Sprinkle each chicken breast on both sides with ¼ teaspoon seasoning rub and pat it in with hands. Refrigerate chicken, covered with plastic wrap, for 1 to 2 hours.

Combine flour in a bowl with remaining 1 tablespoon seasoning rub. In another bowl, beat egg with milk. Place chopped pine nuts in a third bowl. Dredge chicken in seasoned flour, then egg mixture, then pine nuts, pressing nuts thickly onto chicken.

Heat oil in large skillet over medium-high heat and sauté chicken until golden, about 5 minutes on each side. To serve, pour ½ cup poblano sauce onto each of 4 plates. Top with chicken breast and garnish with 1 tablespoon cilantro.

TRY THE SOUTHWEST SEASONING RUB ON THE SHRIMP IN THE RECIPE FOR GRILLED SHRIMP AND BLACK BEAN TOSTADO (PAGE 141).

CHICKEN WITH GOAT CHEESE AND HERBS

SERVES 4

4 ounces fresh goat cheese
1 tablespoon chopped fresh tarragon (divided use)
1 tablespoon chopped fresh Italian parsley (divided use)
1 tablespoon chopped fresh chervil (divided use)
salt and freshly ground white pepper to taste
4 skinless boneless chicken breast halves
4 teaspoons olive oil
1 shallot, minced
1 cup dry white wine
1 cup chicken stock
½ cup heavy cream

Combine goat cheese, half the herbs, salt and pepper in small bowl, mixing well. Insert knife in side of each chicken breast and work to form a pocket without going all the way through.

Fill each pocket with one-fourth of cheese mixture. Season chicken with salt and pepper and sprinkle with olive oil. Roast in oven at 450 degrees for 15 to 20 minutes, or cook on hot grill for 6 to 7 minutes per side. Combine shallot and wine in saucepan. Bring to a boil and reduce to a glaze, about ¼ cup. Add stock and reduce by half. Add cream and continue to reduce until sauce lightly coats back of a spoon. Adjust seasonings and add remaining herbs.

To serve, slice chicken breasts into scallops and place on plates. Spoon sauce over. Serve immediately.

GRILLED ROSEMARY CHICKEN

SERVES 8

8 skinless boneless chicken breast halves

ROSEMARY MARINADE
1 clove elephant garlic, minced
½ cup olive oil
juice of 1 lemon
¼ cup white wine
1 teaspoon freshly ground pepper
1 teaspoon salt
3 tablespoons chopped fresh rosemary

Place chicken breasts between two sheets of waxed paper and pound until about ½ inch thick. Place in large, flat non-metallic pan.

To prepare Rosemary Marinade, combine all ingredients and pour over chicken. Marinate, covered, in refrigerator for 24 hours.

Grill chicken over low coals, about 7 minutes per side.

THIS MARINADE WORKS BEAUTIFULLY FOR SHRIMP AS WELL.

FOR A SPECTACULAR COMBINATION, TOP EACH CHICKEN BREAST WITH A SLICE OF BRIE CHEESE AND HEAT UNDER BROILER UNTIL CHEESE STARTS TO BUBBLE.

MARGARITA CHICKEN

SERVES 8

MARINADE
juice of 2 oranges
juice of 2 limes
¼ cup honey
¼ cup tequila
2 tablespoons triple sec (orange liqueur)
1 teaspoon salt

8 skinless boneless chicken breast halves

SALSA BARACHA
2 cups tomatoes, seeded, diced and drained
¼ cup chopped onion
¼ cup chopped green onion
1 jalapeño, seeded and minced
1 tablespoon chopped cilantro
1 tablespoon tequila
1 teaspoon fresh oregano
1 teaspoon salt
juice of 1 lime

CONDIMENTS
1 cup guacamole
1 cup sour cream
1 orange, cut into wedges (garnish)
1 lime, cut into wedges (garnish)

Combine marinade ingredients and pour over chicken breasts in a non-metallic dish. Marinate for at least 2 hours.

Combine all ingredients for Salsa Baracha. Cover and refrigerate for about 2 hours before serving to meld flavors.

Grill or broil chicken breasts for 4 to 5 minutes per side.

Serve with guacamole, sour cream and Salsa Baracha. Garnish with lime and orange wedges.

INVITE YOUR FRIENDS FOR A MEXICAN BUFFET. START WITH PICADILLO SARITA (PAGE 32) AND PICANTE SAUCE (PAGE 33) WITH CHIPS. ACCOMPANY WITH MARGARITAS OR BEER. SERVE MARGARITA CHICKEN, CORN PIE WITH CHEESE AND GREEN CHILIES (PAGE 175) AND TEXAS BLACK BEANS (PAGE 172) FOR DINNER. FINISH WITH PRALINES.

INSTEAD OF SALSA BARACHA, TRY SERVING THIS CHICKEN WITH CILANTRO PESTO (PAGE 115).

GRILLED CHICKEN WITH PESTO BEAN SAUCE

SERVES 4 TO 6

MARINADE
¼ cup dry white wine
¼ cup basil pesto (purchase or see page 147)
¼ teaspoon salt
¼ teaspoon black pepper

6 skinless boneless chicken breast halves, flattened to ½ inch thick

SAUCE
2 cans (16-ounce) black beans, drained and rinsed
½ cup chicken stock
¼ cup basil pesto
2 tablespoons sour cream

GARNISH
¼ cup sour cream
2 tablespoons basil pesto
2 tablespoons freshly grated Parmesan cheese
fresh herb sprigs such as basil, thyme or parsley

To prepare marinade, combine all ingredients in small mixing bowl and stir until smooth. Arrange chicken in a shallow, large non-reactive dish. Pour marinade over, making sure chicken is coated evenly. Cover and marinate for 30 minutes to 4 hours in the refrigerator.

To prepare sauce, combine beans, chicken stock and pesto in a medium saucepan over low heat. Cook for about 5 minutes. Add sour cream and cook only another minute, or sauce may curdle. For a thinner consistency, add a bit more sour cream or chicken stock.

Prepare barbecue for medium-heat grilling. Remove chicken from marinade and grill about 3 inches from heat for 7 to 10 minutes per side, or until no longer pink.

To serve, place chicken on serving plates and spoon 2 tablespoons bean sauce down center of each breast. Place a dollop each of sour cream and pesto on top. Sprinkle on Parmesan cheese and garnish with herbs. Serve immediately.

FOR A DIFFERENT PRESENTATION, PREPARE A THINNER SAUCE THAT CAN BE POOLED ON THE PLATE. PLACE CHICKEN BREAST ON SAUCE, THEN TOP WITH SOUR CREAM, PESTO, CHOPPED TOMATOES, PARMESAN CHEESE AND CILANTRO LEAVES.

ROASTED CORNISH HENS WITH MADEIRA SAUCE

SERVES 6

MADEIRA SAUCE
5 tablespoons butter (divided use)
½ cup finely chopped shallots
2 cups dry Madeira
2 cups veal stock (page 47)
1 tablespoon salt
½ teaspoon pepper

CORNISH HENS
6 Cornish hens (18 to 20 ounces each)
salt and pepper
3 tablespoons olive oil
2 tablespoons unsalted butter

To prepare Madeira Sauce, melt 2½ tablespoons butter in skillet and sauté shallots for 4 minutes. Add Madeira, veal stock, salt and pepper. Simmer slowly until sauce is reduced by half. Strain and swirl in remaining butter.

Wash and pat dry Cornish hens. Lightly salt and pepper throughout. Heat olive oil and butter in a large roasting pan, until butter begins to brown. Place hens in hot pan, breast side down. Allow to brown on each side of breast for about 1 minute. Transfer to 425-degree oven and bake for 30 minutes. Turn breast side up, pour off fat and brush hens generously with Madeira Sauce. Return to oven for 15 minutes.

Reheat sauce and serve with hens.

MADEIRA SAUCE IS ALSO A WONDERFUL ACCOMPANIMENT TO FILLET OF BEEF.

DUCK WITH ORANGE SAUCE

SERVES 4

RED WINE MARINADE

1½ cups vegetable oil (divided use)

½ cup finely chopped onions

1 shallot, minced

1 clove garlic, minced

1 large stalk celery (top included), diced

1 large carrot, sliced thin

1 tablespoon minced fresh parsley

1 bay leaf

8 peppercorns

8 crushed juniper berries

1 pinch thyme

1 pinch rosemary

3½ cups red wine

DUCKS

2 large ducks (see note)

2 teaspoons salt

2 teaspoons powdered ginger or fresh shredded ginger

½ teaspoon crushed or coarsely ground peppercorns

1 teaspoon dried rosemary

2 oranges, seeded and quartered

1 tablespoon grated lemon peel

2 tablespoons brown sugar

½ cup curaçao (orange liqueur)

6 strips fatty bacon

1 tablespoon cornstarch, dissolved in 2 tablespoons cold water

¼ cup brandy, warmed

To prepare Red Wine Marinade, heat ¼ cup oil in large skillet and add vegetables, herbs and spices. Sauté until onions are clear and golden. Remove from heat and stir in remaining oil and wine. Allow to cool.

Place ducks in non-metallic pan. Pour 2 cups marinade over and marinate 3 to 4 hours, covered, in refrigerator. Drain and reserve marinade. Dry ducks inside and out. Mix together salt, ginger, peppercorns and rosemary. Rub surfaces of ducks with mixture. Divide oranges and insert into cavities. Add ½ tablespoon lemon peel and 1 tablespoon sugar to cavity of each duck.

Place ducks in roasting pan and add 1 cup reserved marinade and the curaçao. Cover breasts of ducks with bacon strips and roast at 350 degrees for 45 minutes.

Transfer ducks to heated platter. Remove and discard cavity contents and bacon. Skim fat from pan drippings. Add cornstarch mixture and simmer, stirring, to thicken slightly. Pour brandy over ducks and ignite. Serve sauce on side.

SERVE WITH ORANGE WILD RICE WITH PINE NUTS, CURRANTS AND APPLES (PAGE 162) AND HERBED ASPARAGUS WITH PARMESAN (PAGE 170).

NOTE: THIS PREPARATION IS IDEALLY SUITED FOR GAME DUCKS.

PHEASANT IN ORANGE WINE SAUCE WITH RAISINS

SERVES 6

3 small young pheasants (about 2 pounds each), dressed and halved lengthwise
1 small lemon, halved
salt and pepper
½ cup (1 stick) butter, softened
2 teaspoons grated lemon rind
juice of 3 medium oranges
1 cup white raisins
1 tablespoon curaçao
½ cup sweet white wine
1 cup chicken stock

Wipe pheasant halves dry with paper towels. Rub all surfaces with cut halves of lemon. Sprinkle lightly with salt and pepper. Place in roasting pan, breast sides up, and coat liberally with butter. Sprinkle with grated lemon rind. Strain orange juice and add to pan. Add raisins, curaçao, wine and stock. Bake at 350 degrees for 45 minutes, basting frequently to keep surfaces moist. Serve with pan mixture poured over.

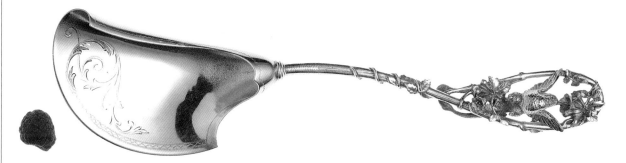

STERLING SILVER SERVING SCOOP, CA. 1875-80, WHITING MFG. CO., NY, 1991.5

DUCK WITH PORT SAUCE AND SHALLOT CONFIT

SERVES 3 TO 4

2 large whole domestic duck breasts, preferably Moscovy

DRY MARINADE

3 shallots, peeled and chopped

2 cloves garlic, peeled and chopped

4 to 5 sprigs of thyme, leaves only

5 to 6 sprigs of flat leaf parsley, chopped

2 dried bay leaves, crumbled

generous amount of coarsely ground peppercorns

sea salt

SAUCE

1 cup port wine

½ cup orange juice

½ cup duck glacé (or demi-glacé, or chicken stock reduced to a thick glaze)

½ cup crème fraîche or heavy cream

salt and pepper to taste

SHALLOT CONFIT

24 large firm shallots

enough chicken stock to cover the shallots in skillet

2 tablespoons butter

2 to 3 tablespoons sugar

1 tablespoon shredded orange zest (optional)

salt and freshly ground pepper to taste

Mix together ingredients for the dry marinade. Set aside. With a sharp knife, slash the skin and fat of duck breasts in a diamond pattern, not penetrating the flesh. Rub with dry marinade, cover with plastic wrap, and refrigerate for several hours.

Place breasts, skin side down, in skillet over high heat and sear for a few minutes to render out some of fat and brown the skin. Transfer breasts to a baking pan, skin side up, and bake at 450 degrees for 8 to 10 minutes. Remove from oven and let sit for a few minutes.

To prepare sauce, skim fat from baking pan and add port to pan juices, stirring up any browned bits in pan. Reduce mixture over high heat by at least half. Add orange juice and reduce again by half. Add duck glacé, reducing a little more; add crème fraîche and reduce until thick. Adjust seasoning with salt and pepper.

To make confit, carefully peel shallots and place in a single layer in skillet. Cover with stock. Add butter and sugar. Place skillet over moderate heat and cook until almost all liquid has evaporated. Add orange zest and continue cooking until rest of liquid is almost completely gone. Season with salt and pepper.

To serve, pool sauce on plates and top each with duck breast accompanied by Shallot Confit.

STERLING SILVER AND SILVERGILT SALAD SERVING FORK, CA. 1866-73, ATTRIBUTED TO J. R. WENDT & CO., NY, 1992.7.11.1

QUAIL WITH CHERRIES

SERVES 4

8 quail
½ cup (1 stick) butter
1 cup beef consommé
½ cup port or Madeira wine
1 tablespoon grated lemon rind
¼ cup tart cherry jelly
1 cup fresh or frozen Bing cherries, pitted
1 tablespoon lemon juice
salt and pepper to taste

Melt butter in heavy skillet and brown birds evenly on all sides. Cover and bake at 375 degrees for 30 minutes. Transfer to a heated serving plate.

Skim pan juices and add consommé, wine and lemon rind. Simmer over medium heat for about 10 minutes, stirring occasionally. Add jelly, cherries and lemon juice. Simmer 15 to 25 minutes longer. (Use longer time if using fresh cherries.) Season with salt and pepper and pour over quail.

SERVE WITH ORANGE WILD RICE WITH PINE NUTS, CURRANTS AND APPLES (PAGE 162) AND VINTNER'S SALAD (PAGE 67).

DOVE STUFFED WITH CHEESE AND JALAPEÑOS

SERVES 4

MARINADE
½ cup olive oil
⅓ cup white wine vinegar
½ teaspoon salt
½ teaspoon pepper
2 tablespoons Worcestershire sauce
½ teaspoon lemon pepper

DOVE
8 dove
8 teaspoons cream cheese
2 jalapeños, seeded and sliced into quarters
8 slices bacon

Mix marinade ingredients thoroughly. Clean birds and place in non-metallic pan. Pour marinade over, cover, and refrigerate for at least 24 hours. Reserve marinade after removing birds.

Cut 2 slits in each breast. Stuff cream cheese in one and jalapeño quarter in the other. Wrap bacon around each bird and place on a skewer (4 birds together). Grill over medium heat, rotating often and basting with reserved marinade as necessary. Cook until well done and bacon is blackened and crisp.

THIS PREPARATION WORKS EQUALLY WELL FOR QUAIL.

ROASTED TURKEY BREAST

A QUICK AND EASY METHOD FOR
COOKING TURKEY THAT IS
PARTICULARLY SUCCULENT.
SERVES 8 TO 12

3 tablespoons vegetable oil
1 turkey breast (4 to 7 pounds), fresh or
   completely thawed
salt and pepper
¾ cup water

CRANBERRY APPLE CHUTNEY (OPTIONAL)

1 pound cranberries
1 cup sugar
½ cup brown sugar, packed
½ cup golden raisins
2 teaspoons cinnamon
1½ teaspoons ground ginger
½ teaspoon ground cloves
¼ teaspoon allspice
1 cup water
1 cup chopped onion
1 baking apple, peeled, cored and chopped
½ cup chopped celery

ITALIAN SAUSAGE DRESSING (OPTIONAL)

1 large onion, chopped
¾ pound Italian sausage links, casings removed
   and cut into ½-inch pieces
2 tablespoons olive oil
½ teaspoon poultry seasoning
¼ teaspoon cayenne pepper
¼ teaspoon garlic powder
½ teaspoon Italian seasoning
1 package (10-ounce) frozen chopped spinach,
   thawed and drained
1 package (8-ounce) herb stuffing
1 can (14½-ounce) chicken broth

Heat oil in a roasting pan over medium heat. Season turkey breast with salt and pepper and brown on all sides in hot oil, about 10 minutes.

Remove pan from heat and carefully pour water over turkey. Place in 450-degree oven and roast for 20 minutes. Reduce oven temperature to 275 degrees and roast an additional 30 to 45 minutes.

Transfer turkey to a platter. Tent with foil to keep warm and allow to stand 15 minutes before carving. Serve with Cranberry Apple Chutney or Italian Sausage Dressing.

To prepare chutney, combine cranberries, sugars, raisins, spices and water in a 2-quart saucepan. Simmer, uncovered, over medium heat, stirring frequently until berries begin to pop. Reduce heat and stir in remaining ingredients. Continue simmering until thickened, about 10 to 15 minutes. (Keeps up to 2 weeks, covered and refrigerated.)

For dressing, sauté onion and sausage in oil for about 5 minutes. Add poultry seasoning, cayenne, garlic powder and Italian seasoning and cook until onion is soft and sausage is no longer pink. Add spinach, stuffing and broth. Stir to combine well. Place in greased pan and bake, uncovered, at 300 degrees for 45 to 55 minutes.

Fish and Seafood

THE ARTFUL TABLE

OPENING PAGE:
STERLING SILVER
AND SILVERGILT
SARDINE SERVER,
CA. 1880-90,
GEORGE W.
SHIEBLER, NY,
1992.7.8

ENAMELED
PORCELAIN
PLATE, CA. 1790-
1810, CHINA,
1954.54.

CRISP PARMESAN CATFISH WITH GARDEN SALSA

SERVES 4

GARDEN SALSA (YIELDS 4 CUPS)
2 cups finely chopped zucchini
2 cups finely chopped yellow squash
3 tomatillos, seeded and chopped
1 tomato, seeded and chopped
½ red onion, finely chopped
1 carrot, peeled and finely chopped
2 jalapeños, seeded and finely chopped
2 tablespoons sherry vinegar
3 tablespoons tequila
2 tablespoons chopped cilantro
1 teaspoon ground cumin
salt, pepper and sugar to taste

FISH
6 catfish fillets (4-ounce)
1 cup plus 2 tablespoons grated Parmesan cheese
6 tablespoons flour
½ teaspoon salt
½ teaspoon freshly ground pepper
¼ teaspoon cayenne pepper, or to taste
1 egg, beaten
2 tablespoons milk
1 tablespoon oil

Combine all vegetables in a bowl. Add vinegar, tequila, cilantro and seasonings, mixing well. Make a day ahead to allow flavors to develop.

Rinse catfish fillets. Pat dry and set aside.

Combine cheese, flour, salt, pepper and cayenne in a shallow dish. Mix egg and milk in another shallow dish. Brush bottom of 9 x 13-inch baking dish with oil.

Dip fillets first in egg mixture, then in flour mixture, coating well. Place fillets, overlapping thinner parts, in prepared baking dish.

Bake at 500 degrees until flesh of fish is opaque and crust is golden, about 6 to 10 minutes. Serve with salsa.

SAUTÉED CRAB CAKES

SERVES 3 AS AN ENTRÉE
(2 CAKES PER PERSON)

CRAB CAKES
1 pound fresh lump crab meat, picked over
½ cup mayonnaise
1 egg, well beaten
1 tablespoon Worcestershire sauce
1 tablespoon fresh lemon juice
1 tablespoon prepared horseradish
¼ cup chopped parsley
1 teaspoon salt
½ teaspoon cayenne pepper
¾ cup bread crumbs (divided use)
¼ cup clarified butter

CILANTRO, CUMIN AND LIME SAUCE (OPTIONAL)

1 cup white wine
2 shallots, chopped
1¼ cups half and half
1 cup fish or chicken stock
1 tablespoon ground cumin
1 tablespoon cornstarch mixed with 2
  tablespoons cold water
½ cup chopped cilantro
juice of 1 lime
salt and pepper to taste

Combine crab meat with mayonnaise, egg, Worcestershire, lemon juice, horseradish, parsley, salt, cayenne and ¼ cup bread crumbs in medium bowl. Stir to blend well. Shape into 6 cakes, about 3½ inches in diameter. Coat lightly with remaining bread crumbs. Sauté in butter, turning once, until lightly browned on both sides.

To prepare sauce, combine wine and shallots in a saucepan; cook over high heat until liquid is reduced to ¼ cup. Add cream and bring to a boil. Reduce until slightly thickened, then add stock and cumin. Continue cooking, adding cornstarch mixture a few drops at a time, until desired consistency is reached. Whisk in cilantro, lime juice, salt and pepper.

SHAPE CRAB MIXTURE INTO 12 SMALL CAKES FOR A WONDERFUL FIRST COURSE OR APPETIZER. SERVE ON A BED OF ARUGULA OR BIBB LETTUCE WITH CILANTRO, CUMIN AND LIME SAUCE.

THE ARTFUL TABLE

Alaskan Grilled Salmon with Honey Marinade

Serves 4

ENAMELED AND GILDED PORCELAIN OYSTER PLATE FROM THE RUTHERFORD B. HAYES WHITE HOUSE SERVICE, DESIGNED BY THEODORE R. DAVIS, HAVILAND & CO., LIMOGES, MAKER, 1991.101.23

HONEY MARINADE

½ cup (1 stick) butter

⅓ cup honey

⅓ cup packed brown sugar

2 tablespoons fresh lemon juice

1 teaspoon liquid smoke flavoring

¾ teaspoon crushed red pepper flakes

SALMON

1 center-cut salmon fillet (about 2 pounds), skin on, in 1 piece

1 large bunch spinach leaves, stemmed

1 papaya, peeled, seeded and cut into ¼-inch thick slices

Combine butter, honey, brown sugar, lemon juice, liquid smoke and red pepper flakes in a saucepan. Cook over medium heat, stirring until smooth, 5 to 7 minutes. Cool to room temperature.

Place salmon in a non-metallic dish just large enough to hold it. Pour cooled marinade over, and let stand at room temperature for 30 minutes, turning once.

Prepare hot coals for grilling. Oil grill well, and cook salmon, skin side up, over medium heat for 5 to 7 minutes. Turn salmon over and cook until fish flakes easily, another 5 to 7 minutes.

Cut salmon into 4 pieces and transfer to a spinach-lined platter. Garnish with papaya slices and serve immediately.

IF YOU PREFER A SLIGHTLY SPICIER FLAVOR, TRY **SOY-HORSERADISH MARINADE** FOR SALMON. COMBINE 2 TABLESPOONS PEANUT OIL, 2 TABLESPOONS SOY SAUCE, 2 TABLESPOONS HORSERADISH, 2 TABLESPOONS BROWN SUGAR, 2 TABLESPOONS FRESH LEMON JUICE AND 2 TABLESPOONS DIJON MUSTARD. USE TO MARINATE 1 TO 2 HOURS BEFORE GRILLING. THIS IS ALSO GOOD FOR TUNA OR SWORDFISH.

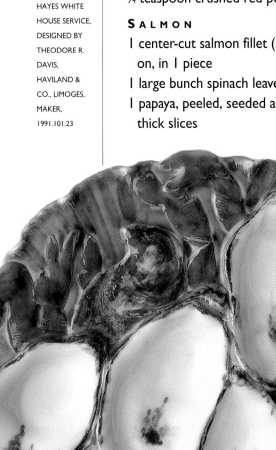

OVEN-BAKED SALMON STEAKS

SERVES 4

4 salmon steaks, 1-inch thick
4 tablespoons butter, melted
1 teaspoon lemon pepper
1 teaspoon garlic salt
paprika
lemon wedges

Place steaks in baking dish large enough to hold them in single layer. Mix butter, lemon pepper and garlic salt together in small bowl. Baste both sides of fish with seasoned butter and sprinkle generously with paprika. Bake at 500 degrees for exactly 10 minutes. Serve with wedges of lemon.

NOTE: YES, YOU REALLY DO BAKE THE FISH AT 500 DEGREES! BE SURE TO TIME IT PRECISELY. THIS PREPARATION ALSO WORKS WELL FOR SWORDFISH, ORANGE ROUGHY OR ANY OTHER THICK FISH.

TRY MANGO MINT SALSA (PAGE 117) OR CILANTRO CUMIN LIME SAUCE (PAGE 133) WITH THE SALMON FOR A SPECIAL TOUCH. COMPLETE THE MEAL WITH ORZO AND RED PEPPER WREATH (PAGE 152) AND MOZZAARELLA AND TOMATOES WITH FRESH BASIL VINAIGRETTE (PAGE 82).

BAKED NORWEGIAN SALMON WITH FRESH ROSEMARY

SERVES 4

4 salmon fillets (6 ounces each)
2 shallots, chopped
½ cup white wine
½ cup fish or chicken stock
1 cup heavy cream or half and half
2 tablespoons chopped fresh rosemary
juice of 1 lemon
salt and pepper to taste

Place salmon, shallots, wine, stock and cream in an ovenproof skillet. Bake at 475 degrees for 10 minutes. Remove salmon to heated platter. Place skillet over high heat and reduce liquid to sauce consistency. Add rosemary, lemon juice, salt and pepper to taste. Spoon sauce over salmon and serve immediately.

Baked Red Snapper with Tomatoes, Herbs and Avocado

Serves 4

4 red snapper fillets

salt and pepper

3 tablespoons olive oil (divided use)

6 green onions, minced

3 cloves garlic, minced

6 to 8 Roma tomatoes, peeled, seeded, chopped and drained

2 tablespoons chopped fresh herbs (basil, thyme, rosemary)

1 avocado

1 tablespoon lime juice

¼ teaspoon Tabasco

lime slices (garnish)

Season fillets with salt and pepper. Heat 2 tablespoons oil in skillet and sauté fillets over high heat, about 2 minutes per side. Arrange fillets in single layer in baking dish. (Can be done early in day, covered and refrigerated.)

Heat remaining tablespoon oil in skillet. Add onions and garlic and sauté until just beginning to brown. Add tomatoes and cook 2 minutes. (Sauce can be prepared early in day. Refrigerate in non-metallic container covered with plastic wrap; reheat before using.) Pour mixture over fish and top with herbs. Bake, uncovered, at 400 degrees for 15 to 20 minutes.

Mash avocado with fork, add lime juice, Tabasco, salt and pepper to taste. (This can be prepared several hours in advance. Place 1 avocado pit in mixture to prevent browning; cover tightly and refrigerate.) Spoon avocado mixture in strip down center of each fillet during last 5 minutes of baking.

Remove fish from oven and serve immediately garnished with slices of lime.

For a simple, mostly "do ahead" meal, serve the snapper with Mediterranean Roasted Vegetable Salad (page 86) and Cheese Bread with Parsley and Poppy Seeds (page 64). Finish with Tarte Tatin (page 194) or Frozen Strawberry Torte (page 212).

Sautéed Prawns with Jalapeños and Cilantro

SERVES 2 AS AN ENTRÉE
OR 4 AS AN APPETIZER

3 tablespoons olive oil
12 large prawns, peeled and deveined
6 cloves garlic, minced
1 to 2 jalapeños, stemmed, seeded and finely chopped
1 bunch cilantro, stemmed and coarsely chopped
½ bunch Italian parsley, stemmed and coarsely chopped
½ cup dry white wine
sea salt and freshly ground pepper to taste
2 tablespoons butter

Heat oil in heavy skillet over high heat. Add prawns and cook for 1 minute, turning at least once. Add garlic and jalapeños and cook for 1 minute. Add cilantro and parsley; cook for 1 minute, stirring constantly. Mix in wine and season to taste with salt and pepper. Stir for 10 seconds until combined. Remove prawns to warm plate.

Reduce wine over high heat, stirring constantly for 1 minute. Remove pan from heat and swirl in butter.

Pour sauce over prawns and serve at once.

STERLING SILVER AND SILVERGILT BERRY SPOON, *NARRAGANSETT* PATTERN, DESIGNED 1884, GORHAM MFG. CO., PROVIDENCE, R. I., 1991.76

Shrimp are divided into two categories, northern (cold water) and tropical. Tropical shrimp are identified by shell color: white, brown, pink, red, striped (tiger). Prawns are a subgroup of freshwater shrimp. On the West Coast, "prawns" refers to large ocean shrimp.

SOLE STUFFED WITH SHRIMP AND ROQUEFORT CHEESE

SERVES 8

1 cup (2 sticks) butter, softened
4 ounces cream cheese, softened
3 ounces Roquefort cheese
2 tablespoons lemon juice
1 teaspoon chopped parsley
1 teaspoon chopped chives
1 green onion, minced
⅛ teaspoon hot pepper sauce
⅛ teaspoon Worcestershire sauce
pepper to taste
salt to taste, if desired
6 ounces raw shrimp, cut into small pieces
8 fillets of sole (6 to 8 ounces each)
2 eggs, beaten
bread crumbs for coating
½ cup (1 stick) butter, melted

Beat butter, cream cheese and Roquefort until thoroughly blended. Add lemon juice, parsley, chives, green onion, hot pepper sauce, Worcestershire sauce and pepper, mixing well. Taste before adding salt, as Roquefort cheese can be salty. Fold in shrimp, blending well. Refrigerate at least 20 minutes.

Pat fish dry. Spread about ¼ cup of chilled filling on skin side (darker side) of each fillet. Roll fillets about halfway, carefully folding in outer edges to hold mixture inside. Finish rolling.

Dip each fillet into eggs and roll in bread crumbs. Place in shallow, buttered baking dish just large enough to hold fillets. Top with remaining filling, if any, and drizzle with melted butter.

Bake at 375 degrees for 20 minutes, or until sole is white and flaky but not overdone. Check frequently after 15 minutes.

FILLETS CAN ALSO BE FILLED, ROLLED AND BAKED WITHOUT DIPPING THEM IN EGG AND BREAD CRUMBS.

Lemon Grass Shrimp with Mushrooms and Snow Peas

SERVES 8

1 tablespoon finely chopped fresh lemon grass

1 tablespoon finely chopped garlic

1½ teaspoons peppercorns, whole or freshly ground

½ teaspoon salt

4 dried red chili peppers, seeded, soaked and coarsely chopped

3 to 4 tablespoons fish sauce (depending on desired saltiness)

1 tablespoon sugar

1 tablespoon cornstarch dissolved in 2 tablespoons water

4 tablespoons oil

2 pounds large shrimp, shelled and deveined

¼ pound button mushrooms, halved

¼ pound snow peas

¼ cup coarsely chopped peanuts (garnish)

2 tablespoons slivered green onion tops (garnish)

Purée lemon grass, garlic, peppercorns, salt and chili peppers to a paste in a blender or food processor. Set aside.

Combine fish sauce, sugar, cornstarch and water. Mix well and set aside.

Heat oil in skillet or wok over medium-high heat. Add lemon grass paste and stir-fry until aroma is released, only a few seconds. Increase heat to high and stir-fry shrimp, mushrooms and snow peas for 3 minutes. Add fish sauce mixture and toss to blend.

To serve, transfer to platter and sprinkle with peanuts and onion tops.

GRILLED SHRIMP AND BLACK BEAN TOSTADA WITH WATERMELON SALSA

SERVES 4

4 corn tortillas
oil for frying

BLACK BEANS
2 cups canned black beans, rinsed, drained and
  puréed
1 teaspoon ground cumin
2 teaspoons chili powder
2 tablespoons sour cream
2 cloves garlic, minced

SHRIMP
1 pound shrimp, cleaned, peeled and deveined
1 tablespoon Creole seasoning
½ teaspoon garlic powder
1 teaspoon ground cumin
1 teaspoon chili powder

CABBAGE SALAD
1 tablespoon Dijon mustard
1 tablespoon sugar
¼ cup red wine vinegar
¾ cup safflower oil
salt and pepper to taste
2 cups shredded Napa cabbage

WATERMELON SALSA
1 cup diced watermelon
2 tablespoons chopped onion
¼ cup minced cilantro
½ habeñero or jalapeño, minced
2 teaspoons lime juice
½ teaspoon salt

Heat oil in skillet and fry tortillas for 1 to 2 minutes, or until crisp. Drain on paper towels. (Can be done early in day.)

Combine bean purée with cumin, chili powder, sour cream and garlic. Mix well. (Can be done several hours ahead.)

Coat shrimp with mixture of Creole seasoning, garlic powder, cumin and chili powder. Grill shrimp 3 to 4 minutes, until just cooked.

Whisk together mustard, sugar, vinegar, oil, salt and pepper. Toss with cabbage.

Combine watermelon, onion, cilantro, habeñero, lime juice and salt. (Ingredients can be chopped early in day, but do not combine more than ½ hour before serving.)

To assemble tostadas, spread each tortilla with black beans, arrange shrimp over beans, top with cabbage and spoon salsa over.

THIS DISH IS EQUALLY GOOD PREPARED WITH GRILLED CHICKEN.

GRILLED MARINATED SWORDFISH WITH AVOCADO BUTTER

SERVES 8

8 small swordfish steaks

MARINADE
½ cup oil
⅓ cup soy sauce
¼ cup fresh lemon juice
1 teaspoon grated lemon peel
1 clove garlic, crushed

AVOCADO BUTTER
½ cup (1 stick) butter, room temperature
1 cup mashed ripe avocado
5 tablespoons fresh lemon or lime juice
2 tablespoons chopped fresh parsley
2 cloves garlic, minced
salt to taste

8 lemon or lime wedges (garnish)
8 sprigs parsley (garnish)

Pierce fish on both sides with fork. Arrange in single layer in shallow baking dish. Mix together oil, soy sauce, lemon juice, lemon peel and garlic. Pour over fish. Marinate 2 hours in refrigerator, turning occasionally.

Beat butter in small bowl until soft and creamy. Mix in avocado, lemon juice, parsley and garlic. Season with salt. Cover and chill until ready to serve.

Prepare grill or preheat broiler. Drain fish, reserving marinade. Grill fish 9 minutes per 1 inch thickness, brushing often with marinade and turning once. Transfer fish to platter. Top each piece with spoonful of avocado butter. Garnish with lemon and parsley.

ENAMELED
PORCELAIN
TUREEN
STAND, CA.
1750-60,
CHINA,
1985.R.855

PEPPERED TUNA STEAKS WITH MINT BÉARNAISE SAUCE

SERVES 4

MINT BÉARNAISE SAUCE
1 bunch fresh mint, stemmed and chopped
   (divided use)
½ cup white wine vinegar
1½ cups (3 sticks) butter (divided use)
3 egg yolks
2 tablespoons water
salt to taste

TUNA
4 tuna steaks
olive oil
1 to 2 tablespoons coarsely cracked green
   peppercorns
¼ teaspoon cayenne pepper (optional)

Place all but 2 tablespoons of mint leaves in a saucepan with vinegar and 2 tablespoons butter. Cook over medium heat until liquid is reduced by half. Set aside.

Melt remaining butter in a separate saucepan, cooking until bubbling but not browned. Combine egg yolks and water in blender. With motor running, add melted butter in a steady stream, blending until thoroughly incorporated and thickened. Blend in mint-vinegar mixture and reserved fresh mint. Season with salt and set aside.

Rub tuna steaks liberally with olive oil and roll in peppercorns, patting to coat. Dust lightly with cayenne. Grill over high heat about 4 minutes per side. Don't overcook. Serve with Mint Béarnaise Sauce.

SERVE ROASTED POTATOES WITH ROSEMARY (PAGE 178) AND SPINACH WITH RAISINS AND PINE NUTS (PAGE 180) TO COMPLETE THE PLATE.

IF YOU USE BLACK PEPPERCORNS INSTEAD OF GREEN, DECREASE THE AMOUNT TO 2 TEASPOONS. BLACK PEPPERCORNS ARE CONSIDERABLY HOTTER THAN THE GREEN.

GRILLED SWORDFISH ORIENTAL

SERVES 4

½ cup oil
3 tablespoons soy sauce
2 tablespoons dry sherry
1 teaspoon grated fresh ginger
2 cloves garlic, minced
4 swordfish steaks (4 ounces each)
lemon slices for garnish

Mix together oil, soy sauce, sherry, ginger and garlic. Arrange fish in shallow glass baking dish. Pour marinade over, turning fish to coat. Cover and refrigerate 4 to 6 hours, turning occasionally.

Prepare grill. Drain fish, reserving marinade. Grill fish 10 to 14 minutes over medium coals, turning once and basting frequently with marinade. Fish is done when it flakes easily with fork. Serve garnished with lemon slices.

GRILLED TUNA STEAKS WITH SWEET SOY AND GINGER BUTTER SAUCE

SERVES 4

MARINADE
¼ cup sherry
2½ tablespoons sesame oil
2 ½ tablespoons soy sauce
1 green onion, finely chopped
1 tablespoon orange zest

TUNA
4 tuna steaks (8-ounce)

SAUCE
½ cup white wine
½ lemon, juiced
¾ cup (1½ sticks) butter, cut in pieces
1 tablespoon minced fresh ginger

4 tablespoons sweet soy sauce

Combine sherry, sesame oil, soy sauce, green onion and orange zest; mix well. Place tuna steaks in glass dish, and pour marinade over. Marinate 1 hour, turning frequently.

To prepare sauce, combine wine and lemon juice in a non-reactive saucepan. Cook over medium heat until liquid is reduced to 2 tablespoons. Remove from heat and whisk in butter a little at a time, returning pan to heat as needed to melt butter. Add ginger and set aside. Reheat sauce just before serving.

Grill tuna over medium-hot coals for 4 to 5 minutes on each side, or until just done.

Place tuna on warmed plates. Spoon sauce over each steak and drizzle with 1 tablespoon sweet soy sauce (or more to taste). Serve at once.

Pasta and Grains

OPENING PAGE:
LEADED GLASS
AND STERLING
SILVER CRUET
AND LABEL
FROM A SET,
1793, HENRY
GREENWAY,
LONDON
(FRAME),
ENGLAND OR
IRELAND
(BOTTLES),
1987.57.
IN THE ERA
WHEN ENGLAND
RULED THE SEAS
WITH ITS GREAT
MERCHANT
FLEET, A SILVER
AND CRYSTAL
CRUET SET OF
THIS
IMPORTANCE
WAS A SYMBOL
OF POWER AND
WEALTH, NOT
ONLY FOR THE
ELEGANCE OF ITS
MATERIALS AND
MANUFACTURE
BUT FOR THE
RARE AND
EXPENSIVE SPICES
IT CONTAINED.

PESTO CHICKEN AND FUSILLI

SERVES 4 TO 6

4 skinless boneless chicken breasts
salt and freshly ground pepper
1 tablespoon butter
2 tablespoons olive oil (divided use)
¼ cup white wine
1 red or green bell pepper, seeded and thinly
   sliced
12 ounces fusilli, cooked according to package
   directions
¼ cup pine nuts, toasted
¼ cup basil pesto (purchase or see page 147)
½ cup mayonnaise

Season chicken breasts with salt and pepper. Heat butter and 1 tablespoon olive oil over high heat in medium skillet. Add chicken breasts and cook until golden brown on both sides. Add wine and continue cooking until chicken is done. Remove from pan and set aside to cool.

Heat remaining tablespoon oil in same pan. Add peppers and sauté, stirring constantly, about 1 minute. Remove peppers and set aside to cool.

Cut chicken into 1-inch wide strips. Combine chicken, peppers, fusilli, pine nuts, pesto and mayonnaise, mixing well. Chill before serving.

LINGUINE WITH SHRIMP AND FETA

SERVES 4

¾ pound shrimp, cooked, peeled and deveined
8 ounces feta cheese, crumbled
6 green onions, chopped (white part only)
4 teaspoons chopped fresh oregano
4 to 6 Roma tomatoes, coarsely chopped
salt and freshly ground pepper to taste
8 ounces linguine
1 tablespoon olive oil

Combine shrimp, feta, green onions, oregano, tomatoes, salt and pepper in large bowl. Let mixture stand at room temperature for at least 1 hour. Cook pasta according to package directions. Drain and toss with olive oil. Add pasta to shrimp mixture and toss to coat. Serve immediately or chill several hours in refrigerator.

SMOKED CHICKEN IS A DELICIOUS ALTERNATIVE TO THE SHRIMP.

PESTO TORTELLINI PRIMAVERA

SERVES 3 TO 4

9-ounce package fresh tortellini or other pasta, cooked and drained

2 carrots, peeled, sliced diagonally and steamed until tender crisp

2 medium zucchini, sliced diagonally and steamed until tender crisp

1 cup sugar snap peas, strings removed and steamed until tender crisp

4 oil-packed, sun-dried tomatoes, drained and sliced

SAUCE

¼ to ½ cup heavy cream

½ cup basil pesto (recipe follows)

¼ cup fresh, shredded Parmesan cheese plus additional cheese to pass

salt and pepper to taste

red pepper flakes to taste (optional)

BASIL PESTO

2 cups fresh basil leaves

3 cloves garlic, peeled

½ cup pine nuts or walnuts

½ cup olive oil (plus additional oil to seal containers)

¾ teaspoon salt

½ cup fresh shredded Parmesan cheese

Heat cream in large skillet. Add drained pasta first, then steamed vegetables and sun-dried tomatoes. Cook over low heat until heated through. Stir in pesto. Remove from heat and add ¼ cup cheese and seasonings. Serve with additional cheese at table.

To make the Basil Pesto, place basil, garlic and nuts in food processor and blend until pulverized. Add oil and salt, processing until smooth. Add cheese and blend briefly. Divide pesto among small containers (leaving a little head room if you are going to freeze). Pour thin film of olive oil over each and seal. Store in refrigerator for a few weeks or in freezer for a year.

VARY THE VEGETABLES ACCORDING TO SEASONAL AVAILABILITY OR, FOR A HEARTIER DISH, ADD SHRIMP OR GRILLED CHICKEN.

STERLING SILVER SERVING SPOON, *MORNING GLORY* PATTERN, CA. 1875, GORHAM MFG. CO., PROVIDENCE, RI, 1991.101.3.

Most pestos can be frozen for later use. Freeze them in ice cube trays and then place the cubes in a plastic bag in the freezer for quick convenient additions to pasta sauces.

GLAZED
STONEWARE
BOWL, C. 1949,
OCTAVIO
MEDELLIN,
DALLAS, 1949.37

FARFALLE WITH FETA

SERVES 6

DRESSING

½ cup olive oil

1 tablespoon sugar

3 tablespoons dry white wine

2 tablespoons lemon juice

1 teaspoon dried basil, crushed

¼ teaspoon ground pepper

several dashes Tabasco

SALAD

4 medium tomatoes, peeled, seeded and chopped (about 3 cups)

1 medium cucumber, peeled, seeded, and chopped

1 small green bell pepper, seeded and chopped

1 slice red onion, chopped

¼ cup snipped parsley

8 ounces farfalle pasta (bowties), cooked al dente and drained

1 cup feta cheese, crumbled

Whisk together all dressing ingredients. Combine vegetables, farfalle and feta in large bowl. Toss with dressing to coat and serve chilled or at room temperature.

LEMON COUSCOUS WITH SPINACH AND DILL

SERVES 6

2¼ cups water

1½ cups couscous

½ teaspoon salt

3 tablespoons fresh lemon juice

grated rind of 1 lemon

¼ cup olive oil

salt and pepper to taste

1 bunch spinach, stemmed and finely shredded (about 2 cups)

3 green onions, thinly sliced

3 to 4 tablespoons finely chopped fresh dill

¼ cup pine nuts, toasted (optional)

Bring water to a boil in a saucepan. Stir in couscous and salt. Remove pan from heat and let couscous stand, covered, for 5 minutes. Fluff couscous with a fork and transfer to a bowl. Stir in lemon juice and rind, oil, salt and pepper. Cool couscous completely.

When cold, stir in spinach, green onions and dill. Chill salad, covered, at least 2 hours or overnight. Add pine nuts just before serving.

Fettuccine with Goat Cheese and Asparagus

Serves 4

¾ pound fresh asparagus
12 ounces fettuccine
2 tablespoons olive oil
2 tablespoons butter
2 teaspoons minced garlic
4 ripe plum tomatoes, peeled, seeded and diced
4 ounces soft goat cheese
4 tablespoons coarsely chopped fresh basil
  leaves
freshly ground pepper to taste
freshly grated Parmesan cheese

Scrape and trim asparagus. Cut on the bias into 1-inch lengths. Cook fettuccine al dente, as directed on package, reserving ¼ cup cooking liquid.

Heat oil and butter in large pot. Add asparagus and garlic, cooking over medium heat for 2 minutes, stirring. Add tomatoes and cook 1 minute. Add fettuccine, goat cheese, basil, reserved cooking liquid and pepper. Toss well over medium heat until just heated through. Serve immediately with Parmesan on top.

Rotini with Gazpacho Dressing

Serves 8 to 10

½ cup olive oil
½ cup red wine vinegar
2 to 3 cloves garlic, minced
½ teaspoon ground cumin
5 tomatoes, peeled, seeded, and chopped
  (divided use)
2 cucumbers, peeled, seeded and chopped
  (divided use)
salt and freshly ground pepper to taste
Tabasco to taste
1 pound rotini, or pasta of choice
2 yellow or green bell peppers, chopped
1 red onion, chopped
1 bunch green onions, thinly sliced
1 cup pitted sliced black olives
1 cup chopped fresh parsley
1 cup chopped fresh mint

Combine oil, vinegar, garlic, cumin, one-half of tomatoes, one-half of cucumbers, salt, pepper and Tabasco in food processor and blend to coarse purée. Set aside.

Cook pasta al dente according to package directions. Drain well. Place in large bowl and toss with dressing. Add remaining tomatoes and cucumbers, peppers, onions, olives, parsley and mint. Serve at room temperature or chilled. (Best if prepared several hours ahead to allow flavors to develop.)

ANGEL HAIR WITH GRILLED CHICKEN AND MACADAMIA-ARUGULA PESTO

SERVES 6 TO 8

BALSAMIC MARINADE
2 tablespoons minced shallots
1 tablespoon minced garlic
½ cup olive oil
¼ cup balsamic vinegar
2 tablespoons chopped fresh basil
1 tablespoon chopped fresh thyme
2 tablespoons honey
½ teaspoon freshly ground pepper
salt to taste

CHICKEN
4 skinless boneless chicken breasts

PASTA
12 ounces angel hair pasta, cooked and chilled
1 mango, sliced

MACADAMIA-ARUGULA PESTO
2 teaspoons minced garlic
¼ cup spinach leaves
¾ cup arugula leaves plus extra for garnish
¾ cup olive oil
1 tablespoon sugar
1 teaspoon freshly ground pepper
salt to taste
½ cup macadamia nuts, toasted
5 tablespoons grated asiago cheese (can use Parmesan)
2 tablespoons dry sack sherry
1 mango, diced

For marinade, sauté shallots and garlic in oil for 3 to 4 minutes. Add vinegar, basil, thyme, honey, salt and pepper, mixing well. Pour over chicken in shallow dish. Cover and refrigerate for 2 to 3 hours.

Grill chicken over medium-hot coals for 3 to 5 minutes per side until cooked through. Cut into julienne strips and refrigerate.

To prepare pesto, purée garlic, spinach, arugula, oil, sugar, pepper and salt in food processor. Add nuts and cheese, blending just until incorporated. Transfer to bowl and stir in sherry and diced mango.

To assemble, toss pasta with three-fourths of pesto, three-fourths of chicken and three-fourths of mango. Allow to sit 30 minutes to meld flavors.

Place on platter and top with reserved chicken strips and mango slices. Drizzle with remaining pesto and garnish with arugula leaves. Serve cold or at room temperature.

TRY THIS SALAD WITH GRILLED SHRIMP.

ANGEL HAIR PASTA WITH SHRIMP IN LEMON PEPPER-TARRAGON SAUCE

SERVES 4

1 tablespoon olive oil
1 teaspoon minced garlic
1 tablespoon lemon pepper
2 tablespoons fresh lemon juice
2 tablespoons white wine
1 teaspoon chopped fresh tarragon
½ cup canned artichoke bottoms, thinly sliced
⅓ cup chopped, oil-packed sun-dried tomatoes, drained
1½ cups heavy cream
1 tablespoon capers (optional)
1 pound medium shrimp, peeled and deveined
8 ounces angel hair pasta, cooked al dente
½ cup freshly shredded Parmesan cheese

Heat oil in skillet over medium heat. Add garlic, lemon pepper, lemon juice and wine. Simmer, stirring frequently, until garlic has softened. Add tarragon, artichokes, sun-dried tomatoes, cream and capers. Simmer until desired consistency.

Heat remaining tablespoon olive oil in separate skillet. Add shrimp and sauté until just pink. Season with salt and pepper.

To serve, toss hot, drained pasta with sauce until well coated. Fold in shrimp. Divide among 4 plates and sprinkle Parmesan over each. Serve immediately.

OMIT SHRIMP AND SERVE THIS SAUCE OVER VEAL SCALOPPINE, GRILLED OR SAUTÉED RED SNAPPER, OR BAKED OR GRILLED CHICKEN BREASTS.

ORZO AND RED PEPPER WREATH

SERVES 8

6 strips bacon
2 cups orzo, cooked according to package directions
½ cup (1 stick) butter (divided use)
1 red bell pepper, chopped
8 ounces fresh mushrooms, sliced
½ cup freshly grated Parmesan cheese plus extra for garnish

Fry bacon until crisp; drain, crumble and set aside. Toss drained orzo with ¼ cup butter. Set aside. Heat remaining ¼ cup butter in skillet. Add pepper and mushrooms; sauté until tender. Add orzo to skillet and toss until well combined and heated through. Add bacon and Parmesan cheese.

When ready to serve, press orzo into greased ring mold. Invert mold onto serving platter. Serve at room temperature topped with an extra sprinkle of Parmesan cheese.

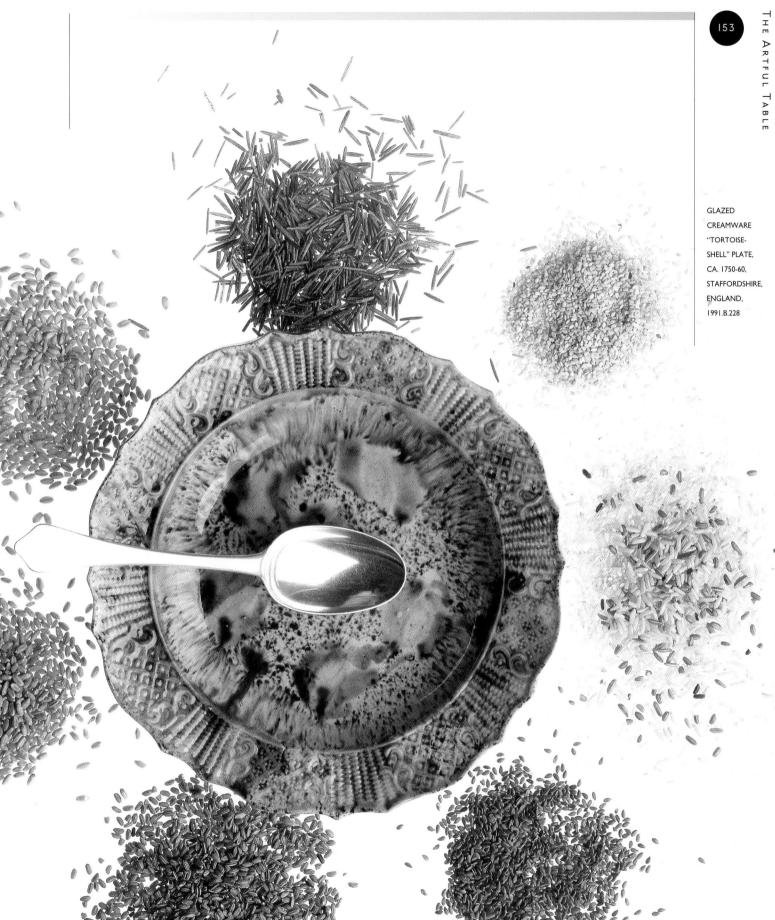

GLAZED
CREAMWARE
"TORTOISE-
SHELL" PLATE,
CA. 1750-60,
STAFFORDSHIRE,
ENGLAND,
1991.B.228

TAGLIATELLE WITH SHRIMP AND WILD MUSHROOMS

SERVES 6 TO 8

1½ pounds shrimp, peeled and deveined
4 tablespoons olive oil
5 cloves garlic, finely minced
⅓ cup oil-packed sun-dried tomatoes, chopped
¾ to 1 pound wild mushrooms
   (any combination you prefer)
⅓ cup white wine
salt and pepper to taste
crushed red pepper flakes (optional)
⅓ cup chopped fresh parsley
⅓ cup chopped fresh basil (or tarragon)
1 pound tagliatelle or linguine, cooked and
   drained
⅓ cup pine nuts, toasted
juice of ½ lemon
freshly shredded Parmesan cheese

Sauté shrimp in olive oil until partially cooked (1 to 2 minutes). Add garlic, tomatoes and mushrooms and continue cooking 2 minutes, or until mushrooms begin to soften. Add wine and season with salt and pepper. When heated through, add herbs and mix well. Toss pasta with shrimp mixture, pine nuts and lemon juice. Serve immediately with Parmesan.

RISOTTO WITH BASIL PESTO

SERVES 4 TO 6

3 tablespoons butter (divided use)
1 tablespoon olive oil
⅓ cup minced onion
1½ cups Arborio rice
5½ cups chicken broth, heated to steady simmer
½ cup pesto (purchase or see page 147)
4 tablespoons pine nuts, toasted (garnish)

Heat 2 tablespoons butter and olive oil in heavy skillet over moderate heat. Add onion and sauté for 1 to 2 minutes, until onion is soft but not brown. Add rice, stirring for 1 minute to coat well. Add broth, ½ cup at a time, stirring frequently. Wait until each addition is almost absorbed before adding next ½ cup. Reserve about ¼ cup broth to add at end. Stir frequently to prevent sticking. After about 18 minutes, when rice is tender but still firm, add reserved ¼ cup of broth and pesto. Turn off heat, add 1 tablespoon butter, and stir to combine. Garnish with pine nuts and serve immediately.

Arborio rice is a starchy, short-grain rice grown in northern Italy. It has the unique ability to absorb 5 times its volume in liquid without becoming mushy. Never rinse Arborio rice because you need the starch for thickening.

VERMICELLI WITH PUTANESCA SAUCE

A CLASSIC SOUTHERN ITALIAN SAUCE. SERVES 4

2 tablespoons olive oil

2 teaspoons minced garlic

2 anchovies chopped (optional)

1 tablespoon capers

¼ cup chopped black olives

½ teaspoon crushed red pepper

1 teaspoon dried oregano

¼ cup finely sliced green onions

1 cup diced Roma tomatoes

1 can (15-ounce) crushed tomatoes

salt and pepper to taste

10 ounces vermicelli or other thin pasta cooked
  al dente

Heat olive oil over medium-high heat. Add garlic and sauté until softened. Add anchovies, capers, olives, red pepper, oregano and green onion; sauté for 2 minutes. Stir in tomatoes. Simmer until desired thickness. Season with salt and pepper. Serve over hot pasta.

KEEP THIS SAUCE IN MIND TO USE FOR PIZZA (REDUCE SAUCE UNTIL VERY THICK), AS WELL AS FOR CHICKEN AND FISH DISHES.

TRANSFER-PRINTED PEARLWARE SOUP PLATE, CA. 1830-50, *ITALIAN SCENERY: BRIDGE AT LUGANO* PATTERN, STAFFORDSHIRE, ENGLAND, 1992.B.234.4

HERB RISOTTO WITH LEEKS AND PARMESAN

A DELICIOUS LOW-FAT VERSION OF THE TRADITIONAL RECIPE.

SERVES 4

1 tablespoon olive oil
2 leeks, finely chopped (about 1 cup)
1 to 2 cloves garlic, minced
1½ cups Arborio rice
½ cup dry white wine
5 to 6 cups chicken broth, heated to simmering
½ cup chopped fresh herbs (chives, basil, oregano, thyme)
½ cup freshly grated Parmesan cheese
salt and freshly ground pepper to taste

Heat oil in a large saucepan over medium heat. Sauté leeks and garlic 3 to 4 minutes, until soft but not brown. Stir in rice and cook for 1 minute until rice is well coated.

Add wine and bring to a boil, stirring constantly. When wine is almost absorbed, reduce heat to simmer. Begin adding broth ½ cup at a time, making sure most of liquid is absorbed before next addition. Stirring steadily, continue adding stock until 5 cups are used. If the rice is still hard, add ½ to 1 cup more broth. Add herbs during last 3 minutes of cooking. (Whole process takes about 18 to 20 minutes.) Rice should be soft and creamy, but individual grains of rice still distinct.

Remove pan from heat and stir in cheese, salt and pepper. Serve immediately.

MICROWAVE RISOTTO

SERVES 4

4 tablespoons (½ stick) butter (divided use)
½ cup chopped onion
1 cup Arborio rice
3 cups chicken broth (divided use)
½ cup water
1 cup freshly shredded Parmesan cheese

All instructions are for using microwave on high power. Place 2 tablespoons butter in covered, 2-quart casserole and cook for 1 minute. Add onion and cook 2 minutes. Add rice and cook 1 minute, stir to coat. Add 2 cups chicken broth and water and cook for 12 minutes. Stir and add ½ cup broth and cook for 5 minutes. Stir and if broth is absorbed, stop cooking. If not, cook 1 or 2 minutes longer. Remove from microwave and add Parmesan cheese and remaining 2 tablespoons butter, stirring to combine. Add remaining broth in small increments until desired creaminess is reached. Serve immediately.

THE AMOUNT OF LIQUID YOU NEED WILL VARY WITH THE BRAND OF CHICKEN BROTH AND ARBORIO RICE YOU USE, AS WELL AS YOUR PERSONAL TASTE. IN GENERAL, THE SALTIER THE BROTH, THE MORE LIQUID YOU'LL NEED. DON'T USE BROTH MADE FROM BOUILLON CUBES FOR THIS REASON.

TO CREATE A MAIN DISH MEAL, STIR FRY 1 POUND OF SHRIMP OR SCALLOPS AND ADD TO RISOTTO AT END OF COOKING. FOR A VEGETARIAN DISH, ADD PEAS, MUSHROOMS, OR ANY VEGETABLE YOU CHOOSE. STIR FRY BRIEFLY AND TOSS WITH COOKED RISOTTO.

MEDITERRANEAN PASTA SALAD

SERVES 6 TO 8

DRESSING
⅔ cup olive oil
3 tablespoons red wine vinegar
2 tablespoons chopped fresh basil
2 tablespoons chopped green onions
2 tablespoons grated Parmesan cheese
¼ teaspoon pepper

SALAD
12 ounces rotini, cooked and drained
1 red bell pepper, cut into thin strips
1 green bell pepper, cut into thin strips
1 yellow bell pepper, cut into thin strips
2 tablespoons chopped fresh basil
1 medium tomato, cut into thin wedges
¼ cup pine nuts, toasted
¼ cup Greek olives, pitted and sliced
8 ounces feta cheese, cubed
¼ teaspoon dried oregano

Combine oil, vinegar, basil, onions, Parmesan and pepper in food processor and purée until smooth.

Combine rotini, peppers, basil, tomatoes, pine nuts and olives in large bowl. Toss with dressing to coat. Mix feta with oregano and add to salad. Serve chilled or at room temperature.

THREE-MUSHROOM LASAGNE WITH GORGONZOLA SAUCE

SERVES 16 TO 24 (2 PANS)

2 ounces dried porcini mushrooms

3 cups boiling water

1 cup (2 sticks) plus 1 tablespoon butter (divided use)

3½ tablespoons olive oil (divided use)

4 shallots, minced (divided use)

2 pounds white domestic mushrooms, minced

1½ teaspoons salt (divided use)

½ teaspoon freshly ground pepper (divided use)

½ teaspoon dried tarragon (divided use)

cayenne pepper to taste

¼ cup fresh lemon juice (divided use)

2 cloves garlic, minced

¾ pound fresh shiitake mushrooms, stemmed, caps sliced ¼-inch thick

½ cup flour

2 cups milk

1 cup heavy cream

6 ounces Gorgonzola cheese

1 cup freshly grated Parmesan cheese (divided use)

1 pound fresh lasagne noodles

COMBWARE
DOUGH
BOWL, CA.
1820-60,
ENGLAND,
1992.B.234

Place porcini mushrooms in bowl, cover with boiling water, and soak for 20 to 30 minutes until softened. Drain mushrooms, reserving liquid. Coarsely chop mushrooms. Strain reserved liquid through double layer cheesecloth and reserve 2 cups.

Melt 2 tablespoons butter and 1 tablespoon oil in heavy skillet over moderate heat. Add 2 tablespoons shallots and half of the domestic mushrooms. Sauté, stirring frequently, until liquid evaporates and mushrooms are lightly browned, 5 to 7 minutes. Season with ¼ teaspoon each of salt, pepper and tarragon. Add generous dash cayenne and 1 tablespoon lemon juice. Set aside. Wipe out skillet and repeat sautéing with 2 more tablespoons butter and 1 tablespoon oil, adding 2 more tablespoons shallots and remaining fresh mushrooms. Sauté and season as before, then set aside with first batch of mushrooms. (This preparation is called mushroom *duxelles*.)

Melt 3 tablespoons butter and remaining 1½ tablespoons oil in same skillet over moderately high heat. Add remaining shallots and garlic and sauté 30 seconds. Add shiitake and porcini mushrooms and sauté 3 minutes, stirring frequently. Reduce heat and cook 5 minutes, stirring. Add 1 cup reserved porcini liquid and simmer, partially covered, 5 to 10 minutes, until mushrooms are tender but still chewy. Uncover and cook, stirring until liquid evaporates. Season with remaining 2 tablespoons lemon juice, salt and pepper to taste. Add to mushroom *duxelles* and set aside.

To prepare sauce, melt ½ cup butter in saucepan over moderate heat. Add flour and cook, stirring, 2 to 3 minutes without letting flour color. Whisk in remaining 1 cup porcini liquid, milk and cream. Bring to boil, whisking constantly, until thickened and smooth. Reduce heat and simmer for 5 minutes, whisking frequently. Add Gorgonzola and ½ cup Parmesan, stirring until melted. Season with 1 teaspoon salt and several dashes cayenne.

Cook lasagne noodles al dente in large pot of boiling salted water. Drain and rinse in cold water. Lay noodles in single layer on kitchen towels to dry.

To assemble lasagne, generously butter two 13 x 9 x 2-inch baking pans. If sauce has cooled, reheat slightly over low heat. Arrange layer of noodles in bottom of each pan, trimming to fit, if necessary, and overlapping edges slightly. Spread thin layer of mushrooms over noodles (using one-fourth of total amount for each pan). Drizzle 1 cup of sauce over mushrooms in each pan. Repeat with another layer of noodles, mushrooms and sauce. Top with final layer of noodles. Divide remaining sauce over noodles and sprinkle ¼ cup Parmesan over top of each pan. Dot each with 1 tablespoon butter. (Can be assembled completely, covered and refrigerated overnight, or frozen up to 2 weeks.)

Bring lasagne to room temperature before baking at 375 degrees, uncovered, for 30 minutes, or until bubbling and lightly browned on top.

Noodles in Peanut Sauce and Sesame Oil

SERVES 4

8 ounces Chinese noodles or thin spaghetti

3 cloves garlic, minced

1 tablespoon red wine vinegar

1 tablespoon brown sugar

6 tablespoons chunky peanut butter

¼ cup low-sodium soy sauce

6 tablespoons sesame oil

2 tablespoons hot chili oil

5 tablespoons sesame seeds, toasted (divided use)

1 pound thin fresh asparagus, ends trimmed and cut in diagonal 1-inch lengths

3 green onions, 1-inch sections cut in julienne strips

1 small cucumber, halved, seeded and diced

Cook noodles according to package directions. Drain, rinse, and set aside in large bowl.

Combine garlic, vinegar, sugar, peanut butter and soy sauce in food processor and purée until smooth, about 1 minute. Slowly add oils and continue processing until smooth. Add to pasta along with 4 tablespoons sesame seeds.

Blanch asparagus in boiling water for 1 minute. Drain, rinse in cold water, and pat dry.

Place pasta on platter and arrange asparagus on top. Sprinkle with green onions, cucumber and remaining tablespoon of sesame seeds. Serve at room temperature.

Multi-Grain Salad with Fennel and Herb Vinaigrette

SERVES 6

FENNEL AND HERB VINAIGRETTE

1 cup olive oil

½ cup champagne vinegar

¼ cup fresh fennel, minced

2 teaspoons fennel seed, crushed

1 tablespoon minced garlic

½ teaspoon red chile flakes

1 teaspoon oregano

1 teaspoon basil

2 teaspoons coarsely ground pepper

1 tablespoon salt

SALAD

4 cups mixed grains (wheat berries, hard-wheat berries, buckwheat groats, barley and millet)

1 cup finely shredded red cabbage

2 cups julienned spinach

1 cup julienned arugula

½ cup diced red onion

salt and freshly ground pepper to taste

1 head red leaf lettuce

3 ounces feta cheese, crumbled

3 or 4 Roma tomatoes, sliced

To prepare vinaigrette, whisk all dressing ingredients together. Refrigerate, covered tightly, in glass container. (This is best made 1 day ahead to allow flavors to develop.)

Bring a large pot of water to a boil and add mixed grains. Lower heat and simmer 20 to 30 minutes or until grains are just al dente. Drain and rinse with cold water. Drain again and chill.

When grains are cold, combine with cabbage, spinach, arugula, onion and 1½ cups vinaigrette. Season to taste, taking into account saltiness of feta to be added later.

To serve, arrange red leaf lettuce leaves on each of 6 salad plates. Divide grain mixture among plates. Sprinkle each salad with feta cheese and garnish with tomatoes.

ORANGE WILD RICE WITH PINE NUTS, CURRANTS AND APPLES

SERVES 12

1 cup wild rice, uncooked
1 cup brown rice, uncooked
1 Granny Smith apple, diced
1 cup dried currants
½ cup orange juice
4 tablespoons chopped cilantro
2 tablespoons grated orange zest
½ cup pine nuts, toasted
2 tablespoons olive oil
salt and freshly ground pepper to taste
⅓ cup freshly shredded Parmesan cheese
2 tablespoons chopped fresh parsley

Cook wild rice according to package directions and set aside. Cook brown rice according to package directions and combine with wild rice. (Rice can be cooked 1 day ahead and stored, covered, in refrigerator. Allow to come to room temperature before proceeding.)

Soak apple and currants in orange juice for 30 minutes; add, undrained, to rice. Add cilantro, orange zest, pine nuts, olive oil, salt and pepper. Toss gently to combine. Place mixture in buttered casserole. (Rice can be prepared to this point up to 2 hours ahead. Cover, but do not refrigerate.)

Bake, covered, at 350 degrees for 30 to 40 minutes until heated through. Toss with Parmesan and parsley before serving.

SAUSAGE GRITS GRATIN

SERVES 8 TO 10

1 pound bulk sausage
1½ cups quick cooking grits
6 cups water
1 pound cheddar cheese, grated
¾ cup (1½ sticks) butter
3 eggs, lightly beaten
2 teaspoons salt
½ teaspoon garlic powder
dash Tabasco

Brown sausage well; drain and set aside. Cook grits in boiling water according to package directions. Beat in cheese, butter, eggs and seasonings until well incorporated and fluffy. Add sausage. Pour into greased, 2-quart casserole. Bake at 350 degrees for 1 hour, or until firm. (Can be prepared ahead and refrigerated or frozen before baking.)

GRITS ARE AN OLD FAVORITE. THEIR POPULARITY MAY BE DUE IN PART TO THEIR VERSATILITY. CONSIDER THE FOLLOWING POSSIBILITIES:

ADD CHOPPED GREEN CHILIES AND A DASH OF CHILI POWDER FOR A SOUTHWESTERN FLAVOR.

FOR A CREAMIER, RICHER TEXTURE USE MILK INSTEAD OF WATER TO COOK THE GRITS.

VARY THE CHEESE TO COMPLEMENT YOUR MENU. TRY GOAT CHEESE, MONTEREY JACK OR A SMOKED GOUDA.

ELIMINATE THE SAUSAGE, OR TRY DIFFERENT VARIETIES.

CRISPED POLENTA CUBES WITH GORGONZOLA WALNUT SAUCE

SERVES 3 TO 4 AS AN ENTRÉE OR

8 AS AN APPETIZER

POLENTA

3 cups water

½ teaspoon salt

1 cup polenta meal, regular or instant type

⅓ cup freshly grated Parmesan, pecorino or
  Romano cheese

2 tablespoons butter

2 to 3 tablespoons olive oil (divided use)

SAUCE

1 medium red onion, peeled and thinly sliced

1 tablespoon olive oil

1 rounded teaspoon flour

1 cup crumbled Gorgonzola cheese

2 cups heavy cream

freshly ground pepper to taste

10 ounces fresh spinach, cleaned, stemmed and
  chopped

1 tablespoon olive oil

½ cup walnut halves, toasted

Bring water and salt to boil in heavy pot. Lower heat and whisk in polenta until smooth. Cover and cook 45 minutes, stirring every 5 minutes with regular polenta (instant must be stirred constantly and will cook in 5 minutes). Add cheese and butter, stirring until well blended. Spoon polenta into lightly oiled, 9-inch square pan. Smooth top and coat lightly with oil. Cool slightly, then cover with plastic wrap and refrigerate several hours until cold and firm. (Can be made up to 2 days in advance to this point.)

For final cooking, cut polenta into 1-inch cubes. Heat 1 tablespoon oil in skillet and add some of polenta cubes (do not crowd pan) and cook for 2 to 3 minutes. Turn and continue sautéing until cubes are golden and crisp on all sides. Remove to warm platter. Repeat with rest of cubes, adding oil as needed. (Polenta can be baked instead of sautéed. Place cubes slightly apart on lightly oiled baking sheet. Bake at 350 degrees for 20 minutes, or until puffed and golden.)

To prepare sauce, sauté onion in oil until soft but not brown. Stir in flour until well blended. Add Gorgonzola, cream and pepper, whisking until sauce is smooth. Simmer 2 minutes to thicken. Keep warm.

Stir fry spinach in oil until just wilted, about 2 minutes.

To serve, place bed of spinach on plate, top with crisped polenta cubes, drizzle with sauce, and top with walnuts.

PENNE WITH PLUM TOMATOES AND CALAMATAS

SERVES 4 TO 6

SAUCE

3 tablespoons olive oil

1½ cups chopped green onion

3 cloves garlic, minced

3 cans (28-ounce) Italian plum tomatoes, drained

2 tablespoons chopped fresh basil

1½ teaspoons crushed red pepper flakes

2 cups reduced-sodium chicken broth

salt and pepper to taste

PASTA

1 pound penne pasta

3 tablespoons olive oil

2½ cups packed, grated Havarti cheese

⅓ cup pitted, sliced Calamata olives

4 tablespoons chopped fresh basil (divided use)

½ cup freshly shredded Parmesan cheese

To prepare sauce, heat oil in large saucepan over medium-high heat. Add onion and garlic and sauté until onion is tender, about 5 minutes. Add tomatoes, basil and pepper flakes, stirring to break up tomatoes with back of spoon. Add broth and bring to boil. Reduce heat and simmer 1 hour and 10 minutes, or until mixture thickens to chunky sauce and is reduced to 6 cups. Stir occasionally. Season with salt and pepper. (Sauce can be prepared 2 days ahead, covered and refrigerated. Reheat sauce over low heat to proceed with recipe.)

Cook pasta in large pot of boiling salted water just until al dente. Drain well. Return pasta to same pot and toss with oil. Pour sauce over and toss gently to blend. Mix in Havarti cheese, olives and 2 tablespoons basil. Transfer pasta to 13 x 9 x 2-inch baking dish. Top with Parmesan. (Can be assembled 1 day ahead, covered with plastic wrap and refrigerated. Allow to come to room temperature before baking.)

Bake at 375 degrees about 30 minutes, or until bubbling and heated through. Sprinkle with remaining basil to serve.

WILD MUSHROOM RISOTTO WITH PINE NUTS

SERVES 4

MUSHROOMS

1 tablespoon butter

1 clove garlic, finely minced

4 ounces fresh wild mushrooms (shiitake, oyster, portabella or other), stemmed and sliced

½ cup heavy cream

salt and pepper to taste

RICE

5 cups broth (beef or chicken)

2 tablespoons butter

1 tablespoon olive oil

2 tablespoons minced onion

1½ cups Arborio rice

½ cup dry white wine

⅓ cup Parmesan cheese

2 tablespoons chopped, fresh parsley

salt and pepper to taste

½ cup pine nuts, toasted (garnish)

Heat butter in skillet; add garlic and sauté 1 minute. Add mushrooms and cook 5 minutes until mushrooms are tender, stirring occasionally. Add cream, salt and pepper; simmer 3 to 5 minutes, or until cream has thickened slightly. Remove from heat and set aside.

Bring broth to steady simmer over medium heat in a separate saucepan. Heat butter and oil in heavy skillet over moderate heat. Sauté onions 2 minutes, or until they begin to soften. Add rice. Using a wooden spoon, stir rice for 1 minute, making sure all grains are well coated. Add wine and stir until completely absorbed. Begin adding simmering broth, ½ cup at a time, stirring after each addition. Wait until liquid is almost completely absorbed before adding next ½ cup of broth. After approximately 18 minutes, when the rice is tender but still firm, add last ½ cup broth, reserved mushroom mixture, Parmesan and parsley. Gently stir into rice and season with salt and pepper. Serve immediately with pine nuts sprinkled on each portion.

YOU CAN SUBSTITUTE 8 OUNCES WHITE MUSHROOMS OR ⅓ OUNCE DRIED PORCINI MUSHROOMS WHICH HAVE BEEN SOAKED IN HOT WATER FOR 30 MINUTES, DRAINED AND CHOPPED.

SLIVERED ALMONDS MAY BE USED INSTEAD OF PINE NUTS.

LASAGNE WITH ROASTED VEGETABLES AND PESTO

SERVES 8 TO 10

ROASTED VEGETABLES

2 tablespoons olive oil

6 zucchini (1½ pounds), sliced into ½-inch rounds

2 red bell peppers, cut into 1-inch pieces

2 leeks, white and light green parts only, thinly sliced

1¼ pounds mushrooms, quartered

salt and pepper to taste

¾ to 1 cup basil pesto (purchase or see page 147)

WHITE SAUCE

3 tablespoons butter

3 tablespoons flour

2 cups hot milk

salt and pepper to taste

¼ teaspoon freshly grated nutmeg

RICOTTA-CHEESE LAYER

1½ pounds ricotta cheese

3 large eggs

1 cup freshly grated Parmesan cheese

2 tablespoons finely chopped parsley

salt and white pepper to taste

1 pound fresh green or white lasagne noodles

1 pound thinly sliced Muenster cheese, diced

⅓ cup freshly grated Parmesan cheese

To roast vegetables, combine oil, zucchini, peppers, leeks and mushrooms in large roasting pan and toss to coat all ingredients. Roast vegetables at 450 degrees until softened, about 45 to 50 minutes, turning occasionally to prevent sticking. (If water accumulates in pan during cooking, pour off excess and continue to roast.) Transfer vegetables to mixing bowl and let cool. Season vegetables with salt and pepper and gently toss with pesto. Set aside.

To prepare sauce, melt butter in saucepan over medium heat. Whisk in flour until blended. Cook 2 minutes, whisking constantly, until bubbling but not changing color. Gradually add hot milk, beating to prevent lumps from forming. Bring to a boil; reduce heat to low and whisk until thickened, about 10 minutes. Add salt, pepper and nutmeg and taste for seasoning. Cover with plastic wrap and set aside.

To prepare ricotta-cheese layer, combine ricotta, eggs, Parmesan, parsley, salt and pepper in medium bowl and mix well. Set aside.

Cook noodles in large pot of salted boiling water until just al dente. Drain and place pasta in mixing bowl; cover with lukewarm water. When the noodles are tepid, lay them in a single layer on paper towels to dry. Blot dry and set aside.

To assemble lasagne, layer ingredients in a deep 13-inch-long ovenproof lasagne pan in the following order:

> one-half white sauce
>
> one-third lasagne noodles
>
> one-half roasted vegetables with pesto
>
> one-half ricotta-cheese mixture
>
> one-half Muenster
>
> one-third lasagne noodles
>
> rest of white sauce
>
> rest of roasted vegetables with pesto
>
> rest of lasagne noodles
>
> rest of ricotta-cheese mixture
>
> rest of Muenster
>
> a sprinkling of Parmesan

To make serving easier, use a serrated knife and cut lasagne into equal squares before baking. (Lasagne can be prepared to this point up to 2 days ahead. Cover in plastic wrap, then foil and refrigerate or freeze.)

Bake lasagne at 375 degrees for 45 minutes, or until bubbling throughout. Serve immediately.

(If lasagne has been refrigerated, bring to room temperature before baking. If frozen, bake lasagne without defrosting for 1 hour at 375 degrees, or until piping hot in center.)

WARM PASTA WITH FETA AND SPINACH

SERVES 6

2 to 3 tablespoons finely chopped fresh herbs (basil, rosemary, parsley or oregano)
freshly ground pepper
1½ cups feta cheese
½ cup olive oil (divided use)
½ pound pancetta, diced and fried, drippings reserved
4 cups (1 pound) spinach leaves, washed, stemmed, cut into ½-inch slices
1 cup seeded, diced fresh tomatoes
2 to 3 cloves garlic, finely chopped
2 tablespoons capers
1 red bell pepper, roasted, peeled, seeded, and cut into ¼-inch strips
1 pound fusilli or other pasta, cooked al dente and drained
salt to taste
¼ cup red wine vinegar
1 cup freshly grated Parmesan cheese

Sprinkle herbs and pepper over feta and drizzle with 1 tablespoon olive oil.

Combine pancetta, spinach, tomatoes, garlic, capers and red pepper in large serving bowl. Place hot pasta on top and toss until spinach wilts. Top with herbed feta and some of reserved pancetta drippings to taste. Season with salt. Add remaining olive oil and vinegar. Toss and sprinkle with Parmesan. Serve warm.

Szechwan Pasta Salad

SERVES 4 TO 6 AS MAIN COURSE

DRESSING
1 cup mayonnaise
⅓ cup soy sauce
1 tablespoon chili oil (hot!)
2 tablespoons sesame oil
1½ teaspoons Dijon mustard
1 clove garlic, minced

SALAD
12 to 16 ounces angel hair pasta
¼ pound snow peas
¼ pound cooked turkey, diced
½ bunch green onions, chopped
1 carrot, diced
½ cup water chestnuts, drained and sliced
1 red bell pepper, diced
1 can (15-ounce) whole baby ears of corn, drained
½ bunch cilantro leaves, chopped
2 tablespoons sesame seeds, toasted

Combine all dressing ingredients in food processor or blender and purée until smooth.

Cook pasta al dente, according to package directions. Drain, rinse with cold water, and drain again.

Stem and string snow peas. Slice diagonally into thin strips.

Combine pasta, snow peas, turkey, green onions, carrot, water chestnuts, pepper and corn in large bowl. Add dressing to coat and toss well. (Salad is best made ahead to allow flavors to develop. Keep refrigerated until serving time.) Garnish with cilantro and sesame seeds.

MANY VARIATIONS ARE POSSIBLE. YOU COULD USE FUSILLI OR PENNE PASTA IN PLACE OF ANGEL HAIR; SHRIMP OR CHICKEN INSTEAD OF TURKEY; ASPARAGUS TIPS INSTEAD OF SNOW PEAS; OR YELLOW PEPPERS INSTEAD OF RED.

IF YOU PREFER A LIGHTER VERSION, TRY USING REDUCED-FAT MAYONNAISE AND REDUCED-SODIUM SOY SAUCE.

"No mean woman can cook well, for it calls for a light head, a generous spirit, and a large heart." —PAUL GAUGUIN

VEGETABLES

HERBED ASPARAGUS WITH PARMESAN

SERVES 6 TO 8

2 pounds asparagus, tough ends removed
4 tablespoons butter, softened
1 tablespoon chopped fresh parsley
1 tablespoon chopped fresh chives
1 tablespoon chopped fresh dill
1 tablespoon chopped fresh rosemary
1 teaspoon freshly ground pepper
¼-pound wedge Parmesan cheese

Blanch asparagus in boiling water for 1½ to 2 minutes until barely tender. Drain and immediately refresh under cold running water. Drain again and pat dry.

Combine butter with parsley, chives, dill, rosemary and pepper. (Recipe can be completed to this point several hours ahead.)

Just before serving, melt herb butter in skillet. Add asparagus and toss gently just to heat through. Place on serving platter and garnish with shaved Parmesan. (Use a vegetable peeler to do this.) Serve immediately.

GREEN BEANS WITH CAPERS AND WATERCRESS

SERVES 4

1 pound small green beans (the tiny French *haricots verts* are wonderful, if you want to splurge)
2 tablespoons butter
2 shallots, minced
¼ cup capers
salt and white pepper to taste
1 teaspoon fresh lemon juice
1 to 2 bunches watercress, stemmed and coarsely chopped
1 tablespoon chopped fresh herbs (oregano, thyme, parsley, basil or combination of your favorites)
⅓ cup pine nuts or walnuts, toasted

Blanch green beans until barely tender, 3 to 5 minutes. Drain and refresh in cold water.

Melt butter and sauté shallots over low heat until softened. Add capers, beans, salt, pepper, lemon juice, watercress and herbs. Toss over medium heat until beans are heated through. Sprinkle with pine nuts before serving.

OPENING PAGE: ENAMELED PORCELAIN PLATE, *MILLENNIUM* PATTERN, CA. 1983, DESIGNED BY HELENA UGLAV, MIKASA CHINA, JAPAN, 12.1991.

GINGERED ASPARAGUS WITH CASHEWS

SERVES 6 TO 8

2 pounds asparagus
2 tablespoons peanut oil
2 teaspoons sesame oil
1 tablespoon grated fresh ginger
1 clove garlic, minced
1 tablespoon finely grated orange peel
1 tablespoon soy sauce
½ cup coarsely chopped cashews, toasted

Trim off tough lower stems of asparagus and discard. Cut each stalk into 2 to 3-inch lengths.

Heat oils in large skillet over high heat. Add asparagus and cook for 2 minutes. Add ginger and garlic, cooking an additional 2 to 3 minutes until tender (being careful not to let garlic burn). Stir in orange peel and soy sauce, sprinkle with cashews, and serve immediately.

CREAMWARE SAUCE TUREEN ON STAND, CA. 1800, JOSIAH WEDGWOOD FACTORY, STAFFORDSHIRE, ENGLAND, 64.1993.23.A-C

HERBED GREEN BEANS WITH TOMATOES

SERVES 8

1½ pounds fresh or frozen green beans
1 large clove garlic, minced
⅔ cup sliced onions
3 tablespoons olive oil
2 cups peeled, seeded and chopped tomatoes
salt and pepper to taste
¼ cup chopped fresh parsley and additional for
  garnish
¼ cup chopped fresh basil
⅓ cup freshly shredded Parmesan cheese

Blanch beans in boiling, salted water for 2 to 3 minutes until not quite tender. Drain, refresh in cold water and dry. (Can be prepared early in day to this point.)

Sauté garlic and onions in oil until tender but not browned. Add tomatoes, beans, salt and pepper. Simmer 2 to 3 minutes until beans are tender crisp. Add fresh herbs and cheese just before serving. Garnish with additional parsley.

WHEN IN SEASON, ZUCCHINI IS AN EXCELLENT SUBSTITUTE FOR GREEN BEANS.

TEXAS BLACK BEANS

SERVES 8

4 cups dried black beans, washed and picked over
1 can (4-ounce) chopped green chilies (or 3 fresh
  green chilies peeled, seeded and chopped)
1 jalapeño, seeded and minced
2 onions, chopped
1 tablespoon minced garlic
2 cups seeded and chopped tomatoes
1 tablespoon dried oregano
2 teaspoons ground cumin
½ teaspoon cayenne pepper
1 teaspoon salt
¼ cup chopped fresh cilantro

CONDIMENTS (OPTIONAL)
grated Monterey Jack cheese
chopped red or green onion
salsa

Place beans in large pot and add water to cover. Bring to boil, then reduce heat and cover. Cook for 1 hour, adding more liquid if necessary.

Add chilies, jalapeño, onions, garlic, tomatoes, oregano, cumin and cayenne to beans. Add more liquid if needed to keep moist. Cook, covered, for 2 to 2½ hours until beans are very soft. Season with salt when beans are done. Stir in cilantro at serving time.

SERVE AS A DIP WITH TOSTADAS, AS A FILLING FOR CHALUPAS OR BURRITOS, OR AS A VEGETABLE.

SESAME BROCCOLI WITH SNOW PEAS

SERVES 6

1 head of broccoli (1½ pounds) separated into florets
½ pound snow peas, trimmed
3 tablespoons sesame oil
2 tablespoons light soy sauce
2 tablespoons rice vinegar
½ cup unsalted cashews, toasted
2 tablespoons sesame seeds, toasted

Cook broccoli in boiling water over moderate heat for 4 minutes. Drain, and refresh immediately under cold running water until cool, about 1 minute. Drain well and gently dry with paper towels. Place in large bowl and set aside.

Blanch snow peas in boiling water for 1 minute. Drain and refresh as before. Add snow peas to broccoli.

Whisk sesame oil, soy sauce and vinegar together until well blended. Pour dressing over vegetables and toss gently to coat. Allow to marinate at room temperature for at least 1 hour and up to 6 hours. Before serving, add cashews and sesame seeds and toss gently to combine.

BROCCOLI WITH SUN-DRIED TOMATOES AND PINE NUTS

SERVES 4

1 pound broccoli, separated into florets
2 cloves garlic, minced
6 oil-packed sun-dried tomatoes, cut into slivers
1 tablespoon olive oil
½ cup pine nuts, toasted
salt and freshly ground pepper

Place broccoli in large saucepan with cold water to cover. Bring to a boil and cook 2 minutes, or until tender crisp. Drain immediately and place in bowl of ice water. When cool, drain again and refrigerate until ready to serve. (This can be done early in day.)

Just before serving time, combine garlic, sun-dried tomatoes and oil in skillet. Sauté over medium heat until garlic colors slightly and becomes aromatic. (Be careful not to burn garlic.) Add broccoli and sauté 1 or 2 minutes to heat through. Add pine nuts and season to taste.

THIS PREPARATION IS WONDERFUL WITH BRUSSELS SPROUTS.

CARROT PUDDING

SERVES 6

1 pound carrots, peeled and cut into 1-inch
pieces
3 eggs
½ to 1 cup sugar (depending on desired
sweetness)
2 heaping tablespoons flour
1 teaspoon baking powder
1 teaspoon freshly grated nutmeg
½ teaspoon cinnamon
3 tablespoons grated orange rind
⅛ teaspoon salt
¼ cup (½ stick) butter
1 cup milk
2 teaspoons vanilla

Cook carrots until tender. Purée in food
processor and set aside to cool to room
temperature.

Beat eggs and sugar together in mixer. Add
carrots. Combine flour, baking powder, nutmeg,
cinnamon, orange rind and salt and add to carrots, mixing well. Add butter, milk and vanilla
and beat until well blended. Pour into buttered
casserole and bake at 350 degrees for 1½ hours, or
until set.

CARROTS WITH PISTACHIOS AND GRAND MARNIER

SERVES 4 TO 6

1½ to 2 pounds carrots, peeled and thinly sliced
1½ cups water
juice of ½ lemon
3 tablespoons butter
¼ cup shelled pistachio nuts
3 tablespoons Grand Marnier
salt and freshly ground pepper to taste

Combine carrots with water and lemon juice in
large pan. Bring to a boil. Cover pan and
reduce heat. Simmer for 10 minutes or until tender
crisp. Drain and refresh carrots in ice cold water.

Melt butter in skillet. Add pistachio nuts and
sauté for 3 minutes. Add Grand Marnier and
cooked carrots. Continue cooking, tossing gently
for 3 to 5 minutes, or until carrots are glazed and
heated through. Season with salt and pepper.

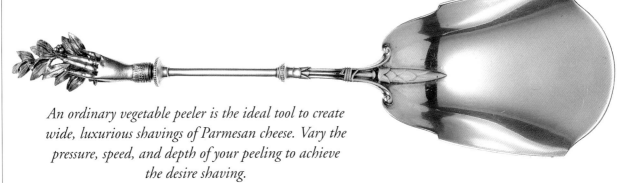

*An ordinary vegetable peeler is the ideal tool to create
wide, luxurious shavings of Parmesan cheese. Vary the
pressure, speed, and depth of your peeling to achieve
the desire shaving.*

CORN PIE WITH CHEESE AND GREEN CHILIES

THIS CAN BE MADE SEVERAL HOURS AHEAD AND SERVED AT ROOM TEMPERATURE. GREAT FOR A BUFFET. SERVES 8 TO 10

2 packages (10-ounce) frozen corn, thawed
1 cup (2 sticks) butter, melted
4 eggs, beaten
1 cup yellow cornmeal
2 teaspoons salt
1 cup sour cream (non-fat may be used)
8 ounces Monterey Jack cheese, diced
2 cans (4-ounce) chopped green chilies

Put corn into blender and mix at low speed until partially puréed but not smooth. Pour into large mixing bowl and add butter, eggs, corn-meal, salt, sour cream, cheese and chilies. Stir to combine thoroughly.

Pour into greased 10-inch deep-dish pie plate. (Do not overfill. You may have a little extra batter which you can bake in custard cups. If doubling recipe, use three 9-inch pie plates.) Bake at 350 degrees for 50 to 60 minutes, or until firm to the touch and golden brown.

BRAISED RED CABBAGE WITH APPLES AND BACON

SERVES 4 TO 6

2 slices bacon, diced
1 Granny Smith apple, diced (unpeeled)
1 medium head red cabbage, shredded
½ cup rice wine vinegar
¼ cup sugar

Cook bacon until slightly crisp. Stir in apple and cabbage and cook 3 to 4 minutes. Add vinegar and sugar. Cover pan and simmer 3 to 4 minutes more until cabbage is tender, but still crunchy. Serve hot.

ROASTED CUCUMBERS WITH DILL

UNUSUAL AND DELICIOUS!

SERVES 6

3 cucumbers, peeled and halved lengthwise
2 tablespoons white wine vinegar
1½ teaspoons salt
1 teaspoon sugar
4 tablespoons butter (½ stick), melted
¼ cup chopped green onions
1 teaspoon fresh dill

Remove seeds from cucumber halves and cut crosswise into ½-inch thick slices.

Combine vinegar, salt and sugar. Pour over cucumber slices and marinate at least 30 minutes. Drain marinade and place cucumbers in shallow baking dish. Add green onions and dill to melted butter. Pour over cucumbers and bake at 375 degrees for 40 minutes.

POTPOURRI OF MUSHROOMS WITH GARLIC AND PARSLEY

SERVES 8

2 tablespoons butter
3 large cloves garlic, minced
½ large Spanish onion, chopped
2 shallots, minced
6 tablespoons chicken stock
8 ounces fresh Italian brown mushrooms, sliced
4 ounces fresh chanterelle mushrooms, sliced
4 ounces fresh shiitake mushrooms, stemmed and sliced
juice of 1 lemon
1 cup minced fresh parsley
salt and pepper to taste

Melt butter in large skillet over high heat. Add garlic, onion and shallots and sauté for 1 minute. Add stock and all mushrooms; cook until all liquid has been absorbed, stirring frequently. Remove from heat and add lemon juice, parsley, salt and pepper. Toss to mix well and serve immediately. (Individual ingredients can be prepared ahead of time, but cooking must be done just prior to serving.)

MUSHROOMS CAN BE VARIED ACCORDING TO AVAILABILITY, BUT ALWAYS BE SURE TO USE 3 VARIETIES.

Swiss and Parmesan Onion Pie

THE ULTIMATE VERSATILE RECIPE! DELICIOUS SIDE DISH WITH BEEF, PORK OR GAME. WONDERFUL AS A FIRST COURSE OR AS A LIGHT ENTRÉE. SERVES 8

4 medium onions, sliced thin
1 cup chicken stock
pastry for 9-inch pie
2 tablespoons minced fresh parsley
1 tablespoon butter, melted
1 tablespoon flour
pinch of salt
½ teaspoon pepper
⅛ teaspoon nutmeg
⅛ teaspoon cayenne pepper
½ cup half and half
¼ cup grated Swiss cheese
½ cup grated Parmesan cheese
⅛ teaspoon paprika
1 tablespoon butter

Simmer onions in chicken stock until tender. Drain, reserving stock. Transfer onions to prepared pie shell and sprinkle with parsley.

Combine melted butter, flour, salt, pepper, nutmeg and cayenne in a bowl. Add ½ cup of reserved stock, half and half, Swiss cheese and half the Parmesan cheese, mixing well. Pour over onions. Sprinkle paprika and remaining Parmesan over top. Dot with butter.

Bake at 450 degrees for 10 minutes. Reduce heat to 350 degrees and bake another 10 minutes. Allow to cool slightly before serving.

Roasted Red and Green Bell Peppers

SERVES 2 TO 4

1 red bell pepper, sliced in strips, seeds and ribs removed
1 green bell pepper, sliced in strips, seeds and ribs removed
8 to 10 cloves garlic, peeled
1 medium red onion, sliced thin
2 tablespoons olive oil
1 teaspoon crushed red pepper
½ teaspoon salt
¼ teaspoon pepper
½ cup fresh shredded Parmesan cheese (optional)

Toss peppers, garlic and onion with olive oil. Season with crushed red pepper, salt and pepper and stir lightly.

Spread pepper mixture on foil-lined baking sheet. Bake at 375 degrees for 20 minutes. Change oven setting to broil and roast 10 minutes more. Add cheese (if desired) during broiling. Be sure to watch carefully to avoid burning.

MASHED POTATOES WITH SAUTÉED GARLIC AND MUSHROOMS

SERVES 6 TO 8

2 pounds Idaho potatoes (about 4 large), peeled
   and quartered
8 ounces fresh mushrooms, sliced
13 tablespoons butter (divided use)
2 large cloves garlic, minced
salt to taste
⅔ cup warm milk
½ cup potato cooking liquid

Place potatoes in large saucepan and fill with cold water to cover by 2 inches. Bring to boil. Reduce heat, partially cover, and cook 20 to 25 minutes, or until tender.

While potatoes are cooking, sauté mushrooms in 2 tablespoons butter for 1 to 2 minutes, or until slightly tender and juices start to appear. Push to one side. Add 1 tablespoon butter and garlic, cooking until garlic is softened but not browned. Combine with mushrooms and cook until juices left in skillet seem slightly thickened. Set aside.

Drain cooking liquid from potatoes, reserving ½ cup. Place potatoes back on heat for about 1 minute to evaporate any remaining liquid. Mash potatoes with mixer, adding 5 tablespoons butter, salt, part of milk and part of cooking liquid. Beat just until light and fluffy, adding remaining milk and cooking liquid as needed for fluffy consistency. Gently fold in mushroom mixture and taste for seasoning. Divide remaining 5 tablespoons butter over potatoes, pushing down slightly. (If necessary, potatoes can be covered at this point and held in 200-degree oven for about 30 minutes.) To serve, gently fold butter into potatoes.

ROASTED POTATOES WITH ROSEMARY

SERVES 6

8 large cloves garlic, minced
2 tablespoons chopped fresh rosemary
2 bay leaves
⅓ cup olive oil
2 pounds large red potatoes
1½ teaspoons salt
1 teaspoon pepper
1 teaspoon crushed red pepper (optional)

Combine garlic, rosemary, bay leaves and oil and set aside for 1 hour. Cut each potato into 6 to 8 wedges and sprinkle with salt and peppers. Pour herb oil over potatoes and mix well to coat evenly. Remove potatoes from oil and place in large, shallow pan. Bake 45 minutes at 375 degrees, or until browned.

GARLIC MASHED POTATOES

SERVES 6

2 pounds russet potatoes, peeled and
  cut into 1-inch cubes
6 tablespoons (¾ stick) butter
¾ cup milk
3 cloves garlic, chopped
salt and pepper to taste

Place potatoes in large saucepan and cover with water. Bring to a boil; reduce heat and simmer, uncovered, for 20 minutes, or until tender. Drain potatoes well. Return to pan and cook over medium heat for 1 to 2 minutes to evaporate any excess liquid.

Bring butter and milk to a boil. Add garlic; reduce heat and simmer for 3 to 4 minutes. Strain liquid, discarding garlic.

Place potatoes in large bowl and whip with electric mixer. Gradually add strained milk mixture until potatoes are light and fluffy. Season with salt and pepper.

TRY DECREASING POTATOES TO 1½ POUNDS AND ADDING ½ POUND TURNIPS. YOU'LL BE AMAZED AT THE WONDERFUL FLAVOR.

GARLIC CAN ALWAYS BE DELETED FOR A MORE TRADITIONAL MASHED POTATO OR ADD 2 TABLESPOONS HORSERADISH FOR ADDED ZIP.

TO ENSURE FLUFFY MASHED POTATOES, REDUCE HEAT IMMEDIATELY WHEN WATER BEGINS TO BOIL. SIMMER POTATOES UNTIL TENDER, NOT ALLOWING WATER TEMPERATURE TO GO ABOVE 185 DEGREES. AT HIGHER TEMPERATURES POTATO CELLS BEGIN TO BREAK DOWN, RELEASING A GLUE-LIKE SUBSTANCE WHICH PRODUCES GUMMY MASHED POTATOES.

HEAVENLY POTATOES

SIMPLE AND SENSATIONAL!

SERVES 10 TO 12

5 pounds red-skinned potatoes
3 cups heavy cream
seasoned salt to taste

Boil potatoes until barely tender, then drain and submerge in cold water. When cool enough to handle, peel and grate coarsely.

Place in 9 x 13-inch greased baking dish. Pour cream over potatoes and sprinkle with seasoned salt. Bake at 350 degrees for 45 minutes, or until lightly browned.

FOR A DELICIOUS VARIATION, TRY **BOURSIN POTATOES**. THINLY SLICE 3 POUNDS RAW, UNPEELED RED POTATOES. LAYER IN 9 x 13-INCH BAKING DISH AND SEASON WITH SALT AND PEPPER. COMBINE IN SAUCEPAN 2 CUPS HEAVY CREAM AND 5 OUNCES BOURSIN CHEESE WITH GARLIC AND HERBS. HEAT UNTIL CHEESE MELTS AND MIXTURE IS SMOOTH. POUR OVER SEASONED POTATOES. BAKE AT 400 DEGREES FOR 1 HOUR, OR UNTIL GOLDEN BROWN.

Spinach with Raisins and Pine Nuts

SERVES 4

2 pounds fresh spinach
2 tablespoons olive oil
2 cloves garlic, minced
⅓ cup golden raisins
⅓ cup pine nuts, toasted
salt and pepper to taste

Wash spinach and trim stems, but do not drain. Put spinach in frying pan large enough to hold it all. Cook over high heat just until spinach begins to wilt. Remove spinach to colander, squeezing out any remaining liquid, and set aside.

Dry frying pan and add olive oil and garlic. Heat garlic until tender, but do not let it brown. Add raisins and pine nuts and sauté for 1 minute. Add spinach, taste for seasoning, and sauté until flavors are blended and spinach is heated through, about 3 to 4 minutes.

YOU CAN SUBSTITUTE BROCCOLI FOR SPINACH. PARBOIL IT FIRST, THEN PROCEED WITH INSTRUCTIONS FOR SAUTÉING.

FOR A MORE MEDITERRANEAN FLAVOR, ADD ⅓ CUP CALAMATA OLIVES.

Sweet Potato Custard with Pecans

SERVES 10 TO 12

6 large sweet potatoes, cooked, peeled and sliced
½ cup (1 stick) butter
1 teaspoon baking powder
1 teaspoon vanilla
1 teaspoon cinnamon
¾ cup sugar
2 eggs
¾ cup buttermilk

TOPPING
⅓ cup butter, melted
1 cup brown sugar
½ cup flour
1 cup chopped pecans

Place hot sweet potatoes in large bowl of electric mixer. Add butter, baking powder, vanilla, cinnamon, sugar, eggs and buttermilk; mix until smooth. Spoon mixture into buttered 2-quart casserole. (Can be prepared to this point 1 day in advance and refrigerated. Allow to warm to room temperature before proceeding.)

To prepare topping, add butter to sugar and flour, mixing well. Stir in pecans. Sprinkle mixture over sweet potatoes. Bake for 30 minutes at 350 degrees, or until lightly browned.

TO VARY THIS RECIPE, ADD ½ CUP BOURBON IN PLACE OF BUTTERMILK. INSTEAD OF PECAN TOPPING, ADD MARSHMALLOWS DURING LAST 10 MINUTES OF BAKING.

SOUTHWESTERN WHIPPED SWEET POTATOES

SERVES 4

2 large sweet potatoes, peeled and diced
1 white potato, peeled and diced
4 tablespoons maple syrup
½ teaspoon salt
¼ to ½ teaspoon cayenne pepper
2 to 3 teaspoons chili powder
4 tablespoons butter

Boil potatoes for 15 minutes, or until soft. Drain, and purée in food processor. Add syrup, salt, cayenne and chili powder. Continue to process for 1 minute, adding 1 tablespoon of butter at a time.

THE PIQUANT FLAVOR OF THESE POTATOES IS A DELICIOUS COMPLEMENT TO GRILLED MEAT, ESPECIALLY PORK TENDERLOIN OR FLANK STEAK.

CAPERED TOMATOES

IDEAL FOR ENTERTAINING — MAKE AHEAD AND SERVE AT ROOM TEMPERATURE. SERVES 6 TO 8

5 tablespoons olive oil (divided use)
6 large, firm tomatoes, cored and cut into thick slices
¼ cup chopped fresh oregano or basil
⅓ cup capers
salt and freshly ground pepper
¼ cup bread crumbs

Oil a large, shallow baking dish with 1 tablespoon olive oil. Arrange half the tomatoes in dish. Sprinkle with all the oregano and half the capers. Season with salt and pepper and drizzle with 2 tablespoons olive oil. Repeat layers with remaining tomatoes and capers. Top with bread crumbs, season again and drizzle with remaining olive oil.

Bake for 20 minutes at 450 degrees, or until crumbs are lightly browned. Let cool. Serve chilled or at room temperature.

Baked Mushroom, Eggplant and Zucchini Parmesan

SERVES 8 TO 10

SAUCE
2 tablespoons olive oil
¾ cup chopped onion
2 cloves garlic, minced
2 tablespoons white wine
1 tomato, chopped
3 cans (14½-ounce) Italian-style tomatoes
3 to 4 fresh basil leaves, sliced (optional)
½ teaspoon dried oregano (optional)
1 teaspoon dried basil
salt and pepper to taste

MUSHROOMS
3 tablespoons olive oil
½ cup chopped leeks, white part only
2 tablespoons chopped green bell pepper
¼ cup chopped red bell pepper
1 clove garlic, minced
1 pound mushrooms, sliced
salt and pepper to taste

EGGPLANT AND ZUCCHINI
1 medium eggplant, peeled and sliced lengthwise in ⅛-inch slices
1 egg mixed with 3 tablespoons water (for egg wash)
1 cup flour
1 teaspoon paprika
salt and pepper to taste
oil for frying
2 large zucchini, sliced lengthwise in ⅛-inch slices
1 cup grated Parmesan cheese (divided use)
1¾ cups shredded mozzarella cheese (divided use)

To prepare sauce, heat oil in large saucepan. Add onions and garlic and sauté until softened. Add wine and fresh tomato, cooking 2 minutes. Add canned tomatoes and bring to boil over medium-high heat. Simmer, stirring occasionally, about 30 minutes, or until sauce has thickened. Cut up tomatoes as they are cooking. Add herbs and season with salt and pepper. Remove from heat and set aside. (Can be prepared one day in advance.)

For mushrooms, heat oil in skillet. Add leeks, peppers and garlic and sauté until softened. Add mushrooms and cook about 5 minutes, or until tender. Season with salt and pepper and set aside.

Salt eggplant on both sides of slices, place in one layer on paper towels, and set aside for 30 minutes. Pat dry with additional paper towels.

Place egg wash and flour seasoned with paprika, salt and pepper in 2 flat dishes. Dip eggplant and zucchini slices in flour mixture, then in egg wash, and once again in flour mixture. Heat oil in skillet over medium-high heat and fry vegetables until browned. Drain on paper towels.

Layer ingredients in 10 x 9 x 4-inch pan in following order: ½ cup of sauce in bottom, eggplant, ½ cup Parmesan cheese, ½ cup mozzarella cheese, 1 more cup sauce, mushroom mixture, zucchini, ½ cup Parmesan cheese, remaining 2 cups of sauce, and finally 1¼ cups shredded mozzarella cheese.

Cover and bake at 375 degrees for 15 minutes. Remove cover and bake an additional 30 minutes.

TUSCAN WHITE BEANS WITH SAGE

DELICIOUS ACCOMPANIMENT TO
LAMB. SERVES 4 TO 6

2 ounces proscuitto or pancetta, chopped fine
1 small onion, sliced
3 cloves garlic, minced
½ cup olive oil (divided use)
8 leaves fresh sage, chopped, plus whole leaves
  for garnish
2 cans (16-ounce) cannellini beans, rinsed and
  drained
salt and pepper to taste

Sauté proscuitto, onion and garlic in 1 table-spoon olive oil for 8 to 10 minutes or until onion is tender. Stir in sage and cook 1 minute. Add beans, remaining oil, salt and pepper. Toss gently, taking care to keep beans whole. (Can be prepared 1 day ahead to this point.)

To serve, heat through and garnish with sage leaves.

FOR A FIRMER BEAN, USE DRIED BEANS THAT HAVE
BEEN SOAKED OVERNIGHT AND COOKED TO DESIRED
CONSISTENCY.

ZUCCHINI AND EGGPLANT SAUTÉ WITH TARRAGON

SERVES 4

1 tablespoon butter
2 tablespoons olive oil
1 pound zucchini, sliced ¼-inch thick
1 pound small Japanese eggplants, sliced ¼-inch
  thick
2 teaspoons flour
⅓ cup milk
salt to taste
1 tablespoon dried tarragon
1 egg yolk, lightly beaten
½ cup freshly grated Parmesan cheese
¼ cup freshly grated Romano cheese

Heat butter and olive oil in skillet. Add zucchini and eggplant and sauté until tender crisp. Combine flour, milk, salt, tarragon and egg yolk, mixing well. Stir into hot vegetables. Remove from heat, add cheeses and serve.

IN PLACE OF TARRAGON, TRY 1 TABLESPOON DRIED
BASIL OR ¼ CUP FRESH BASIL.

VEGETABLE GOUGÈRE

A VERY DRAMATIC PRESENTATION!

SERVES 6 TO 8

PÂTE À CHOUX
1 cup water
½ cup (1 stick) butter
1 cup flour
salt and pepper to taste
4 eggs
½ pound sharp Cheddar cheese, grated (reserve
   small amount for topping)

FILLING
¼ cup (½ stick) butter
1 cup chopped leeks
½ pound mushrooms, sliced
1½ tablespoons flour
1 teaspoon salt
¼ teaspoon pepper
1 chicken bouillon cube
½ cup boiling water
2 zucchini, sliced
1 pound tomatoes, peeled, cut into wedges,
   seeded and drained
1 tablespoon chopped fresh thyme
1 tablespoon chopped fresh basil
chopped fresh parsley, garnish

To make choux pastry, bring water and butter to a boil in small saucepan. Add flour, salt and pepper. Remove from heat and stir until mixture forms large ball. Cool at least 5 minutes. Put in food processor and mix for 15 seconds using steel blade. Add eggs and process for 35 seconds. Add cheese, processing 15 seconds. Put dough in greased, 9-inch springform pan, covering bottom, pushing dough up on sides. (Can be made to this point 1 hour in advance. Keep covered with plastic wrap.)

For filling, melt butter and sauté leeks until barely soft, about 2 minutes. Add mushrooms, sauté 1 minute, and sprinkle with flour, salt and pepper. Dissolve bouillon cube in water and add to vegetables, mixing well. Add zucchini; bring to a boil and simmer 2 minutes. Add tomatoes, thyme and basil. (Filling can be made early in day, but be sure to drain any liquid that may have accumulated before proceeding. Assemble only when ready to bake.)

Place filling in center of prepared ring and sprinkle with reserved cheese. Bake at 400 degrees for 40 minutes, or until puffed and brown. To serve, remove sides of pan and sprinkle with parsley.

VEGETABLES CAN BE VARIED TO SUIT MENU OR SEASONAL AVAILABILITY, OR FOR A CHANGE TRY MONTEREY JACK CHEESE INSTEAD OF CHEDDAR.

Desserts

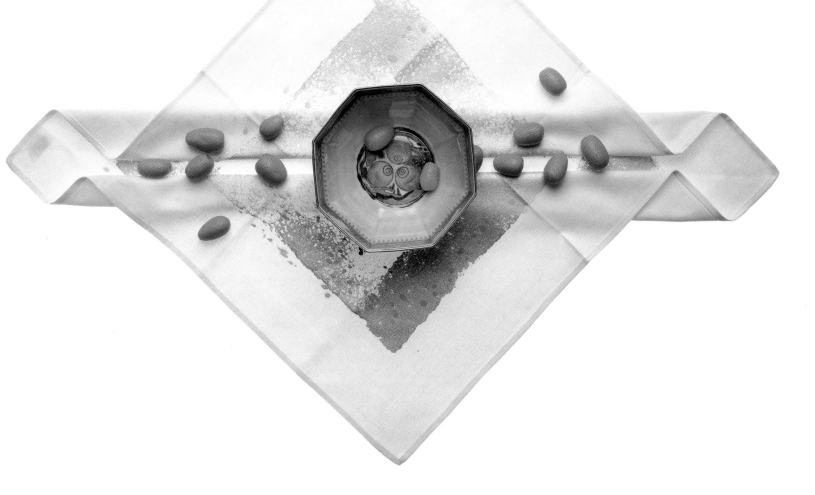

RASPBERRY CHOCOLATE MOUSSE CAKES

SERVES 4

3 ounces unsweetened chocolate
4 tablespoons unsalted butter, softened
⅔ cup sugar
2 eggs, separated, room temperature
4 tablespoons seedless raspberry preserves
1 tablespoon framboise
6 tablespoons flour
1 pint fresh raspberries (divided use)
2 tablespoons sugar or to taste

Melt chocolate in top of double boiler over simmering water. Set aside.

Cream butter and sugar until smooth. Beat in egg yolks and stir in raspberry preserves, framboise and melted chocolate. Stir in flour. Beat egg whites until they hold soft peaks. Stir a little into the chocolate mixture to lighten the batter, then fold in the remaining egg whites.

Butter four ½-cup ramekins and line bottoms with buttered waxed paper or parchment paper. Divide batter among ramekins and place in a larger pan, filling it with enough hot water to come halfway up sides of ramekins. Bake at 325 degrees for 40 minutes. Remove from oven and let cool in water.

Set aside ½ cup fresh raspberries and purée the rest in food processor. Force through wire sieve to remove seeds and sweeten to taste.

When ready to serve, run knife around inside of ramekins, invert onto individual plates, and peel off paper. Surround each cake with pool of sauce and scatter with fresh raspberries. Serve at room temperature.

CHOCOLATE TRUFFLE DESSERT

SERVES 10 TO 12

8 ounces semisweet chocolate
½ cup strong coffee
1 cup (2 sticks) butter
1 cup plus 2 tablespoons sugar (divided use)
4 eggs, beaten
1 cup heavy cream
2 to 3 teaspoons brandy

Melt chocolate in coffee in top of double boiler. Add butter and 1 cup sugar, stirring until butter is melted. Allow mixture to cool. Beat in eggs, 1 at a time.

Pour mixture into 9 x 5-inch glass loaf pan lined with buttered foil. Bake at 350 degrees for 35 to 45 minutes, or until crust forms on top.

Set loaf pan in enough cool water to come halfway up sides of pan. Dessert will rise and fall as it cools. When cool, wrap pan well and refrigerate for at least 2 days, or up to 2 weeks.

When ready to serve, beat cream with remaining 2 tablespoons sugar until stiff. Stir in brandy. Unmold loaf and cut into thin slices. Garnish with whipped cream.

PEANUT BUTTER AND CHOCOLATE DELIGHTS

YIELDS 32 SQUARES

¾ cup plus 2 tablespoons (1¾ sticks) butter
1 cup smooth or crunchy peanut butter
1 pound powdered sugar
1½ cups semisweet chocolate chips

Melt butter in large saucepan. Add peanut butter, stirring to mix well. Remove from heat and stir in powdered sugar. When mixture becomes thick and doughy, pat into an oiled 9 x 13-inch pan.

Melt chocolate until soft (2 to 3 minutes in microwave). Stir gently and spread over peanut butter mixture. Cool and cut into small squares.

GLASS
FINGER
BOWL, CA.
1880,
PROBABLY
ENGLAND,
1992.482

CHOCOLATE CHEESECAKE WITH RASPBERRIES

SERVES 10

8 ounces chocolate wafer or icebox cookies
5 tablespoons unsalted butter, melted
½ cup plus 2 tablespoons sugar (divided use)
1½ pounds cream cheese, room temperature
6 ounces bittersweet chocolate, melted
½ cup raspberry liqueur
4 large eggs
½ cup heavy cream
1 cup sour cream
½ cup powdered sugar
1 pint fresh raspberries

Grind wafers into fine crumbs in food processor. Add melted butter and 2 tablespoons sugar; blend thoroughly. Press evenly into bottom and partway up sides of a generously buttered, 9-inch springform pan.

Beat cream cheese with electric mixer at high speed until smooth and creamy, about 5 minutes. Add melted chocolate and remaining ½ cup sugar, beating until thoroughly blended. Add liqueur and continue beating until mixture is very smooth, about 4 minutes.

Set mixer at low speed and add eggs, 1 at a time. Beat each until just incorporated, being careful not to overbeat. Blend in cream.

Pour mixture into crust and bake for 50 minutes at 350 degrees, or until firm. Filling should seem soft in middle; don't overbake. Remove from oven and allow to cool to room temperature.

Whisk sour cream with powdered sugar until smooth and creamy. Spread over cake and refrigerate for at least 4 hours before removing springform ring.

Top cake with raspberries before serving.

RUM POUND CAKE

SERVES 12 TO 16

3 cups (6 sticks) margarine, softened
3⅓ cups sugar
10 eggs
4 cups flour
½ teaspoon salt
1 teaspoon cream of tartar
1 bottle (1-ounce) rum flavoring
2 teaspoons vanilla

Cream margarine in large bowl of electric mixer. Add sugar and beat until light and fluffy. Add eggs, one at a time, beating well after each addition. Sift flour, salt and cream of tartar together and add slowly to batter. Add rum flavoring and vanilla, blending well. Pour batter into greased and floured 10-inch tube pan. Bake at 300 degrees for 1 hour and 15 to 20 minutes or until wooden pick tests clean. Remove from oven and let stand for 5 minutes before turning out on rack to cool. (Keeps at least a week covered and refrigerated. Freezes well.)

TOULOUSE-LAUTREC CAKE

THE PERFECT DESSERT FOR A
SERIOUS "CHOCOHOLIC."
SERVES 8 TO 10

1 pound semisweet chocolate
10 tablespoons (1¼ sticks) unsalted butter, softened
4 eggs, separated
1 tablespoon flour
1 tablespoon sugar

RASPBERRY COULIS (OPTIONAL)

2 packages (10-ounce) frozen raspberries, defrosted
2 teaspoons cornstarch
2 tablespoons water
sugar to taste
2 tablespoons raspberry liqueur (optional)

Butter bottom and sides of 8-inch springform pan. Place baking parchment, cut to size, on bottom of pan and butter it too. Melt chocolate and stir in butter gradually. Cool slightly. Beat egg yolks 5 to 7 minutes until pale yellow. Stir in flour. Add yolk mixture to chocolate. Beat egg whites until frothy. Gradually add sugar and beat until whites form firm, but not stiff, peaks. Do not overbeat. Gently fold egg whites into chocolate mixture until combined. Pour into prepared pan and bake at 425 degrees for 20 minutes. (Cake will look underdone.) Chill well for several hours or overnight. When chilled, remove ring from pan and invert onto serving plate.

To prepare coulis, force raspberries through a fine-mesh strainer to remove seeds. Mix cornstarch with water and add to raspberries. Cook over medium heat until slightly thickened, adding sugar if desired for more sweetness. Add raspberry liqueur, mixing well. Allow to cool. To serve, spoon small amount of coulis on plate and place slice of cake on top.

IN PLACE OF THE COULIS, TOP THE CAKE WITH A DOLLOP OF WHIPPED CREAM AND GARNISH WITH FRESH RASPBERRIES OR STRAWBERRIES.

SILVER AND SILVERGILT SERVING SPOON, *BIRD'S NEST* PATTERN, CA. 1875, U.S., 1991.101.13

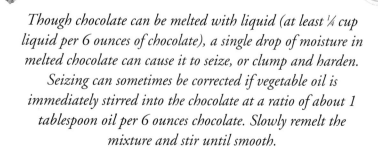

Though chocolate can be melted with liquid (at least ¼ cup liquid per 6 ounces of chocolate), a single drop of moisture in melted chocolate can cause it to seize, or clump and harden. Seizing can sometimes be corrected if vegetable oil is immediately stirred into the chocolate at a ratio of about 1 tablespoon oil per 6 ounces chocolate. Slowly remelt the mixture and stir until smooth.

TORTA DI FRUTTA SECCA

SERVES 12

1 cup coarsely chopped hazelnuts
1¼ cups flour
4 teaspoons baking powder
3 eggs
⅔ cup sugar
⅓ cup slivered almonds
¾ cup dried figs, coarsely chopped
3 ounces bittersweet chocolate, coarsely
  chopped
¾ cup diced candied orange peel
powdered sugar for dusting (optional)

CHOCOLATE GLAZE (OPTIONAL)

1 ounce unsweetened chocolate
3 ounces semisweet chocolate
2 tablespoons honey
4 tablespoons unsalted butter
chopped nuts or orange peel (garnish)

Roast hazelnuts at 350 degrees for 10 minutes. Rub between dish towels to remove most of skins.

Sift flour with baking powder. Beat eggs; add sugar and continue beating until fluffy. Mix in nuts, figs, chocolate and orange peel, then stir in flour mixture lightly but thoroughly.

Grease 9-inch springform pan. Place circle of baking parchment in bottom. Pour mixture into pan and bake at 350 degrees for 45 minutes. Do not open door during first 30 minutes of baking so cake will rise properly. Cool slightly in pan, then turn out onto rack. Top with chocolate glaze if desired, or simply dust with powdered sugar.

To prepare glaze, melt chocolates in top of double boiler. Stir in honey and butter. Cool 10 minutes until slightly thickened. Pour over top of cake and smooth over top and sides. Garnish with chopped nuts or orange peel.

TORTA CAVOUR

SERVES 10 TO 16

MERINGUE
8 egg whites
½ teaspoon cream of tartar
¼ teaspoon vanilla
pinch of salt
2 cups superfine sugar

FILLING
4 cups whipping cream, chilled
1 cup plus 2 tablespoons sugar
½ cup chopped almonds, toasted
6 tablespoons coarsely grated dark sweet chocolate

In bowl of electric mixer, beat egg whites until frothy. Add cream of tartar and continue beating until somewhat stiff. Add vanilla and salt to taste. Gradually add ½ cup sugar and continue beating until mixture stands up in soft peaks. Continue beating on high speed while gradually adding remaining sugar, continuing until whites become glossy and very thick.

Line two baking sheets with parchment paper. Trace two 10-inch circles with pencil. Fill pastry bag with meringue and pipe onto traced circles, working in a spiral from outside to center. Or, use a spatula to spread meringue evenly over traced circles. Spread some of meringue into smaller shapes which will be crushed later to cover sides of torta.

Bake meringues at 200 degrees for 3 hours, or until crisp and firm. Turn off oven and leave meringues overnight to dry out completely.

Whip cream in several batches, gradually beating in sugar. Place 1 meringue circle on serving plate. Spread with ⅓ of whipped cream, smoothing top. Sprinkle with 3 tablespoons each of almonds and chocolate. Place second meringue circle on top. Coat sides and top with remaining whipped cream, smoothing with spatula. Roughly chop remaining meringue pieces and press onto sides of torta. Garnish top with remaining almonds and chocolate. Freeze several hours or longer before serving.

Pecan Cake with Raisins and Brandy

YIELDS THREE 4 x 8-INCH LOAVES

½ pound golden raisins
4 cups flour, plus 3 tablespoons for dredging
¼ teaspoon salt
1 nutmeg, grated
1 cup (2 sticks) butter, room temperature
2 cups sugar
6 eggs
3 tablespoons brandy
1 pound pecans

Dredge raisins in 3 tablespoons flour. Toss well to coat and shake off excess. Set aside.

Combine remaining 4 cups flour with salt and nutmeg in large bowl. Cream butter and sugar with electric mixer. Add ½ cup flour mixture and beat well; then add 1 egg, beating well. Continue to add flour mixture in ½ cup amounts, alternating with eggs, 1 at a time. Beat thoroughly after each addition.

Fold in brandy, nuts and raisins, mixing well. Divide batter into 3 greased and floured 4 x 8-inch pans. Bake at 300 degrees for 45 to 60 minutes, or until wooden pick inserted in center comes out clean. Cool on rack. Serve thin slices accompanied by a glass of port.

Fresh Apple Cake with Caramel Glaze

SERVES 10 TO 12

CAKE
3 eggs
2 cups sugar
1 cup oil
2 teaspoons vanilla
2¾ cups flour
1 teaspoon baking soda
1 teaspoon salt
2 teaspoons cinnamon
4 cups peeled chopped apples
1 cup chopped pecans

GLAZE
½ cup (1 stick) butter
1 cup brown sugar
¼ cup evaporated milk
1 teaspoon vanilla

Beat eggs with electric mixer until thick and pale. Gradually add sugar, oil and vanilla, beating at low speed. Combine flour, baking soda, salt and cinnamon, and stir into egg mixture until blended. Fold in apples and pecans. Bake in greased and floured 10-inch tube pan at 350 degrees for 1 hour and 25 minutes, or until wooden pick tests clean. Allow to rest in pan for 5 minutes before turning out on rack to cool.

To prepare glaze, melt butter and sugar over low heat. Add milk and cook for 2 minutes. Remove from heat, add vanilla, and beat until creamy. Spread over warm cake.

FRENCH APPLE TART

SERVES 6 TO 8

CRUST

Prepare dough for single pie crust (page 195),
  using 1 tablespoon sugar in place of salt

FILLING

6 to 7 firm Granny Smith apples (divided use)
1 tablespoon butter
grated rind of 1 lemon
¼ cup sugar
1 to 2 tablespoons Calvados, rum or brandy
  (optional)

TOPPING

¼ cup sugar
1 tablespoon butter
½ cup apricot preserves

Roll out pastry and fit into 9-inch tart pan with removable bottom. Place in refrigerator or freezer until ready to use.

Peel and core 3 apples and chop coarsely. (Should have about 2 cups.) Heat butter in skillet and add apples. Sprinkle with lemon rind and sugar. Stir and shake apple mixture in pan and cook for about 10 minutes. Add Calvados and mash apples lightly with fork. Chill.

Peel remaining apples. Cut each apple in half vertically and remove core. Place cut side down and cut crosswise into ⅛-inch thick slices.

Spoon cooked apples over bottom of prepared crust. Arrange uncooked apple slices over filling, making overlapping circles on top. Sprinkle with topping sugar and dot with butter. Bake at 400 degrees for 40 to 45 minutes, or until pastry is lightly browned.

Heat and strain preserves. Brush over tart. Cool before serving.

FOR AN ELEGANT TOUCH, CUT LEAVES FROM PASTRY SCRAPS AND ARRANGE IN CENTER OF TART BEFORE BAKING.

SERVE WITH WHITE CAMBOZOLA CHEESE.

LEMON TART WITH BUTTER PECAN CRUST

SERVES 8 TO 10

BUTTER PECAN CRUST
1¼ cups flour
1 egg yolk
⅓ cup finely chopped pecans
3 tablespoons powdered sugar
½ cup (1 stick) butter, softened
¼ teaspoon salt

FILLING
3 eggs, beaten
1 cup sugar
1 tablespoon flour
3 tablespoons lemon juice
grated rind of 1 lemon
powdered sugar (optional)

RASPBERRY TOPPING (OPTIONAL)
1½ pints fresh raspberries
12 ounces currant jelly

Combine all crust ingredients in large bowl. Blend with a fork until dough forms a ball. Press dough evenly into bottom and sides of greased 9-inch pie plate or tart pan. Bake at 350 degrees for 10 minutes. Set aside to cool.

Combine eggs, sugar, flour, lemon juice and rind; stir until smooth. Pour mixture into crust and bake at 350 degrees for 20 to 25 minutes, or until filling is set. Remove to rack to cool. Dust with powdered sugar or cover with Raspberry Topping to serve. Store, covered, in refrigerator.

To prepare topping, arrange raspberries on top of cooled tart, starting at outside and working toward center. Raspberries should cover tart completely. Melt jelly over low heat until liquid. Brush melted jelly over each raspberry with a pastry brush. Jelly must be very hot to glaze well. Let cool until glaze is set before cutting.

TARTE TATIN

A LEGENDARY UPSIDE-DOWN

APPLE TART. SERVES 6

4 to 5 large Granny Smith apples, peeled, cored and quartered
½ cup (1 stick) unsalted butter
1 cup sugar
1 prepared single pie crust, unbaked (see note)

Melt butter over medium heat in extra-heavy 10-inch round cake pan or straight sided skillet. Add sugar and stir until it melts. Place apples in pan, round side up, squeezing them in tightly. Cook over low to medium heat letting mixture bubble for 10 to 15 minutes. Top with prepared pie crust, folding sides of pastry in.

Bake at 375 degrees for 30 minutes. Let cool for about 10 minutes before carefully inverting onto serving platter. (If pie is allowed to cool too long, it will not release from pan.)

NOTE: THE PREPARED PIE CRUST (NOT FROZEN) IN THE DAIRY SECTIONS WORKS WELL OR YOU CAN MAKE YOUR OWN.

TARTE TATIN IS A CLASSIC FRENCH DESSERT THAT WAS INVENTED YEARS AGO BY THE DEMOISELLES TATIN IN THEIR RESTAURANT AT LAMOTTE-BEUVRON ON THE LOIRE RIVER. THIS IS A BEAUTIFUL PRESENTATION BUT SIMPLE TO PREPARE. YOU CAN ASSEMBLE THE TART EARLIER IN THE DAY, BAKE IT DURING DINNER, AND SERVE IT WARM TO VERY IMPRESSED GUESTS.

BASIC PIE CRUST

YIELDS 1 OR 2 CRUSTS FOR 9-INCH PIE

DOUBLE CRUST

1⅓ cups flour

¼ to ½ teaspoon salt

⅔ cups solid vegetable shortening or butter

⅓ cup flour mixed with ⅓ cup cold water

SINGLE CRUST

1 cup less 2½ tablespoons flour

¼ teaspoon salt

⅓ cup solid vegetable shortening or butter

2½ tablespoons flour mixed with 2½ tablespoons cold water

Mix flour and salt in food processor. Cut shortening into small pieces and add to flour. Process with a pulsing action until mixture resembles coarse meal. Add flour and water mixture; process until dough just starts to cling together (not until it forms a ball).

Turn dough out onto a floured board and press into a ball using fingers. Shape ball into 1 or 2 flattened circles about 1 inch thick (2 if making double crust). Dust rolling pin with flour and roll dough out to form an even 12-inch circle. Lightly dust bottom of pie plate with flour and transfer pastry to pan. (It helps to gently fold dough into quarters before picking it up, or drape it over rolling pin.) Fold edges under to fit pan and flute with fingers to give finished look.

If pie recipe calls for pre-baked crust, line pastry with foil and fill bottom with pie weights, dried beans or rice. Bake at 400 degrees for 10 to 15 minutes. Remove weights and foil and prick crust with a fork. Bake an additional 5 to 10 minutes, or until crust is a pale golden color.

TO MAKE A SWEETER PASTRY, USE 1 OR 2 TABLESPOONS SUGAR IN PLACE OF SALT.

USING A ROLLING PIN COVER MINIMIZES THE AMOUNT OF FLOUR NEEDED DURING ROLLING; TOO MUCH FLOUR TOUGHENS THE CRUST. ROLL PASTRY LIGHTLY BECAUSE TOO MUCH HANDLING WILL ALSO TOUGHEN CRUST. BE CAREFUL NOT TO STRETCH PASTRY WHEN FITTING IT INTO PIE PLATE; IF STRETCHED, CRUST WILL SHRINK DURING BAKING.

PEAR AND GINGER TART

SERVES 8 TO 10

SWEET PASTRY
2 cups flour
2 tablespoons sugar
¼ teaspoon salt
11 tablespoons butter, very cold
2 egg yolks
2 tablespoons ice water

FILLING
10 ripe but firm Comice or Anjou pears, about
   4 pounds (divided use)
⅔ cup sugar
1 teaspoon ground ginger
½ cup water
6 tablespoons apricot preserves
whipped cream (optional)

Combine flour, sugar and salt. Cut butter into ½-inch pieces and add to flour. Mix together, using pastry cutter, just until texture resembles coarse meal.

Beat yolks and water together and add to flour mixture, mixing until all liquid is incorporated and dough is starting to hold together. Do not overmix or pastry will be tough. Gather dough into a ball and wrap in plastic wrap. Chill 1 hour.

Place dough on a floured surface. Dust rolling pin with flour and roll dough out, forming an even 12-inch circle. Dust bottom of 9-inch tart pan with small amount of flour and transfer pastry to pan. (To ease transfer, dough can be folded before it is picked up, or can be partially rolled over the rolling pin and placed in pan.) Trim pastry to fit pan, making sure it is large enough not to stretch dough.

Line pastry with foil and fill bottom with pie weights or dried beans. Bake at 400 degrees for 10 minutes. Remove weights and foil and set aside to cool.

Peel and core 6 pears; cut each into 8 wedges. Place pear wedges in saucepan with sugar, ginger and water. Cover and simmer until tender, but still firm, 8 to 10 minutes. Turn pears during cooking so pieces cook evenly. (Pears should not be mushy.) Reserve 4 tablespoons of pear liquid and drain the rest. Chill pears thoroughly.

Arrange pear wedges close together in pastry shell. Peel, core and thinly slice remaining 4 pears. Arrange slices symmetrically over cooked pears.

Combine preserves with reserved pear liquid. Bring to a boil, then strain. Brush tart with half the apricot glaze and bake at 425 degrees for 30 minutes. Remove from oven and brush with remaining glaze. Serve warm. Garnish with whipped cream if desired.

MIXING OF DOUGH CAN BE DONE IN ELECTRIC MIXER OR IN FOOD PROCESSOR. BE CAREFUL NOT TO OVERMIX. TURN MACHINE OFF JUST BEFORE MIXTURE COMES TOGETHER IN BALL.

MIXED BERRY AND KIWI TART

SERVES 6 TO 8

CRUST
½ cup (1 stick) butter, melted
1 cup flour
⅓ cup sugar
½ teaspoon vanilla

CUSTARD
2¼ cups milk
1 teaspoon vanilla
½ cup plus 1 tablespoon sugar (divided use)
3 egg yolks
⅛ cup flour
⅛ cup cornstarch

FRESH FRUIT TOPPING AND GLAZE
raspberries, strawberries and/or blueberries
sliced kiwi
⅓ cup red currant jelly

Combine butter with flour, sugar and vanilla in medium bowl, blending well. Press dough on bottom and sides of 10-inch fluted tart pan with removable bottom. Prick with fork. Bake at 375 degrees for 10 minutes. Set aside to cool. (This can be done 1 day ahead.)

Slowly heat milk, vanilla and ¼ cup sugar, stirring constantly. Whisk remaining sugar with egg yolks. Sift flour and cornstarch into egg yolk mixture and stir until smooth. Slowly whisk in hot milk mixture. Return to pan and bring to a boil, stirring with whisk. Reduce heat and simmer 10 minutes. Remove from heat. Place waxed paper on surface of custard and allow to cool. (Custard can be prepared 1 day ahead.)

To assemble tart, remove crust from pan and place on flat serving plate. Pour custard into crust. Top with desired fruit. Berries may be mounded on filling or arranged in an attractive design. Be creative! Melt jelly in microwave and brush onto fruit with pastry brush. Refrigerate until serving time.

SUGAR-SEARED CRÈME BRULÉE

SERVES 8

3 cups heavy cream
pinch of salt
2 teaspoons vanilla
6 egg yolks
½ cup plus 6 tablespoons sugar (divided use)

Combine cream, salt and vanilla in saucepan and heat to simmering. Mix together egg yolks and 6 tablespoons sugar. Slowly add cream mixture to egg mixture, stirring lightly to mix. Pour through a strainer into eight ½-cup ramekins. Place ramekins in larger pan filled halfway with hot water. Bake at 300 degrees for 35 minutes. Do not overbake. Remove from oven and allow to cool in pan. (Cooking will continue while the water cools.) Chill thoroughly.

Before serving, sprinkle ½ cup sugar on top of ramekins (1 tablespoon per ramekin). Shake to distribute sugar evenly. Set ramekins on bed of ice in larger pan, then place under broiler for approximately 2 minutes to caramelize sugar. Watch carefully so sugar doesn't burn. If it does, gently remove the burnt sugar and start again.

BE SURE TO USE GRANULATED WHITE SUGAR. BECAUSE BROWN SUGAR HAS A HIGH MOISTURE CONTENT IT DOESN'T WORK AS WELL FOR CARAMELIZING.

LOW-FAT CRÈME BRULÉE

SERVES 6

2 cups skimmed evaporated milk
2 tablespoons non-fat dry milk powder
¾ cup pasteurized egg substitute
⅓ cup plus 2 tablespoons sugar (divided use)
1 teaspoon vanilla
30 fresh raspberries

Combine ½ cup skimmed evaporated milk with milk powder. Stir until well blended. Add remaining milk, egg substitute, ⅓ cup sugar and vanilla.

Place 5 raspberries in bottom of each of six 6-ounce ramekins. Pour custard mixture over, dividing equally. Place ramekins in larger pan and fill halfway with hot water. Bake at 325 degrees for 35 minutes, or until custard is set. Remove from oven and water bath. When cooled, refrigerate to chill.

Sprinkle ½ teaspoon sugar over top of each ramekin. Broil, 4 inches from heat, until sugar is caramelized.

CRANBERRY WALNUT TART

SERVES 8

CRUST

1¼ cup flour

3 tablespoons sugar

¼ teaspoon baking powder

⅛ teaspoon salt

6 tablespoons (¾ stick) cold unsalted butter, cut into small pieces

1 large egg, beaten with 1 tablespoon water

FILLING

¾ cup brown sugar

1 tablespoon cornstarch

grated zest of 1 orange

juice of 1 orange

2½ cups cranberries, washed and culled

¾ cup golden raisins

¼ teaspoon salt

½ cup coarsely chopped walnuts or pecans (optional)

1 egg, beaten with 1 tablespoon water

1 tablespoon sugar

Combine flour, sugar, baking powder and salt in food processor. Mix for several seconds. Add butter, processing until mixture resembles coarse meal. Add egg mixture and process until mixture just begins to cling together. Turn out onto work surface and press together to form a ball. Flatten ball into 6-inch circle, cover with plastic wrap and chill several hours. (Can be prepared 1 day ahead.)

To prepare filling, combine brown sugar, cornstarch, orange zest and juice, cranberries, raisins and salt in saucepan. Bring to a boil. Reduce heat to medium-low and cook until half the cranberries have popped. Stir in nuts. Remove from heat and pour into a bowl. Chill several hours or overnight.

Sprinkle work surface and rolling pin with flour. Roll dough out to at least 12 inches in diameter. Using a large plate for a pattern, cut dough into a 12-inch circle. Carefully transfer circle to a cookie sheet.

To assemble tart, heap cooled cranberry filling onto center of dough circle. Gently spread filling outward to form an 8-inch circle. Carefully fold outer edges of dough toward center to leave a 4-inch circle of uncovered filling in the center. Brush dough with egg wash and sprinkle sugar on top. Cover exposed filling with foil and bake at 425 degrees for 10 minutes. Remove foil and bake an additional 10 minutes. Let cool before transferring to serving platter.

BOURBON STREET BREAD PUDDING

SERVES 8

1 cup sugar
½ cup (1 stick) butter
5 eggs, beaten
2 cups heavy cream
dash cinnamon
1 tablespoon vanilla
½ to ¾ cup raisins

day-old French bread, sliced 1 inch thick
   (enough to fit 9 x 9-inch pan in a single layer)

HOT BOURBON SAUCE

1 cup sugar
1 cup heavy cream
1 tablespoon butter
dash cinnamon
½ teaspoon cornstarch dissolved in ¼ cup water
¼ cup bourbon

Cream sugar and butter in a mixer until light and fluffy. Add eggs, cream, cinnamon, vanilla and raisins, mixing well. Pour into greased 9-inch square pan. Arrange sliced bread in egg mixture in single layer to fit pan. Let stand for 5 minutes. Turn bread over and let stand for 10 minutes. Push bread down so that mixture is well-absorbed by bread. Set pan in larger pan and fill larger pan halfway with hot water. Cover smaller pan with foil and bake at 350 degrees for 30 minutes. Remove foil and bake 15 to 20 minutes longer. Custard should be soft, not firm, when done.

To prepare sauce, combine sugar, cream, butter and cinnamon in saucepan. Bring to a boil and add cornstarch mixture. Continue stirring until sauce is translucent. Remove from heat and stir in bourbon.

Serve pudding with Hot Bourbon Sauce spooned over top.

BREAD PUDDING NEEDS TO BE MADE WITH VERY LIGHT, DAY-OLD FRENCH BREAD. (SOURDOUGH BREAD IS TOO DENSE AND CHEWY TO ABSORB LIQUID AND PUFF.) THE CREOLES, BEING VERY PRACTICAL, USED THEIR LEFTOVER BREAD TO MAKE BREAD PUDDING. SINCE THIS WAS BREAD THAT HAD NO OTHER USE (ITS VALUE WAS LOST), IT WAS CALLED *PAIN PERDU*, OR "LOST BREAD."

BREAD PUDDING WITH PRALINE SAUCE

SERVES 16

1½ pounds country-style Italian or French bread, thinly sliced and lightly toasted (or dried overnight in oven with light on)

5 eggs

3 cups milk

1½ cups plus 3 tablespoons sugar (divided use)

¼ teaspoon salt

3 tablespoons vanilla

1½ cups raisins

1 cup chopped pecans, lightly toasted

1 teaspoon cinnamon

½ teaspoon freshly grated nutmeg

½ cup (1 stick) butter, cut into small pieces

PRALINE SAUCE

1 cup (2 sticks) unsalted butter

1 cup brown sugar

1 cup heavy cream

Tear bread into bite-size pieces and place in large bowl. In another bowl, whisk eggs with milk, 1½ cups sugar, salt and vanilla. Pour over bread and set aside until liquid is completely absorbed.

Fold raisins and pecans into the moistened bread. Place mixture in buttered 9 x 13-inch glass baking dish and pat down evenly.

Combine remaining 3 tablespoons sugar with cinnamon and nutmeg; sprinkle over bread. Dot with butter and cover with foil. Set baking dish in a larger pan and fill halfway with hot water. Bake at 350 degrees for 50 to 60 minutes or until firm. (A knife inserted into center should come out clean.) Remove foil and let stand for 10 minutes.

To make Praline Sauce, combine butter, sugar and cream in saucepan and bring to a boil over high heat. Reduce heat and simmer for 5 minutes. Serve warm over bread pudding.

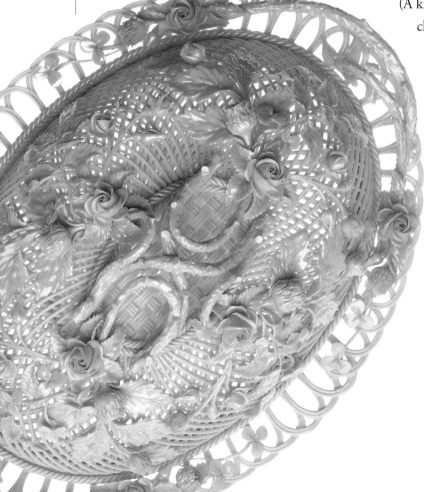

PORCELAIN COVERED BASKET, CA. 1925, BELLEEK FACTORY, COUNTY FERMANAGH, IRELAND, 17.1991.A-B

STEAMED PERSIMMON PUDDING

A MOIST AND DELICIOUS DESSERT SURE TO BECOME A HOLIDAY FAVORITE. SERVES 12

3 ripe persimmons (about 1 cup), skinned and puréed (see note)
2 teaspoons baking soda
½ cup (1 stick) butter
1½ cups sugar
2 eggs
1 teaspoon lemon juice
2 teaspoons vanilla
2 tablespoons brandy (optional)
1 cup flour
2 teaspoons cinnamon
1 teaspoon ground ginger
½ teaspoon nutmeg
dash of cloves
¼ teaspoon salt
1 cup raisins
½ cup coarsely chopped pecans

HARD SAUCE (OPTIONAL)

1 cup powdered sugar
5 tablespoons butter, softened
⅛ teaspoon salt
1 teaspoon vanilla
1 tablespoon brandy

LEMON SAUCE (OPTIONAL)

¼ to ½ cup sugar (depending on desired sweetness)
1 tablespoon cornstarch
1 cup water
2 tablespoons butter
1 teaspoon grated lemon rind
2 tablespoons lemon juice
⅛ teaspoon salt

Add baking soda to persimmon purée and let stand at least 10 minutes. (Mixture should be very gelatinous. If it hasn't jelled, baking soda may be too old and pudding will not work.) Set aside.

Cream together butter, sugar, eggs, lemon juice, vanilla and brandy. Add persimmons and mix well. Sift together flour, cinnamon, ginger, nutmeg, cloves and salt. Add to persimmon mixture and blend well. Fold in raisins and pecans. Grease and flour a 2-quart mold and lid. (Place buttered baking parchment, cut to fit, in top and bottom of mold to help prevent sticking when unmolding.) Pour pudding into mold.

Position a rack in large stockpot several inches from bottom. Pour in boiling water just to bottom of rack. Place covered mold on rack. Cover and steam for 2½ hours. Water should be simmering, but not boiling. Add more hot water if necessary during steaming.

Cool 20 minutes and unmold carefully, gently loosening edges with sharp knife. Serve plain or with Hard Sauce or Lemon Sauce.

To prepare Hard Sauce, sift powdered sugar. Beat butter until soft and blend in sugar gradually. Add salt, vanilla and brandy, mixing well.

To prepare Lemon Sauce, combine sugar and cornstarch in top of double boiler. Add water and cook until translucent. Remove from heat and stir in butter, lemon rind, lemon juice and salt. Mix well.

NOTE: YOU CAN RIPEN PERSIMMONS BY PUTTING THEM IN A BROWN PAPER BAG ALONG WITH A SLICE OF APPLE. IF THIS PUDDING BECOMES YOUR FAMILY'S FAVORITE, YOU'LL WANT TO KEEP AN EYE OUT FOR PERSIMMONS IN THE GROCERY STORE. SLICE AND SCOOP OUT THE PULP, SEEDS AND ALL. PURÉE AND FREEZE. YOU CAN ALSO FREEZE THE PERSIMMONS WHOLE. WHEN DEFROSTED, THEY WILL SLIP OUT OF THEIR SKINS EASILY.

SET OF GLASSES ON STAND, CA. 1775-1825, LA GRANJA FACTORY, SAN ILDEFONSO, SPAIN, 1985.R.199; "THE PICNIC" FAN, CA. 1775,. FRANCE, SKIN, MOTHER-OF-PEARL, PAINT, 1985.R.514

203 THE ARTFUL TABLE

HAZELNUT BISCOTTI

THESE COOKIES STAY FRESH FOR 4 WEEKS. THEY ARE DELICIOUS DIPPED IN SHERRY, RED WINE OR COFFEE. YIELDS 3 DOZEN

1 cup hazelnuts (divided use)
2¼ cups flour
1 cup sugar
1 teaspoon baking soda
pinch of salt
1 teaspoon vanilla
3 eggs (divided use)

Blanch ¼ cup hazelnuts (see note). Roast both blanched and unblanched nuts for 5 to 8 minutes at 350 degrees, until slightly golden. Remove blanched nuts and pulverize in food processor. (Do not over-process or nuts will turn to butter.) Return whole nuts to oven for another 2 to 3 minutes. Chop coarsely and set aside. (This can be done 1 day ahead. Store nuts tightly covered or they will re-absorb moisture from atmosphere.)

Combine flour, sugar, baking soda, salt and pulverized hazelnuts in large bowl. Beat vanilla with 2 eggs and blend into flour mixture, mixing well to incorporate all the ingredients. (Dough will be stiff. If it is too stiff to hold together, add small amounts of water.) Add chopped nuts and knead them into dough.

Beat remaining egg and set aside to use for glaze. Divide dough into 3 portions and roll to form logs about 1½ inches in diameter. Place logs on greased and floured baking sheet and brush with beaten egg. Bake at 300 degrees for 45 to 50 minutes. Remove from oven and cool completely. Cut logs diagonally with serrated knife into ¼-inch slices. Lay flat on cookie sheets and return to oven. Bake at 275 degrees for 20 to 30 minutes, or until light brown. Turn over halfway through baking time. Cool completely before storing in airtight containers.

YOU CAN ALSO MAKE BISCOTTI WITH ALMONDS OR WALNUTS. ADD ¼ TEASPOON ALMOND EXTRACT IF YOU USE ALMONDS.

NOTE: TO BLANCH NUTS, SHELL THEM FIRST. COVER WITH BOILING WATER AND LET STAND 3 TO 5 MINUTES. DRAIN AND REMOVE OUTER HUSK WITH FINGERS. DRY COMPLETELY BEFORE USING OR STORING.

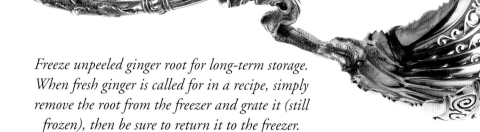

Freeze unpeeled ginger root for long-term storage. When fresh ginger is called for in a recipe, simply remove the root from the freezer and grate it (still frozen), then be sure to return it to the freezer.

CAPPUCCINO BROWNIES

YIELDS 18 TO 24 BROWNIES

1 pound dark brown sugar
¾ cup (1½ sticks) unsalted butter
2 tablespoons instant coffee powder
2 tablespoons hot water
3 eggs
2 tablespoons vanilla
1½ cups flour
2 teaspoons baking powder
½ teaspoon salt
1 cup chopped pecans
1 cup semi-sweet chocolate chips

Cook brown sugar and butter in saucepan over medium heat until butter melts. Dissolve coffee powder in hot water and stir into butter mixture. Let cool to room temperature.

When mixture is completely cool (important because chocolate chips will melt if too warm), beat in eggs and vanilla. Sift flour, baking powder and salt together; stir into butter mixture. Fold in pecans and chocolate.

Spread mixture evenly in buttered 9 x 13-inch baking pan. Bake at 350 degrees for 25 to 30 minutes, or until lightly browned. Do not over-bake.

Cool completely before cutting into squares.

FOR A DECADENT TREAT, SERVE THESE BROWNIES WITH ICE CREAM AND HOT CARAMEL FUDGE SAUCE (PAGE 213).

FRESH GINGER SNAPS

THESE COOKIES CAN BE SERVED ALONE OR WITH A COMPLEMENTARY CHEESE SUCH AS MASCARPONE OR GOURMANDISE. YIELDS 60 COOKIES

⅓ cup butter, softened
⅓ cup solid vegetable shortening
1¼ cups sugar (divided use)
1 egg
2 tablespoons dark corn syrup
1 heaping tablespoon grated fresh ginger
2 cups flour
1 teaspoon ground cloves
1½ teaspoons baking soda
½ teaspoon salt
1 teaspoon cinnamon

Cream together butter, shortening and 1 cup sugar in electric mixer. Add egg and mix well. Stir in syrup and ginger. Sift together flour, cloves, baking soda and salt; add to butter mixture. Continue to mix until well blended. Chill dough for 1 hour to overnight.

Combine cinnamon and remaining ¼ cup sugar. Form dough into 1-inch balls and roll in cinnamon-sugar mixture until evenly coated.

Place balls 2 inches apart on greased cookie sheets. Bake at 350 degrees for 10 to 12 minutes, or until lightly browned and beginning to crackle on top.

CHILLED BERRIES IN CREAM WITH COINTREAU

EASY AND ELEGANT. SERVES 4

1 cup sliced strawberries

1 cup raspberries

2 tablespoons orange juice

1 tablespoon Cointreau (orange liqueur)

1 cup heavy cream

¼ cup powdered sugar

Combine berries, orange juice and Cointreau in large bowl. Beat cream with sugar until stiff. Fold into berries. Chill in serving bowl or in individual parfait glasses.

GARNISH WITH CRUSHED MACAROONS AND COCONUT AND/OR SHAVINGS OF CHOCOLATE.

STERLING SILVER ICE BOWL AND SPOON, DESIGNED 1870, MADE 1871, GORHAM MFG. CO., PROVIDENCE, R.I., 1989.5.1-2.MCD

DESIGNS IN THE "ARCTIC" OR "GLACIAL" STYLE WERE POPULAR IN THE 1870S BECAUSE OF THE NOVELTY AND ELEGANCE OF SERVING ICE AND ICE CREAM, AND ALSO BECAUSE OF THE PUBLICITY SURROUNDING AMERICA'S PURCHASE OF ALASKA IN 1867. THIS HIGHLY ROMANTIC ICE BOWL AND SPOON DEPICT A POLAR BEAR CUB CAPTURED IN TRAPPERS' ROPES, WHILE ITS PARENTS ROAR IN GRIEF FROM THEIR ICE FLOE.

SUMMER BERRY CRISP

SERVES 10

5 cups sliced strawberries
2 cups blueberries
2 cups raspberries
1 cup sugar
5 tablespoons quick-cooking tapioca
½ teaspoon cinnamon
½ teaspoon freshly grated nutmeg

TOPPING
1½ cups flour
½ cup oats
1½ cups brown sugar
1 teaspoon cinnamon
1 teaspoon freshly grated nutmeg
⅛ teaspoon salt
½ cup (1 stick) butter, melted

Combine berries with sugar, tapioca, cinnamon and nutmeg, tossing gently to mix. Spoon into buttered 9-inch square baking pan.

Combine topping ingredients and mix with a fork until crumbly. Sprinkle over berries. Bake at 350 degrees for 1 hour. Serve at room temperature or chilled.

CRANBERRY APPLE CRUMBLE

SERVES 6 TO 8

FILLING
2 cups peeled, cored and sliced apples
2 cups cranberries
¼ cup packed brown sugar
½ teaspoon cinnamon
2 tablespoons lemon juice
⅛ teaspoon nutmeg

CRUMBLE TOPPING
¼ cup sugar
¼ cup packed brown sugar
½ cup rolled oats
5 tablespoons flour
¼ teaspoon cinnamon
¼ teaspoon nutmeg
pinch of salt
5½ tablespoons butter, cold

Place apples and cranberries in buttered 9-inch square pan or pie plate. Sprinkle with brown sugar, cinnamon, lemon juice and nutmeg.

To make crumble topping, combine sugars, rolled oats, flour, cinnamon, nutmeg and salt in bowl. Gradually cut pieces of butter into mixture until it resembles coarse meal. Spread topping over the fruit and pat it flat with palm of hand. Bake at 350 degrees for 45 to 50 minutes, or until fruit is fork-tender and topping is browned and crisp.

PINE NUT CRISPS WITH CARDAMOM

YIELDS 24 TO 30 CRISPS

½ cup plus 2 tablespoons pine nuts
¼ cup (½ stick) unsalted butter
¼ cup solid vegetable shortening
½ cup powdered sugar
2 tablespoons granulated sugar plus extra for topping
1 teaspoon vanilla
1 cup flour
½ teaspoon ground cardamom
¼ teaspoon baking powder
¾ teaspoon salt

Toast pine nuts in 350-degree oven for 10 minutes, or until golden. Set aside 2 tablespoons for later use. Grind remaining nuts in food processor until finely textured.

Mix butter, shortening, sugars and vanilla until well combined. Sift together flour, cardamom, baking powder and salt. Add flour mixture along with ground nuts, mixing until well combined. Chill for 30 minutes or longer.

Place 1-inch balls of dough on cookie sheet 2 inches apart. Flatten balls with bottom of glass which has been dipped in granulated sugar. Decorate with reserved pine nuts.

Bake at 325 degrees for 15 to 20 minutes, or until just beginning to color around edges. Leave on cookie sheet for 2 to 3 minutes before removing to rack. Store in airtight container when completely cooled.

TOFFEE DIAMONDS

YIELDS 24 PIECES

1 cup (2 sticks) butter, softened
1 cup brown sugar
1 egg
1 cup flour
6 ounces semisweet chocolate chips
½ cup chopped pecans

Cream together butter, sugar, egg and flour. Press into jelly roll pan. Bake at 350 degrees for 15 to 20 minutes or until lightly browned.

Immediately after removing from oven, sprinkle chocolate chips evenly over top. Allow to melt, then spread over entire surface with spatula. Sprinkle with chopped pecans. Let cool completely before cutting.

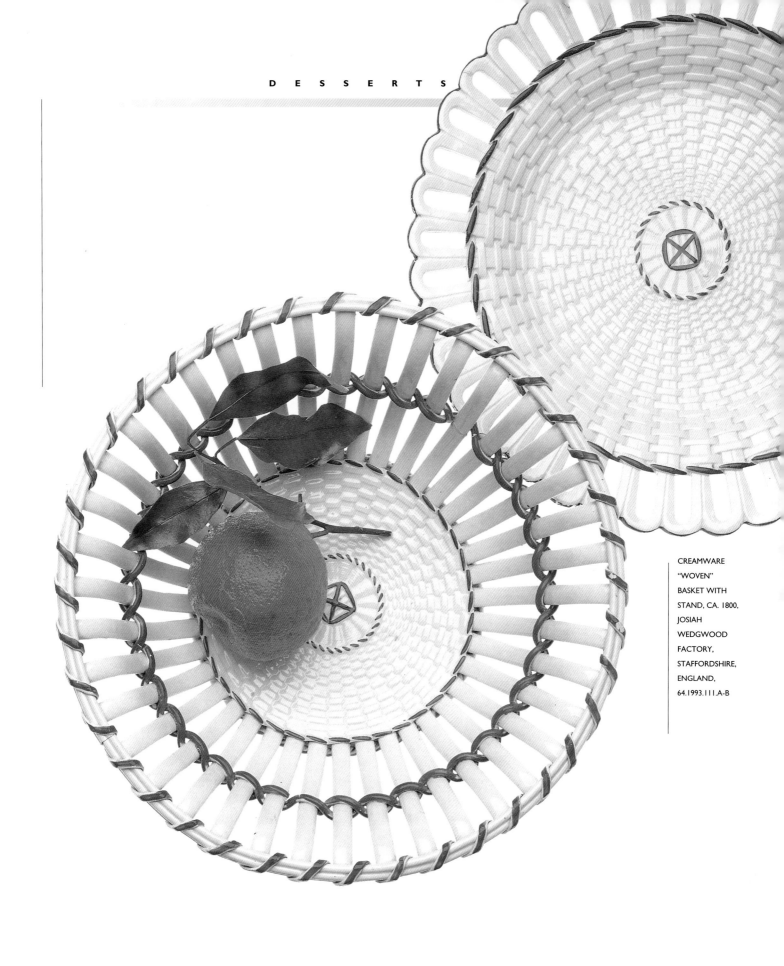

CREAMWARE
"WOVEN"
BASKET WITH
STAND, CA. 1800,
JOSIAH
WEDGWOOD
FACTORY,
STAFFORDSHIRE,
ENGLAND,
64.1993.111.A-B

Blend all ingredients in large bowl, adding peaches last. Pour into 4-quart freezer and freeze according to manufacturer's instructions.

NOTE: TO MAKE VANILLA SUGAR, PLACE 2 WHOLE VANILLA BEANS IN 4 CUPS SUGAR AND LET SIT, COVERED, AT LEAST 1 WEEK, OR AS LONG AS YOU WANT. ONCE YOU'VE TASTED THIS, YOU'LL WANT TO KEEP SOME ON HAND TO USE IN OTHER RECIPES.

DEPENDING ON YOUR TASTE PREFERENCES, THE CRYSTALLIZED GINGER CAN BE INCREASED UP TO 8 OUNCES. IT IS AVAILABLE IN BULK AT MOST ASIAN GROCERY STORES.

SERVE THE ICE CREAM WITH FRESH GINGER SNAPS (PAGE 205).

PEACH RUM ICE CREAM WITH CRYSTALLIZED GINGER

YIELDS 1 GALLON

6 tablespoons fresh lemon juice
4 cups vanilla sugar (see note)
2 quarts sour cream
4 ounces crystallized ginger, finely chopped
¼ cup dark rum
6 to 8 ripe peaches, peeled, pitted and puréed

DOUBLE FUDGE PIE

SERVES 10 TO 12

CRUST
1½ cups graham cracker crumbs
1 tablespoon sugar
6 tablespoons (¾ stick) butter, melted

FUDGE LAYER
6 tablespoons flour
½ teaspoon baking powder
⅛ teaspoon salt
½ cup (1 stick) butter, cut into 8 pieces
4 ounces semisweet chocolate, chopped
1 ounce unsweetened chocolate, chopped
½ cup sugar
1 egg
1 egg yolk
1 teaspoon vanilla

2 cups (½-inch pieces) Snickers bars (about 8½ ounces)

CREAM CHEESE LAYER
10 ounces cream cheese, softened
⅓ cup sugar
1 egg
1 teaspoon vanilla

TOPPING
2 ounces milk chocolate, chopped
2 tablespoons cream or milk

For crust, combine graham cracker crumbs and sugar in medium bowl. Add melted butter and stir until well incorporated. Press mixture evenly into buttered 10-inch pie plate. Bake at 350 degrees until crust is set, about 5 minutes. Cool on rack.

To prepare fudge layer, sift flour, baking powder and salt into medium bowl. Combine butter and chocolates in top of double boiler set over simmering water. Stir until melted and smooth. Remove from heat and cool slightly. Beat sugar, egg and egg yolk with electric mixer until slightly thickened, about 1 minute. Add vanilla and cooled chocolate mixture, stirring until well blended. Add dry ingredients and mix just until combined.

Pour fudge mixture into crust. Bake at 350 degrees until almost set and tester inserted into center comes out with moist batter still attached, about 17 minutes. (Cover crust with foil if browning too quickly.) Cool on rack 10 minutes. Arrange Snickers bar pieces evenly over fudge layer.

For cream cheese layer, beat cream cheese and sugar with electric mixer until smooth. Add egg and vanilla and beat just until smooth. Carefully spread mixture on top of Snickers pieces. Bake at 350 degrees until cream cheese layer is set, about 15 minutes. Cool on rack. Cover cooled pie with plastic wrap and freeze until firm. (Can be made up to 3 days ahead.)

Before serving, combine milk chocolate and cream in top of double boiler set over simmering water. Stir until just melted and smooth. Remove from heat. Serve pie on individual dessert plates and drizzle chocolate topping decoratively over each piece.

INSTEAD OF FREEZING THIS PIE, YOU MAY CHOOSE TO SERVE IT CHILLED. PREPARE CHOCOLATE TOPPING AND DRIZZLE IT OVER ENTIRE PIE, THEN REFRIGERATE UNTIL WELL CHILLED. IT'S DELICIOUS BOTH WAYS!

FROZEN STRAWBERRY TORTE

SERVES 10 TO 12

CRUST

1 cup graham cracker crumbs

3 tablespoons sugar

½ cup finely chopped nuts

¼ cup butter, melted

FILLING

2 cups sliced fresh strawberries

1 cup sugar

2 egg whites

1 tablespoon lemon juice

1 teaspoon vanilla

⅛ teaspoon salt

½ cup whipping cream, whipped

RASPBERRY SAUCE (OPTIONAL)

2 packages (10-ounce) frozen raspberries, thawed

1 tablespoon cornstarch

2 tablespoons lemon juice

2 tablespoons kirsch or framboise

Combine crust ingredients, mixing well. Press mixture into bottom of a 10-inch springform pan. Bake at 350 degrees for 10 minutes. Set aside to cool.

Combine strawberries, sugar, egg whites, lemon juice, vanilla and salt in large bowl of electric mixer. Beat, starting at low speed to blend, then at high speed for about 15 minutes until firm peaks form when beaters are withdrawn. Gently fold in whipped cream. Pour into cooled crust. Cover and freeze about 12 hours. Serve drizzled with Raspberry Sauce, if desired.

To prepare sauce, purée berries. Force through fine sieve (using a metal or plastic spoon). Mix cornstarch with lemon juice and add to purée. Pour into saucepan and bring to a boil. Reduce heat and simmer, stirring frequently, until slightly thickened. Add kirsch. Keeps up to 2 weeks in refrigerator.

WHOLE FROZEN, UNSWEETENED STRAWBERRIES MAY BE USED IF FRESH BERRIES ARE NOT AVAILABLE.

IRISH COFFEE ICE CREAM CAKE

SERVES 8

3 cups macaroon crumbs

½ cup (1 stick) butter, melted

½ cup chopped pecans

1 cup finely chopped semisweet chocolate

2 tablespoons Irish Cream liqueur

2 pints vanilla ice cream, softened

2 pints coffee ice cream, softened

hot fudge sauce (optional)

Combine crumbs, butter, nuts and chocolate, tossing with a fork until blended. Spread ⅓ of crumb mixture in bottom of an 8-inch springform pan. Mix liqueur into vanilla ice cream and spread evenly over crumb layer. Top with another ⅓ cup crumb mixture and freeze until firm. Add layer of coffee ice cream and top with remaining crumb mixture. Freeze until firm.

Remove from freezer 5 minutes before slicing. Serve as is or top with hot fudge sauce.

HOT CARAMEL FUDGE SAUCE

Y I E L D S   2 ½   C U P S

1 pound caramels
⅓ cup whole milk
½ pound milk chocolate
1 cup vanilla ice cream
1 teaspoon vanilla
2 teaspoons kahlua

Melt caramels and milk in top of double boiler or in microwave (3 to 4 minutes on high). Add chocolate to hot caramel mixture, stirring until melted. Mix in ice cream, vanilla and kahlua. Sauce will keep several weeks in refrigerator. Reheat to serve.

11.1991 Plate, Lent by David T. Owsley

12.1991 Plate, Lent by David T. Owsley

17.1991.a-b Basket, Lent by the Alvin and Lucy Owsley Collection

64.1993 All objects, Lent by Barbara Wedgwood

1949.29 Bowl, Gift of Contemporary House

1949.31 Bowl, Gift of the artists

1949.37 Bowl, Dallas Art Association Purchase

1954.54 Plate, Helen Woolworth McCann Collection

1954.85 Platter, Helen Woolworth McCann Collection

1974.77 Bowl, Gift of Conan West

1981.179 Plate, Anonymous gift

1981.196 Bowl, Gift of Donald and Florence S. Lewis

1983.8.1-2 Fingerbowl and Plate, Gift of Mr. and Mrs. Nelson Waggener

1983.13.3 Goblet, Gift of Mr. and Mrs. Nelson Waggener

1983.13.15 Goblet, Gift of Mr. and Mrs. Nelson Waggener

1983.26 Bowl, Gift of Mr. and Mrs. Nelson Waggener

1985.7 Bowl, Gift of Mrs. James H. Agnew in memory of L. A. Bickel

1985.R. All objects, The Wendy and Emery Reves Collection

1986.249 Dish, Gift of Margaret Sutherland Coleman

1987.57.a-s Cruet Set, The Karl and Esther Hoblitzelle Collection. Gift of the Hoblitzelle Foundation.

1988.46.a-b Pottery, General Acquisitions Fund

1988.66 Ice Cream Slice, Gift of Phyllis Tucker in honor of Charles R. Masling

1989.4.1-2.MCD Salad Serving Set, The Eugene and Margaret McDermott Fund

1989.5.1-2.MCD Ice Bowl and Spoon, The Eugene and Margaret McDermott Fund

1989.18.1-3 Glasses, Gift of the Dallas Antiques and Fine Arts Society

1989.22.1-2 Tea Set, Gift of the Cleaver Family in memory of James Stuart Cleaver and Mr. and Mrs. Charles Thornton Cleaver and an anonymous gift in honor of Mrs. James Stuart Cleaver

1989.123 Spoon, Gift of Robert E. Miller, Jr.

1989.136 Ice Cream Server, Gift of the Tri Delta Charity Antiques Show in honor of Henry S. Coger

1990.148.a-b Salad Serving Set, Anonymous gift

1990.183 Charger, Gift of the 1990 Dallas Symposium

1990.231 Bowl, Gift of the Craft Guild of Dallas

1991.5 Serving Scoop, Gift of Nicholas Harris Gallery

1991.10.1-4 Tea Set, Anonymous gift

1991.76 Berry Spoon, Gift of Loyd Taylor and Paxton Gremillion

1991.101 All objects, The Charles R. Masling & John E. Furen Collection. Gift of Mr. and Mrs.William Rubin, the Arthur A. Everts Co., and Arthur and Marie Berger by exchange.

1991.113.a-b Tureen, Gift of the Alvin and Lucy Owsley Foundation in memory of Lucy Ball Owsley

1991.412.9 Bowl, Anonymous gift

1991.412.42.a-c Butter Dish and Plate, Anonymous gift

1991.412.86 Charger, Anonymous gift

1991.B.228 Plate, The Faith P. and Charles L. Bybee Collection, Gift of Faith P. Bybee

1992.7 All flatware, The V. Stephen Vaughan Collection, Gift of the 1991 Silver Supper

1992.B.28 Plate, The Faith P. and Charles L. Bybee Collection, Gift of Faith P. Bybee

1992.338 Rolling Pin, Dallas Glass Club Collection

1992.404 Glass, Dallas Glass Club Collection

1992.445.a-b Cup and Saucer, Dallas Glass Club Collection

1992.451 Plate, Dallas Glass Club Collection

1992.482 Bowl, Dallas Glass Club Collection

1992.494 Bowl, Dallas Glass Club Collection

1992.501.1-2 Cream and Sugar, Dallas Glass Club Collection

1992.522.1-3 Place Setting, 20th-Century Design Fund

1992.526.1-3 Place Setting, Gift of Sylvia and Charles Venable

1992.B.224 Charger, The Faith P. and Charles L. Bybee Collection, Gift of Faith P. Bybee

1992.B.234 Dough Bowl, The Faith P. and Charles L. Bybee Collection, Gift of Faith P. Bybee

1992.B.234.4 Soup Plate, The Faith P. and Charles L. Bybee Collection, Gift of Faith P. Bybee

1992.B.225 Plate, The Faith P. and Charles L. Bybee Collection, Gift of Faith P. Bybee

1992.B.244 Pottery, The Faith P. and Charles L. Bybee Collection, Gift of Faith P. Bybee

1993.40 Pottery Plate, 20th-Century Design Fund

1993.53 Jelly Server, The V. Stephen Vaughan Collection, Gift of the Dallas Antiques and Fine Arts Society

1993.54 Serving Spoon, The V. Stephen Vaughan Collection, Gift of the Dallas Antiques and Fine Arts Society

1993.57.1 Salad Serving Spoon, The V. Stephen Vaughan Collection, Gift of the 1992 Silver Supper and Mr. and Mrs. John H. Chiles

1993.62.a-c Game Dish, Anonymous gift in memory of Sophia Taubman

1994.21 Plate, Gift of the Decorative Arts Guild of North Texas 1994 Connoisseurship Class

1994.229.1-3 Tea Set, 20th-Century Design Fund

MASTER TESTERS

APPETIZERS

Chairman
SHANNON CALLEWART

Committee
Jean Anne Cheatham
Puddin Evans
Sarah Jo Hardin
Teri Kramer
Kathy LeBolt
Barbara Macari
Barbara Paschall
Sarah Rathjen

BREADS AND SOUPS

Chairmen
NANCY CURREY
MARTY DALE

Committee
Rebecca Barnum
Julie Benigo
Brenda Brand
Barbara Busker
Gene Coker
Linda Coleman
Beth Heckert
Christine Heimerman
Martha Kean
Shelly Koeijmans
Carol McConnell
Dorothy Newell
Barbara Scott
Allen Segal
Kay Smith
Salle Stemmons
Kathy Weaver
Tina Young

SALADS

Chairmen
SARAH HAWN
BARBARA PLETCHER

Committee
Genie Bentley
Holly Chamness
Bev Freeman
Susan Granberry
Marty Nichols
Shirley Sloan

MEAT AND GAME

Chairmen
MELISSA AND GENE COKER
SALLY AND REN MAGUIRE
LIBBY AND MORRIS ORR

Committee
Carmen Clausse
Carol Collins
Cathy Cox
Kelli Maguire
Carol McEachern
Aleta McGhee
Bunny McWhorter
Sharon Protzman
Ann Schooler
Caryn Tebbe
Jane Thayer
Cindy Turner
Karen Wahl
Kathy Weaver

ACCOMPANIMENTS

Chairmen
ROSE MARIE SIEBS
SHARON SWEENEY

Committee
Mary Cass
Janice Finks
Nancy Ryan
Katie Siebs
Carolyn Watson

FISH AND POULTRY

Chairmen
ELLEN GRIMES
CAROLYN MARQUEZ

Committee
Nancy Bass
Betty Black
Jean Bowie
Barbara Franklin
Dawn Gibson
Elaine Henrion
Julie Hubach
Polly Kelly
Ruth Langdon
John Lutton
Mary Alice Murski
Christine Spencer
Shirley Tart

PASTA

Chairmen
CLAIRE GREENBERG
MARILYN SEGAL

Committee
Pat Bennison
Robyn Carafiol
Carol Campbell
Cecelia Feld
Lori Finkelston
Carol Graham
Lorraine Gurun
Betty May
Adrienne Rosenberg
Andrea Rosenberg
Joyce Saunders
Priscilla Sebel
Betty Seltzer
Judy Smith
Salle Stemmons
Paula Zeitman

VEGETABLES

Chairman
BLAINE BOLTON
NANCY TAYLOR

Committee
Fran Bennett
Alicia Cheek
Jane Eaton
Susan Jaffer
Ruth Langdon
Barbara Macari
Meredith Rugg

DESSERTS

Chairmen
ROSANN GUTMAN
JOANNA PISTENMAA

Committee
Jane Eaton
Susan Jaffer
Susan Johnson
Susan Kaminsky
Shirley Kochman
Betsy Lawson
Barbara Shellist
Pat Snoots
Eileen Steensen
Katherine Suttill
Joanna Townsend

MARKETING

Beverly Freeman
Joanna Pistenmaa
Susan Gates
Carol Resnick
Carole Graham
Marilyn Hailey
Sue Padgett
Nan Alexander
Genie Bentley
Laurie-Jo Straty
Muffin Lemak
Barbara Pletcher
Shirley Sloan
Wendy Robinson

THE DALLAS MUSEUM OF ART LEAGUE would like to recognize all who have contributed so generously of their talents and resources in creating *The Artful Table*. Our deepest gratitude goes to those listed here and to anyone we may have inadvertently failed to mention.

Virginia Abdo
Betty Ablon
Dick Allen
Marge Allen
Bob Baker
Kitzi Ball
Ed Bamberger
Joan Barnette
Rebecca Barnum
Marilyn Barr
Barbara Barrett
Dolores Barzune
Nancy Bass
Bobbie Baumgarten
Carole Beasley
Genie Bentley
Beth Beran
Nathaniel Berry
Linda Blackburn
Lida Light Blue
Chong Boey
Blaine Bolton
Flo Braeker
Ann Braithwaite
Sharon Brener
Deborah Brown
Sara Virginia Burrell
Jayne Buskuhl
Patricia Ann Callahan
Shannon Callewart
Beverly Campbell
Carol Campbell
Angelina Carros
Margaret Carter
Holly Chamness
Jean Anne Cheatham
Alicia Cheek
Dorothy Cheek
Melanie Cheek
Marie Chiles
Lillian Clark
Sue Clark
Carmen Clausse
Fran Clem
Patsy Cline

Julie Cochran
Gene Coker
Melissa Coker
Polly Colaw
Frances Collins
Cheryl Coney
Annette Corman
Mark Cox
Kathy Crow
Margaret Anne Cullum
Marianne
  Cunningham
Nancy Currey
Marty Dale
Joyce Day
Karen Dickerman
Ann Drees
Pat Ducayet
Kelly Duff
Elsie Dunklin
Susan Dyer
Glen Eaton
Jane Eaton
Karen Ehni
Louise Eiseman
Fran Enslein
Ilse Entenmann
Puddin Evans
JoJo Ewing
Stella Fail
Diane Farber
Krista Farber
JoAnn Feikes
Cecelia Feld
Gertrude Ferguson
Sherry Ferguson
Corinna Flores
Tootsie Fonberg
Eileen Freed
Beverly Freeman
Marvin Freid
Liz Friedman
Harris Garrett
Ann Geich
Sandra Gengler
Estelle George
Elizabeth Gibbens
Joy Ginsberg
Jo Goyne
Carole Graham
Teel Gray
Claire Greenberg
Rebecca Greenblatt
Gail Greene
Joan Greiner
Ellen Grimes
Elaina Gross
Marsha Guckenheimer
Rosann Gutman

Mary Haase
Marilyn Hailey
Charles Hale
Hope Hallis
Cheri Hamilton-Smith
Linda Hampton
Karen Hansen
Carol Haralson
Marilyn Harbison
Sarah Jo Hardin
John F. Hardison
Mary Anne Hardison
Hope Harris
Kathryn Harris
Jody Hawn
Sarah Hawn
Doris Haynes
Beth Heckert
Kelly Hendrix
Scott Hendrix
Elaine Henrion
Ruth Holberg
Nancy Howley
Mary Hull
Helen Ann Hurst
Alice Ingle
Linda Jackson
Susan Jaffer
Beverly James
Tom Jenkins
Marilyn Johnson
Susan Johnson
Mabel Johnston
Candace Jones
Biddie Jordan
Louise Kahn
Susan Kaminsky
Lylia Kaplan
Burdette Katzen
Martha Kean
Sylvia Keizer
Trudy Kennedy
Elizabeth Ann Ketz
Martha Kimmerling
Stella Klein
Shirley Kochman
Bill Komodore
Teri Kramer
Billie Krausse
Sunny Krutz
Robert Kuhner
Beverly Lambert
Myra Lancaster
Ruth Langdon
Gloria LaRovere
Betsy Lawson
Daniele Lea
Kathy Leake
Schatzie Lee

Jimmie Leeson
Nancy Lemmon
Mary Lois Leonard
Ann Levell
Chandler Lindsley
Nancy Longo
Barbara Macari
Selma Macari
Ren Maguire
Sally Maguire
Carolyn Marquez
Joan Mason
June Mattingly
Michael McAdams
Pat McBride
Carole McConnell
Pat McConnell
JoAnne McCullough
Margaret McDermott
Carol McEachern
Brenda McHugh
Joan McIlyar
Amanda Meiler
Su-Su Meyer
Irene Miller
Mary Ann Miller
Ann Mills
Shannon Mitchell
Melinda Moore
Kit Morris
Chris Mosley
Jean Muller
Amy Mumma
Virginia Murphy
Tom Nabors
Kay Nakamoto
Carolyn New
Lucky Newfeld
Lynda Newman
Marty Nichols
Jeanne Nisenson
Carol Norwood
Elaine Notestine
Caroline Nusloch
Renee Olds
Libby Orr
Morris Orr
Wanda Otey
Chris Overcash
Sue Padgett
Eric Pamperin
Mary Carol Pamperin
Barbara Paschall
Jody Phelps
Susie Phillips
Emilyn Pinnell
Joanna Pistenmaa
Barbara Pletcher
Shirley Pollock

Nicole Porges
Sally Posey
Martha Price
Ron Price
Sondra Price
Vin Prothro
Sharon Protzmann
Alice Quigley
Virginia Ramsey
Sarah Rathjen
Linda Jones Rayes
Ginger Reeder
Carol Resnick
Dan Rizzie
Diane Roberts
Sharon Roberts
Carolyn Cole Rogers
Jean Rogers
Deedie Rose
Merle Rosenberg
Meredith Rugg
Luwanna Russell
Nancy Ryan
Cathy Sack
Dan Sanders
Lynda Sanders
Mary Jo Schneider
Dorothy Schoeneman
Barbara Scott
Allen Segal
Marilyn Segal
Oona Settembre
June Sherman
Nancy Shutt
Rose Marie Siebs
Ginger Simmons
Joan Skibell
Kay Smith
Pamela Smith
Geraldine Sobel
Elissa Sommerfield
Christine Spencer
Kathryn Stanley
Eileen Steensen
Laurie-Jo Straty
Katherine Suttill
Barbara Swearingen
Sharon Sweeney
Frances Syphers
Shirley Tart
Carter Taylor
Judy Taylor
Nancy Taylor
Caryn Tebbe
Ann Terry
Jere Thompson
Susan Tribble
Katherine Troendle
Katherine Tyson

Susie Underhill
Mary Margaret
  Underkofler
Cheryl Vogel
William K. Wallace
Chris Walters
Marilyn Wangsnes
Mimi Ward
Mary Watson
Kathy Weaver
Sue Weaver
Charlotte Webberman
Karoline Webster
Karen Weiner
Terry West
Janet Whitney
Barbara Wiggens
Nancy Wilbur
Coe Williams
Ruth Wiseman
Michele Wolff
Elaine Xeros
Grace Young
Mary Ann Young
Tina Young
Paula Zeitman
Tillie Zuber